Dublin

DIRECTIONS

ARD OIFIS AN PUIST

WRITTEN AND RESEARCHED BY

Paul Gray and Geoff Wallis

ROUGH GUIDES

NEW YORK • LONDON • DELHI

www.roughguides.com

Contents

Introduction to

Dublin

Although physically a compact city, more than a quarter of the Republic of Ireland's population of just over four million lives within Dublin's boundaries, a figure swelled by more than a million tourist arrivals each year. While for centuries it was the fulcrum of Ireland's fight for independence from Britain, today celebrated in the numerous memorials that pay homage to the revolutionary struggle, the cit y has developed into a thriving modern metropolis, which embraced the European ideal far more readily than anyone ever expected.

◄ Georgian door

◄ Grattan Bridge

Bisected by the River Liffey, the city's geographical and spiritual core, Dublin boasts an impressive architectural heritage, vividly represented by cathedrals and churches, castles and bridges, grand Georgian squares and townhouses.

The city's richly textured history – which runs the gamut from Viking to Norman to, finally, English invasion – provides a suitably redolent backdrop, but Dublin is very much a modern-day city. A large part of the centre has

When to visit

Unless you're planning your trip to coincide with a major festival (see p.206), Dublin is definitely at its best in the spring and early autumn when the temperature remains generally mild and rainfall is often lower. Though the hottest months, July and August are also often the wettest, the tourist crowds are at their peak at this time and the city can sometimes seem oppressive.

▲ Liffey at night

been redeveloped over the last few decades, leaving one wag to comment that "the city's only sights are building sites" as it – literally – builds upon Ireland's economic boom. So, alongside the city's historic buildings and monuments, you'll discover grand new, hotels and clubs, stunning modern architecture and a state-of-the-art tramway system. It's this meeting of the old and the new, and the constant sense of anticipation, that gives the city its edge.

Dublin is constantly changing in subtle ways, too, as its population becomes less homogeneous. Ever-growing Chinese, African and Eastern European communities are nudging the city slowly towards multiculturalism, bringing welcome variety to the city's restaurants, shops and street markets, as well as fresh impetus to its music and arts scenes.

▼ Sunlight Chambers

An increasingly style-conscious city, Dublin once looked inwards for inspiration, but today it is ever glancing both east and west, to Europe and America, catching new trends – and bringing a decidedly Irish slant to bear upon them. Much of that trendsetting reveals itself in the flourishing shops, bars, clubs, cafés, restaurants and galleries of the fashionable Southside, centring especially on and around Grafton Street and the redeveloped arts

Opening hours

City-centre **shops** tend to open from 9.30am or 10am until 6pm Monday to Saturday, with many staying open until 8pm on Thursday. Some also open roughly noon–6pm on Sunday. Where shops are closed for one or more days of the week, this is noted in the listings. Standard opening times for **pubs** are Monday to Thursday 10.30am–11.30pm, Friday and Saturday 10.30–12.30am and Sunday noon–11pm. **Cafés** tend to open Monday to Saturday 8am–6pm, with most in the city centre opening on Sunday from around 9am or 10am until 6pm. **Restaurants** generally serve lunch from noon until 3pm and dinner from 6pm onwards. Exceptions to these hours are detailed in the listings section of each chapter.

quarter Temple Bar. Rising against its erstwhile image as dowdy, occasionally seedy and somewhat down-at-heel, the Northside is also smartening up, and you'll find a plethora of new, chic bars, cafés and restaurants here, in particular around the quays of the Liffey. East of the centre, on both sides of the river, the former docklands are forming the nexus for the latest stage of regeneration.

Renowned for its literary tradition, the city has produced celebrated writers such as George Bernard Shaw, Oscar Wilde, Samuel Beckett, Brendan Behan and, of course, James Joyce, the author whose novels and short stories most incisively and intensely capture the life and spirit of the city. Added to this is its theatrical pedigree, once focused mainly on the Abbey and the Gate theatres, but nowadays encompassing all manner of experimental shows and events.

Inseparable from its musical heritage, the city nurtures emerging talent in its numerous cutting-edge venues covering all manner of musical genres. Traditional music lovers are particularly well catered

▲ Doheny and Nesbitt

for by a wealth of pubs hosting regular, often excellent sessions. Dublin boasts a vibrant nightlife, too, with enough clubs to keep the hardiest party animal spoilt for choice.

For a taste of Ireland at large, it's very easy to slip out of Dublin to visit a host of nearby attractions, from fascinating Neolithic and monastic sites to opulent mansions once occupied by Ireland's ruling elite. Alternatively, cliff-top walks and exhilarating mountain vistas will bring the fresh air rushing into your lungs.

However, there's no escaping the reality that Dublin has become one of Europe's most expensive cities; in particular, the cost of eating and drinking has risen sharply in recent years. Despite this seeming exorbitance, it's still relatively easy to experience this invigorating city to the full without incurring the wrath of your bank manager. Accommodation, at least, is one area you can save, by booking in advance and keeping abreast of midweek bargains, and the city also offers an array of free attractions.

Dublin
AT A GLANCE

KILDARE STREET AND MERRION SQUARE

With its main entrance on Kildare Street, Leinster House, seat of the Irish Parliament, is neatly bordered at its four corners by the country's main cultural and touristic institutions: the National Museum, the National Library, the National Gallery and the Natural History Museum (currently closed). To the east, the lawns of Merrion Square are a pleasant, quiet spot, surrounded by well-preserved Georgian terraces.

▼ The National Gallery

▲ Temple Bar

Temple Bar somehow manages to remain the city's hub both for boisterous nightlife and for art. With bars and clubs, cosmopolitan restaurants, stylish shopping, galleries and arts centres, it's likely that you'll end up here at some stage.

▲ Museum of Modern Art, Kilmainham

TEMPLE BAR

Hemmed in by the river and the former dam that is Dame Street,

KILMAINHAM

Just west of the city, the suburb of Kilmainham offers a taste of

Ireland both old and new in the form of the Irish Museum of Modern Art, housed in the imposing Royal Hospital, and through the austere penal conditions on view at Kilmainham Gaol, a building with an iconic status in Ireland's struggle for freedom.

▼ Farmleigh Gardens

PHOENIX PARK

Whether you just fancy a stroll, watching sports such as hurling, polo, or, perhaps surprisingly, cricket, or taking a trip to the zoo, this sprawling parkland offers plenty of scope for relaxation and entertainment. The adjacent Farmleigh mansion, sumptuous former home of the Guinness family, should be included in everyone's agenda.

THE INNER NORTHSIDE

Alongside some of Dublin's most renowned traditional music pubs, this much-regenerated area offers swish new clubs, bars and cafés, chain stores and bustling streets,

▼ Buses on O'Connell Street

historic monuments and edifices, a thriving street market and famous theatres, museums and galleries – something for everyone, in fact.

▲ The Old Library, Trinity College

GRAFTON STREET

In the centre of the city, Trinity College happily opens its doors to casual visitors to enjoy its grand architecture, wonderful collection of illuminated manuscripts and restful parkland. The main gate stands at the bottom (or, some say, the top) of Grafton Street, a pedestrianized arena for purposeful shoppers by day, rambling carousers by night.

▲ Dublin Castle

AROUND DUBLIN CASTLE

The relics of British rule – Dublin Castle, City Hall, Christ Church and St Patrick's cathedrals – can be found in the former Anglo-Norman city centre, with the area's highlight the global treasure-house of the Chester Beatty Library. Alongside the castle, South Great George's Street is home to cafés and restaurants, hip shops and some great pubs, old and new.

Ideas

The big six

Wandering the streets of Dublin without a fixed plan, taking in street performances, Georgian squares and traditional pubs as the mood takes you, is one of this compact city's great pleasures. But there are a number of things you really shouldn't leave town without seeing, ranging from stark reminders of Ireland's colonial past at Kilmainham Gaol to the unexpected Oriental beauties of the Chester Beatty Library.

▲ Kilmainham Gaol

The notorious Gaol was where Ireland's revolutionaries were often incarcerated and, in some cases, executed. Tours provide a chilling evocation of nineteenth-century penal conditions.

P.126 ▶ THE LIBERTIES AND KILMAINHAM

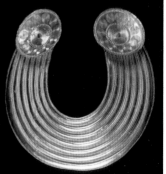

▲ The National Museum

Dazzling hordes of prehistoric gold and beautifully wrought Christian treasures to make your jaw drop.

P.79 ▶ KILDARE STREET AND MERRION SQUARE

▼ Chester Beatty Library

An elegant, world-renowned display of manuscripts, prints and *objets d'art* from Europe, the Middle East and the Far East.

P.108 ▸ DUBLIN CASTLE AND AROUND

▲ The National Gallery

A graceful showcase of European art since the fifteenth century – don't miss the vibrant Jack B. Yeats collection.

P.81 ▸ KILDARE STREET AND MERRION SQUARE

▶ Trinity College

The gorgeously illustrated *Book of Kells* and the magnificent Long Room in the Old Library justly take pride of place amongst the treasures of Dublin's famous college.

P.66 ▸ TRINITY COLLEGE, GRAFTON STREET AND AROUND

▶ The Liffey

Bisecting the city, the river lies at the very heart of Dublin and has inspired many a writer and artist. A stroll along the Quays is an essential part of any trip to the city.

P.129 ▸ AROUND O'CONNELL STREET

Literary Dublin

Ireland has a rich and vivid literary heritage, much of it centred upon the capital. Many of the nation's greatest works were written by authors in sometimes self-imposed exile, including Samuel Beckett and James Joyce (see p.142). Contemporary writers like Roddy Doyle and Joseph O'Connor (brother of singer Sinéad) have continued to explore the city's vibrant life, often to great comic effect.

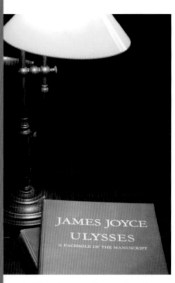

▲ The James Joyce Centre

Devoted to all things Joycean, the Centre celebrates both the author's life and his literary achievements.

P.143 ▸ NORTH FROM PARNELL SQUARE

▲ Dublin Writers Museum

The best place to begin your literary explorations of the capital and its authors.

P.142 ▸ NORTH FROM PARNELL SQUARE

▲ James Joyce Tower, Sandycove

A quirky collection of Joycean artefacts in the imposing Martello tower that was home to *Ulysses'* Buck Mulligan.

P.161 ▸ THE SOUTHERN OUTSKIRTS

▲ George Bernard Shaw

The playwright spent most of his life in England but lived in Synge Street during his early years.

P.90 ▸ ST STEPHEN'S GREEN TO THE GRAND CANAL

▲ Jonathan Swift

The author of the great satirical novel *Gulliver's Travels* was once Dean of St Patrick's Cathedral, and is buried there.

P.113 ▸ DUBLIN CASTLE AND AROUND

◀ Bloomsday

Fans of Joyce annually celebrate the day on which *Ulysses* is set, many following in the footsteps of the central characters and some even dressing for the part.

P.142 ▸ NORTH FROM PARNELL SQUARE

Dublin tastes

Dublin's culinary reputation is fast improving, though prices can sometimes be off-putting. The pleasures of modern Irish cuisine (as well as the finer points of Guinness) are dealt with elsewhere, but there are plenty of traditional tastes that won't break the budget and will leave you with an evocative memory of the city.

▲ Hot port

Drop into a traditional pub off Grafton Street, or indeed any Dublin bar worth its salt, for this fine winter warmer, spiked with lemon and cloves.

P.75 ▶ TRINITY COLLEGE, GRAFTON STREET AND AROUND

▲ Leo Burdock's

The crisply battered fish and perfectly fried potatoes from Dublin's best-loved chipper are hard to beat.

P.117 ▶ DUBLIN CASTLE AND AROUND

▼ The Old Jameson Distillery

Learn the secrets of whiskey-making and sample a drop of the hard stuff.

P.150 ▸ FROM CAPEL STREET TO COLLINS BARRACKS

▼ The Porterhouse

Sample an award-winning range of home-brewed stouts, lagers and bitters.

P.103 ▸ TEMPLE BAR

▲ Sheridan's

Savour the tastes and aromas of Dublin's finest display of Irish cheeses.

P.72 ▸ TRINITY COLLEGE, GRAFTON STREET AND AROUND

▲ King Sitric's Fish Restaurant, Howth

Local oysters, mussels, lobsters and fish – a great way to round off the Howth Cliff Walk.

P.171 ▸ THE NORTHERN OUTSKIRTS

Musical Dublin

Whatever your musical tastes, you're bound to find something to suit in Dublin. There are plenty of pubs hosting traditional music sessions, often of astonishingly high quality, while many others, from the tiny to the mega-bar, offer jazz, blues and up-and-coming rock bands. There's also a plethora of places for gigging and ligging, from small events to major concerts, as well as several classical music venues.

▲ J.J. Smyth's

The Aungier Street bar is the Southside's focus for Dublin's blues and jazz-fusion scene.

P.121 ▸ DUBLIN CASTLE AND AROUND

▲ Temple Bar Music Centre

A purpose-built venue with a justifiably lauded reputation for hosting left-field bands and singers.

P.104 ▸ TEMPLE BAR

▼ Crawdaddy

One of the best of the city's smaller venues, featuring a diverse range of live bands and singers.

P.205 ▸ ST STEPHEN'S GREEN TO THE GRAND CANAL

▼ National Concert Hall

Home to the city's major classical music concerts and other important musical events.

P.94 ▸ ESSENTIALS

▲ U2

Unquestionably Ireland's most successful musical export, and singer Bono has become one of the country's most powerful political ambassadors. In its early days the band played at many small venues in the city, including the Project Arts Centre.

P.98 ▸ TEMPLE BAR

▲ The Cobblestone

One of the best places to catch a traditional session in the city, and also to sample locally produced brews.

P.153 ▸ FROM CAPEL STREET TO COLLINS BARRACKS

Georgian Dublin

During a period of great prosperity in the eighteenth century, Dublin enjoyed its architectural heyday: from 1757 the Wide Streets Commissioners oversaw the building of tree-lined squares and boulevards that were worthy of a modern European capital. Famous architects and craftsmen were brought in to design both public set-pieces and intimate residences. Hard times, however, followed the complete transfer of political power to London in 1801, though this economic stagnation helped to ensure the survival of extensive areas of Georgian architecture to this day.

▲ Fitzwilliam Square

This late-Georgian square, built on a more intimate scale than other examples in the city, was home to W.B. Yeats, among other notables.

P.91 ▸ ST STEPHEN'S GREEN TO THE GRAND CANAL

▲ The Custom House

Dominating the waterfront, the design of Gandon's magnificent edifice features numerous intricate exterior details and a grand dome.

P.133 ▸ AROUND O'CONNELL STREET

▲ The Casino at Marino

Probably Ireland's finest Neoclassical building, executed with beautiful craftsmanship and witty sleight of hand.

P.168 ▶ THE NORTHERN OUTSKIRTS

▼ Newman House

Fabulous stucco-work adorns what became Ireland's first Catholic university.

P.88 ▶ ST STEPHEN'S GREEN TO THE GRAND CANAL

▲ No. 29 Fitzwilliam Street Lower

An absorbing tour of a re-created Georgian townhouse on the corner of Merrion Square.

P.84 ▶ KILDARE STREET AND MERRION SQUARE

Guinness pubs

Few visitors leave Dublin without trying the hometown drink, the stout Guinness, even if it's just a "glass" (a half-pint). It really does taste better here, and locals argue about exactly which pub pours the best drop (is the travel-shy liquid better at *Ryan's*, just across the river from the brewery, than downstream at *Mulligan's*?). It's always granted the requisite two minutes' settling time halfway through pouring, and no matter how thirsty you are, you should let it settle again once it's fully poured.

▲ Ryan's

A long-time challenger to the claim that *Mulligan's* serves the best pint of the black stuff, this Parkgate Street bar is also a handy watering hole en route to Phoenix Park.

P.158 ▸ PHOENIX PARK

▲ The Palace Bar

Sip some of the finest Guinness in Dublin at the sociable bar or in the easy-going, glass-roofed back room.

P.77 ▸ TRINITY COLLEGE, GRAFTON STREET AND AROUND

▼ Mulligan's

Characterful, rambling haunt of *Irish Times* hacks, and who's to doubt their view that it purveys the best pint in the city?

P.77 ▶ TRINITY COLLEGE, GRAFTON STREET AND AROUND

▲ The Long Hall

Friendly staff, atmospheric decor and careful handling of the black stuff.

P.121 ▶ DUBLIN CASTLE AND AROUND

▼ The Gravity Bar

Perched on the seventh storey of the Guinness Storehouse, *The Gravity Bar* offers the chance – literally – to get high and enjoy a pint that's travelled the shortest distance in Dublin.

P.124 ▶ THE LIBERTIES AND KILMAINHAM

Dead Dublin

In few capital cities in the world are you made so vividly aware of local, and therefore national, history as in Dublin. Events and their colourful protagonists are each firmly rooted and commemorated in their location, evoking the diverse strands – Catholic, Anglo-Irish and even French Protestant – of the city's past.

▲ Glasnevin Cemetery

Tour Ireland's poignant national cemetery, followed by the traditional drink round the corner at *Kavanagh's*, also known as *The Gravediggers*.

P.167 & P.172 ▸ THE NORTHERN OUTSKIRTS

▲ Monuments in St Patrick's Cathedral

Eclectic reminders of the city's Protestant history, from a cast of Jonathan Swift's skull to a grandiose memorial to the mother of physicist Robert Boyle.

P.113 ▶ DUBLIN CASTLE AND AROUND

▼ Huguenot Cemetery

A small, well-tended tribute to these industrious seventeenth-century immigrants.

P.87 ▶ ST STEPHEN'S GREEN TO THE GRAND CANAL

▲ St Michan's Church

Take a tour of the spooky crypt and its mummified remains.

P.148 ▶ FROM CAPEL STREET TO COLLINS BARRACKS

▲ Irish Famine Memorial

Rowan Gillespie's stark bronze figures were commissioned to commemorate the 150th anniversary of the worst year of the Great Famine. More than a million people died between 1845 and 1849 and many others were forced to emigrate.

P.134 ▶ AROUND O'CONNELL STREET

Bars and clubs

Dublin has a multitude of stylish, modern bars, some featuring startlingly idiosyncratic decor, with the Quays and surrounding streets one of the best areas to head for. The club scene is thriving too, though reflecting popular tastes some of the mega-clubs have closed in recent years, and chic, smaller venues have sprung up in their stead. The streets west of Grafton Street, and Harcourt Street, south of St Stephen's Green, are the centres of the action.

▲ Sin É

The bar's name means "that's it" in Irish – enough said. If you're looking for a dark and seductive atmosphere, this is the place to go.

P.153 ▸ FROM CAPEL STREET TO COLLINS BARRACKS

▲ Gaiety Theatre

A weekend makeover sees this renowned theatre transformed into one of the city's largest clubs with plenty of DJs and a very late licence.

P.77 ▸ TRINITY COLLEGE, GRAFTON STREET AND AROUND

▲ 4 Dame Lane

Landmark braziers herald this stylish bar-club, which has DJs and late opening every night.

P.120 ▸ DUBLIN CASTLE AND AROUND

▲ Anséo

This unpretentious watering hole on Camden Street is Dublin's DJ bar of the moment.

P.93 ▸ ST STEPHEN'S GREEN TO THE GRAND CANAL

▲ Dice Bar

Don't be deterred by the dark and brooding interior – there's plenty of life here, and some great sounds.

P.152 ▸ FROM CAPEL STREET TO COLLINS BARRACKS

▼ Rí Rá

A vibrant and long-standing venue – Monday's "Strictly Handbag" is the night to hit.

P.93 ▸ DUBLIN CASTLE AND AROUND

Dublin churches

Dublin city is not in truth a magnet for connoisseurs of religious architecture. Though Christianity has had a strong presence here since the fifth century, when St Patrick baptized converts in a well near his present-day cathedral, the area's finest early Christian remnants are well to the south of the city at Glendalough. However, the compelling interest of Dublin's churches lies in the stories that the stones and artefacts tell, from the wildly oscillating fortunes of St Audoen's to the miraculous survival of Our Lady of Dublin.

▲ Whitefriar Street Carmelite Church

This Catholic church enshrines Our Lady of Dublin, one of the few pre-Reformation wooden statues to survive in Ireland, and the remains of St Valentine.

P.115 ▸ DUBLIN CASTLE AND AROUND

▲ Glendalough

The ninth-century cathedral is just one of several important remains on view at this monastic site, gloriously set against the backdrop of the Wicklow Mountains.

P.177 ▸ DAY TRIPS

▲ Christ Church Cathedral

Originally built in the twelfth century but substantially reconstructed in the nineteenth, with an interesting display of treasures in the huge crypt.

P.111 ▸ DUBLIN CASTLE AND AROUND

▲ St Audoen's

Dublin's longest-functioning parish church bears witness to the troubled history of the city and the Church of Ireland.

P.122 ▸ THE LIBERTIES AND KILMAINHAM

▼ St Mary's Pro-Cathedral

The renowned Palestrina Choir celebrates Latin Mass here every Sunday morning.

P.133 ▸ AROUND O'CONNELL STREET

▲ St Patrick's Cathedral

A quirky array of memorials adorn the national Anglican cathedral.

P.113 ▸ DUBLIN CASTLE AND AROUND

Pub snugs

Blissfully resisting the pressures of modernization and conformity, many Dublin pubs have kept their snugs. Partitioned off by carved wood and cut-glass screens, these havens often have a private hatch to the bar and are perfect for making and breaking confidences. The pubs described here are all congenial places to drink, even if you can't take up residence in their coveted snugs.

▲ The Octagon Bar

The stylish bar at *The Clarence* bathes in artificial daylight, from which you can hide, if you wish, in the secretive, pew-like, modern snug.

P.103 ▶ TEMPLE BAR

▲ Toners

Efficient service and one glass-partitioned booth by the bar at this Spartan, sociable pub.

P.94 ▶ ST STEPHEN'S GREEN TO
THE GRAND CANAL

▼ Kehoes

This former grocery-pub has a fine mahogany bar and plenty of cosy nooks and crannies.

P.76 ▶ TRINITY COLLEGE, GRAFTON STREET AND AROUND

▼ Doheny and Nesbitt

Atmospheric pub with a small, packed front bar, roomier back bar and two large snugs to choose from.

P.93 ▶ ST STEPHEN'S GREEN TO THE GRAND CANAL

▲ The Stag's Head

Ornate, stag-themed decor and good Guinness, but you'll have to come early to get a table in the large, dark snug.

P.121 ▶ DUBLIN CASTLE AND AROUND

Rebellious Dublin

Wherever you tread in Dublin you're bound to encounter some connection with Ireland's 700-year struggle for independence. Monuments recalling the past abound in the city: in statues, notably those of Daniel O'Connell and Charles Parnell on O'Connell Street; in buildings inextricably linked to key moments in the country's history, such as Dublin Castle and the General Post Office; and in memorials to those who fell during the process in Parnell Square and at the Croppy's Acre.

▲ Daniel O'Connell

A key figure in the struggle for Catholic Emancipation, O'Connell is celebrated in several notable Dublin monuments, including this one at City Hall.

P.109 ▸ DUBLIN CASTLE AND AROUND

▲ Robert Emmet

Romantic nationalist hero, hanged after the failed rebellion of 1803, who is remembered for his powerful speech from the dock.

P.127 ▸ THE LIBERTIES AND KILMAINHAM

▼ Kilmainham Gaol

The leaders of the Easter Rebellion were executed here – an event that, alongside many other incidents in Ireland's political history, is recounted in the Gaol museum's galleries.

P.126 ▸ THE LIBERTIES AND KILMAINHAM

▲ General Post Office

The locus of the 1916 Easter Rebellion, the GPO's portico still bears bullet marks.

P.131 ▸ AROUND O'CONNELL STREET

▲ Wolfe Tone

Leader of the unsuccessful French-supported Rebellion of 1798, who killed himself in prison and became the martyr figure for later revolutionary nationalism.

P.87 ▸ ST STEPHEN'S GREEN TO THE GRAND CANAL

Indulgent Dublin

It's easy to get through a lot of money during a stay in Dublin, one of Europe's most expensive cities. Some of the treats described here, however, won't break the bank – though you'll probably want to be on rock-star royalties to stay in The Clarence's penthouse. A growing number of the city's hotels open their spas to non-residents, with treatments and massages an optional extra.

▲ Horse and carriage ride

See the sights in style.

P.87 ▸ ST STEPHEN'S GREEN TO THE GRAND CANAL

▲ Tethra Spa at the Merrion Hotel

A luxurious escape offering wide-ranging treatments, a gym, a swimming pool decorated with murals of Neoclassical landscapes, and a marble steam room.

P.190 ▸ ACCOMMODATION

▲ Restaurant Patrick Gilbaud

A top-class French restaurant, using the best of seasonal Irish produce, with a good-value lunch time menu.

P.85 ▶ KILDARE STREET AND MERRION SQUARE

▼ The penthouse suite at The Clarence

The heights of indulgence . . . your own piano, outdoor hot tub and peerless views of the Liffey.

P.191 ▶ ACCOMMODATION

▲ Black Velvet

This champagne cocktail is a waste of good Guinness, some say. Enjoy it at *The Morrison* overlooking the river, or in any of the major hotel bars.

P.137 ▶ AROUND O'CONNELL STREET

Outdoor Dublin

With attractive public gardens, elegantly designed squares and the sprawling expanse of Phoenix Park, Dublin provides a wealth of green space, with plenty of opportunities for a stroll or an alfresco picnic. Outside the city, the shores of Dublin Bay offer bracing walks, while hardier souls might fancy a dip in the sea.

▲ The Forty Foot Pool

A popular bathing place, summer and winter – brace yourself.

P.162 ▸ THE SOUTHERN OUTSKIRTS

'AEOLUS - the offices of the Evening Telegraph (Ulysses, Episode 7)

▲ St Stephen's Green

Bang in the centre, the Green is great for people-watching and gives an outdoor history lesson through its fascinating monuments.

P.86 ▸ ST STEPHEN'S GREEN TO THE GRAND CANAL

▲ Walking Tours

Whether it involves treading in the footsteps of James Joyce and his characters or a historical guided tour such as "Rebellious Dublin", the city offers plenty of peripatetic pleasures.

P.203 ▸ ESSENTIALS

▲ North Bull Island

A stroll along the island and its three-mile beach, Dollymount Strand, will reveal a rich diversity of birds – especially in winter – and flowers.

P.170 ▸ THE NORTHERN OUTSKIRTS

▲ The Botanic Gardens

Exotic gardens, rockeries and arboreta to explore – and you can duck into the Victorian glasshouses if it rains.

P.166 ▸ THE NORTHERN OUTSKIRTS

▼ Phoenix Park

Europe's largest walled park, developed as a deer enclosure for Charles II, offers vast scope for investigation – visit the People's Garden, enjoy the zoo or take a tour of the magnificent grounds and mansion at Farmleigh.

P.154 ▸ PHOENIX PARK

Sporting Dublin

Sport is an integral part of Irish life and nowhere more so than in the capital. Gaelic football, hurling, soccer and rugby matches feature on pub TV screens and as a prominent part of daily conversation, and newspaper coverage seems boundless. There's also that well-known Irish fondness for a flutter, be it on the horses or the dogs.

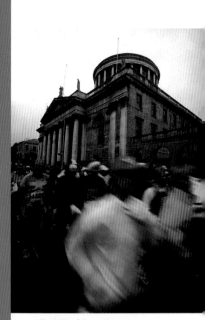

▲ Dublin Marathon
The event is Ireland's largest road-race and takes place every October.
P.208 ▸ ESSENTIALS

▲ Rugby at Donnybrook
Watch the best of Irish rugby as Leinster take on top European sides at the Donnybrook stadium.
P.206 ▸ ESSENTIALS

▲ Shelbourne Park

See the dogs in action and catch the trackside banter.

P.206 ▸ ESSENTIALS

▶ Croke Park

The national stadium for Gaelic games hosts several matches during the summer and the All-Ireland finals in September.

P.206 ▸ NORTH FROM PARNELL SQUARE

▼ Leopardstown races

Home of the Irish Gold Cup in February, the closest racetrack to the city is a great place to experience local passion for the horses.

P.206 ▸ ESSENTIALS

Gay and lesbian

Though attitudes to homosexuality have become more tolerant in recent years, Dublin's gay and lesbian scene remains relatively small – reflecting centuries of Catholic teaching and hardened attitudes – and is now almost entirely focused on a few Southside bars. *Outhouse* and *GCN* (see p.209) are the best sources of information.

▲ The George

Ireland's oldest and most popular gay bar offers plenty of entertainment, as well as a relaxed area for a quiet pint.

P.120 ▸ DUBLIN CASTLE AND AROUND

▲ Centre Stage Café

Small, easy-going, new venue, with suitably theatrical decor.

P.103 ▸ TEMPLE BAR

▼ The Front Lounge

This sophisticated and long-standing café-bar attracts an easy-going, mixed crowd.

P.103 ▸ TEMPLE BAR

▲ Dragon

Plush, vaguely Oriental reincarnation of a grand old bank, with a dance floor, booths and a large terrace.

P.120 ▸ DUBLIN CASTLE AND AROUND

Modern art and architecture

Though small, Dublin's modern-art scene is thriving, thanks to a range of exhibition spaces, both public and commercial. Major shows tend to focus upon international artists, though native Irish art is gaining increasing coverage. In architecture, recent trends have seen a shift away from a merely functional modernism and there's a graceful eloquence present in many new constructions, as well as a striking range of "street sculpture", the most impressive example being the Dublin Spire, also known as The Spike.

▲ The Spike

The Northside's premier landmark, Ian Ritchie's 120-metre needle catches the sunlight during the day and broods ominously at night.

P.130 ▶ AROUND O'CONNELL STREET

▲ The Gallery of Photography

It's always worth checking out the exhibits of Irish and international photo-works here.

P.98 ▶ TEMPLE BAR

▲ Irish Museum of Modern Art

IMMA displays a regularly changing selection of temporary exhibitions as well as those drawn from its own extensive collection of modern art from Ireland and beyond.

P.125 ▸ THE LIBERTIES AND KILMAINHAM

▼ The Francis Bacon studio

Though London-based, the painter Francis Bacon was Irish-born. Part of the Hugh Lane Gallery recreates his studio and displays a selection of striking paintings.

P.141 ▸ NORTH FROM PARNELL SQUARE

▲ The Douglas Hyde Gallery

An attractive and prestigious venue for contemporary art in Trinity College.

P.67 ▸ TRINITY COLLEGE, GRAFTON STREET AND AROUND

Shoppers' Dublin

Dublin boasts some excellent book and CD shops, the most notable of them specializing in Irish literature and music. Fashionistas are well catered for too, with plenty of boutiques, jewellery shops and department stores stocking the best of Irish and global design. On a fine day, consider heading for a food market or deli and picnicking in one of the city's attractive squares.

▲ Hodges Figgis

Behind this ornate facade lies the city's finest bookshop, particularly strong on Irish literature, history and culture.

P.71 ▸ TRINITY COLLEGE, GRAFTON STREET AND AROUND

▲ Temple Bar food market

Saturday finds Dublin's foodies shopping here, for everything from cheese to oysters, and it's well worth joining them to pick up a take-away lunch.

P.100 ▸ TEMPLE BAR

▼ Moore Street market

Browse among the stalls and shops at this eclectic, esoteric and, nowadays, fundamentally ethnic market.

P.135 ▸ AROUND O'CONNELL
STREET

▲ Avoca

Chic Irish clothes, woollen goods and gifts, with an excellent deli in the basement.

P.70 ▸ TRINITY COLLEGE,
GRAFTON STREET
AND AROUND

▲ Brown Thomas

BT's is the city's flagship department store, the place to go for anything from Irish designer labels to a haircut.

P.70 ▸ TRINITY COLLEGE,
GRAFTON STREET
AND AROUND

▼ Claddagh Records

The best traditional-music store in Dublin.

P.99 ▸ TEMPLE BAR

Children's Dublin

There's plenty in Dublin for kids to enjoy. As well as the attractions shown here, there's fun to be had exploring the great outdoors, with trips to Phoenix Park or the seaside. Most attractions and activities offer significant discounts to children.

▼ **The Ark**

Book your kids in for a performance or activity at this purpose-built cultural centre for children.

P.98 ▶ TEMPLE BAR

▲ Viking Splash

Amphibious vehicles take in the major sites by land before heading to the river in probably the city's most exciting tour.

P.203 ▸ ESSENTIALS

▼ Dublinia & The Viking World

A long roster of imaginative activities, especially in the summer, bring medieval and Viking Dublin to life.

P.112 ▸ DUBLIN CASTLE AND AROUND

▼ Lambert Puppet Theatre

High-quality puppet shows for kids throughout the year and performances for adults during the international festival in September.

P.205 ▸ ESSENTIALS

▼ Dublin zoo

As well as the chance to see animals as various as hippos and meerkats, Dublin's major child-friendly attraction features a City Farm specifically geared towards younger kids. The zoo's breeding programme offers the chance to see newborn arrivals.

P.154 ▸ PHOENIX PARK

Modern Irish cooking

Over the last fifteen years or so, the quality of local ingredients, often supplied by artisanal, organic producers, has been rediscovered in a way that has transformed Irish cooking. Irish meat has a justly famous reputation; excellent fish and all manner of seafood are freshly available; while the country's dairy produce and baking traditions are of the highest standards. The stress is on cooking techniques, whether based on traditional recipes or drawing on influences from around the world, that allow the ingredients to speak for themselves.

▲ Avoca Café

Top-flight, creative cooking, gracious service and reasonable prices at this bright and bustling café.

P.72 ▶ TRINITY COLLEGE,
GRAFTON STREET
AND AROUND

▲ Ely Wine Bar

An informal, good-value spot to sample excellent, carefully sourced food, some of it from the family farm in County Clare.

P.92 ▶ ST STEPHEN'S GREEN
TO THE GRAND CANAL

▼ Eden

Traditional Irish weather permitting, sit outside on Meeting House Square and tuck into West Cork scallops with potato and bacon salad.

P.101 ▶ TEMPLE BAR

▼ The Tea Room

Haute cuisine employing the best of Irish seasonal produce, in modernist surroundings.

P.102 ▶ TEMPLE BAR

▲ Chapter One

An acclaimed basement restaurant offering a delicious blend of Irish and French cuisines.

P.145 ▶ NORTH FROM PARNELL SQUARE

Dublin views

Dublin has few tall buildings, so the backdrop of the Wicklow Mountains to the south is often visible from the city centre. And, if you do get up high, there aren't many obstructions to your bird's-eye view, which is often bisected by the River Liffey and its diverse bridges. The city's location at the centre of the magnificent sweep of Dublin Bay is undervalued, but can be fully appreciated by a journey on the DART, particularly to the south of the centre.

▲ O'Connell Bridge

The bridge provides one of the city's most expansive views, whether it's looking east towards the Custom House and the developing docklands, west along the Quays to the Four Courts, north up bustling O'Connell Street or south towards Trinity College – a great place to get your bearings.

P.129 ▶ AROUND O'CONNELL STREET

▲ Powerscourt

The pleasing geometry of the formal gardens, with their fine statues and fountain lake, is echoed in the neat triangular backdrop of Sugarloaf Mountain.

P.176 ▶ DAY TRIPS

▲ Smithfield Observation Chimney

The heart of the city captured in miniature, with stunning views looking east to Dublin Bay.

P.150 ▶ FROM CAPEL STREET TO COLLINS BARRACKS

▼ The Guinness Storehouse

Sup your pint of the black stuff at the top of the seven-storey Guinness Storehouse tower and survey the panoramic vista of the city.

P.124 ▶ THE LIBERTIES AND KILMAINHAM

▲ Dalkey and Killiney hills

An easy walk between DART stations, offering glorious views of Killiney Bay, the Wicklow Mountains and the city.

P.164 ▶ THE SOUTHERN OUTSKIRTS

Dublin cafés

The Irish drink even more tea per head than the English, so it's not surprising that Dublin has long had a thriving café society – strongly supported by the widespread temperance movement and the churches. Nowadays you're almost as likely to find baklava as brack (a delicious traditional Irish sweet bread with spices and dried fruits), accompanied by a delicate speciality tea or a frothy cappuccino.

▲ Caffe Cagliostro

This tiny Italian café serves up splendid coffee and delicious pastries with outside tables for watching the world pass by.

P.135 ▶ AROUND O'CONNELL STREET

▼ Silk Road Café

The stylish café in the Chester Beatty Library serves mostly Middle Eastern food, from delicious moussaka and falafel to filo pies and baklava.

P.177 ▸ DUBLIN CASTLE AND AROUND

▲ Queen of Tarts

A mouthwatering display of cakes, tarts and all things yummy.

P.40 ▸ TEMPLE BAR

▼ The Merrion Hotel

The drawing rooms here are the place to come for sumptuous afternoon tea, sitting beneath a fine collection of Irish art, overlooking impressive gardens.

P.190 ▸ ACCOMMODATION

▲ La Maison des Gourmets

Excellent traditional French patisserie with an elegant and airy salon de thé on the first floor.

P.73 ▸ TRINITY COLLEGE, GRAFTON STREET AND AROUND

Theatre and film

Lovers of the theatre are spoilt for choice in Dublin where, alongside Irish classics and newer works by dramatists such as Brian Friel, numerous smaller theatres and arts centres offer more experimental productions. There are also major festivals in September and October (see p.207). Film fans are also well catered for in numerous mainstream cinemas as well as a major centre for independent releases. An international film festival is held in February, and the lesbian and gay-focused GAZE in August (see p.207).

TICKETS

▲ Abbey Theatre

Ireland's most renowned theatre offers a varied programme of classic and contemporary drama.

P.132 › AROUND O'CONNELL STREET

▲ The Helix

Operating at the populist end of the spectrum, this modern theatre offers everything from musicals and ice shows to rock bands and ballet.

P.172 ▸ THE NORTHERN OUTSKIRTS

▼ Gate Theatre

The Abbey's main rival also stages striking theatrical productions of European drama.

P.139 ▸ NORTH FROM PARNELL SQUARE

▲ Project Arts Centre

Originating as an arts project in the foyer of the Gate Theatre, the flagship of the contemporary arts scene hosts experimental theatre, film, music and dance.

P.98 ▸ TEMPLE BAR

▲ Irish Film Institute

Dublin's best cinema, showing the pick of releases from around the world, and a busy social hub.

P.98 ▸ TEMPLE BAR

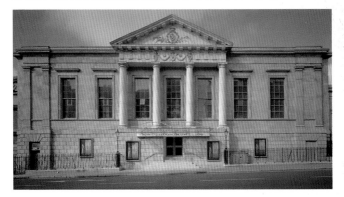

Festivals

Dublin stages numerous festivals during the year. The arts are particularly well catered for, with major events devoted to theatre, film, music and literature an established part of the calendar. There's plenty for children to enjoy as well, such as the St Patrick's festival and numerous events in Temple Bar.

▲ St Patrick's Day

Five days of fun and frolics around March 17, featuring a parade on the day itself and a *céilí mór* day of traditional dancing.

P.206 ▸ ESSENTIALS

▼ Docklands Maritime Festival

Tall ships visit Dublin and there's lots of quayside enjoyment too, such as a street market and plenty of events for children.

P.207 ▸ ESSENTIALS

▼ Summer events in Temple Bar

"Diversions" is Temple Bar's summer series of free events, and includes outdoor film shows and live music.

P.207 ▸ ESSENTIALS

▲ Dún Laoghaire Festival of World Cultures

A packed programme of international events spread across the last weekend in August brings new dimensions to the seaside town.

P.207 ▸ ESSENTIALS

▼ Dublin Horse Show

This five-day show-jumping event in August features top international stars.

P.207 ▸ ESSENTIALS

Free Dublin

Though Dublin is an expensive city, there are plenty of free attractions that won't burden your pocket or purse. Some major sites, such as the National Gallery (see p.81) and National Museum (see p.79), charge no entrance fee except for special events. There's also plenty of street and outdoor entertainment, especially in summer.

▲ The House of Lords

It's well worth coming on a Tuesday for the free guided tour, to learn the fate of the eighteenth-century Irish Parliament, now a bank.

P.68 ▶ TRINITY COLLEGE, GRAFTON STREET AND AROUND

▲ Smithfield horse sales

Smithfield has been hosting a horse fair for more than three hundred years. Catch it on the first Sunday of the month, spot a bargain and sample the *craic*.

P.149 ▶ FROM CAPEL STREET TO COLLINS BARRACKS

▼ Collins Barracks

Home to the National Gallery's collection of decorative arts, Collins Barracks offers plenty to enthral and entertain.

P.151 ▶ FROM CAPEL STREET TO COLLINS BARRACKS

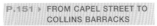

▼ The National Library

Richly endowed literary exhibitions and a stately and historic reading room.

P.80 ▶ KILDARE STREET AND MERRION SQUARE

▲ Farmleigh

This splendid conservatory features amongst the delights of Farmleigh mansion, one of the city's most sumptuous buildings.

P.157 ▶ PHOENIX PARK

▲ Grafton Street buskers

You're as likely to come across a man with a *bodhrán* as a string quartet, and it's all free – apart from a penny or two in the hat, perhaps.

P.68 ▶ TRINITY COLLEGE, GRAFTON STREET AND AROUND

Places

Trinity College, Grafton Street and around

Like a walled village of scholars, Trinity College takes up a surprisingly large tract of Dublin's city centre. Visitors are free to stroll through its tranquil quads and parkland, though its overarching draw is the glorious Book of Kells. Opposite, near the site of the flat-topped mound that was Dublin's Viking assembly, sits the poignant former House of Parliament, now a particularly ornate branch of the Bank of Ireland. Just a stone's throw from these august institutions, the city's most frenetic commercial street, Grafton Street, marches off towards St Stephen's Green. Here and in the surrounding streets, you'll find Dublin's most stylish shops and boutiques, notably in the elegantly converted Georgian mansion of Powerscourt Townhouse shopping centre. With the city's best concentration of traditional pubs, as well as a wide variety of fine cafés and restaurants, the area's only marginally less lively by night.

College Green

Open fields beyond the city walls when Trinity College was founded, College Green is today one of Dublin's most frantic junctions. Hemmed in by Trinity's grandiose west front and the curving facade of the Bank of Ireland, cars and pedestrians flow past a fine array of monumental **statues**, mostly depicting old boys of the college: from the eighteenth century, philosopher and politician Edmund Burke and writer Oliver Goldsmith stand on either side of the college's main entrance; politician Henry Grattan (1746–1820) by the bank; and, in the thick of the traffic at the top of Dame Street, nineteenth-century

▼ EDMUND BURKE

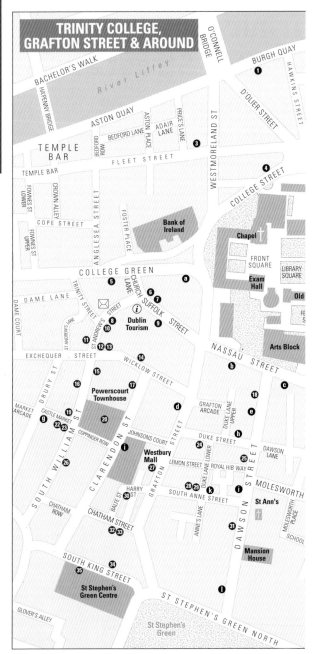

TRINITY COLLEGE, GRAFTON STREET & AROUND

PLACES

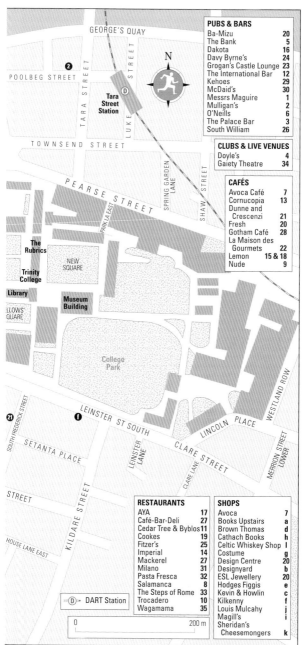

GEORGE'S QUAY

POOLBEG STREET

TARA STREET
LUKE STREET
Tara Street Station

N

TOWNSEND STREET

SPRING GARDEN LANE
SHAW STREET

PEARSE STREET

PARK LA EAST

The Rubrics

NEW SQUARE

Trinity College

Library

LLOWS' QUARE

Museum Building

College Park

WESTLAND ROW

LEINSTER ST SOUTH

LINCOLN PLACE

SOUTH FREDERICK STREET

SETANTA PLACE

LEINSTER LANE

CLARE STREET

CLARE LANE

MERRION STREET LOWER

STREET

KILDARE STREET

HOUSE LANE EAST

PUBS & BARS	
Ba-Mizu	20
The Bank	5
Dakota	16
Davy Byrne's	24
Grogan's Castle Lounge	23
The International Bar	12
Kehoes	29
McDaid's	30
Messrs Maguire	1
Mulligan's	2
O'Neills	6
The Palace Bar	3
South William	26

CLUBS & LIVE VENUES	
Doyle's	4
Gaiety Theatre	34

CAFÉS	
Avoca Café	7
Cornucopia	13
Dunne and Crescenzi	21
Fresh	20
Gotham Café	28
La Maison des Gourmets	22
Lemon	15 & 18
Nude	9

RESTAURANTS	
AYA	17
Café-Bar-Deli	27
Cedar Tree & Byblos	11
Cookes	19
Fitzer's	25
Imperial	14
Mackerel	27
Milano	31
Pasta Fresca	32
Salamanca	8
The Steps of Rome	33
Trocadero	10
Wagamama	35

SHOPS	
Avoca	7
Books Upstairs	a
Brown Thomas	d
Cathach Books	h
Celtic Whiskey Shop	l
Costume	g
Design Centre	20
Designyard	b
ESL Jewellery	20
Hodges Figgis	e
Kevin & Howlin	c
Kilkenny	f
Louis Mulcahy	j
Magill's	i
Sheridan's Cheesemongers	k

═Ⓓ═ DART Station

0 ────── 200 m

nationalist and poet Thomas Davis, who penned some of the most popular Irish ballads. Among these was *A Nation Once Again*, which explains the nickname of the fountain in front of him, depicting the heralds of the four provinces of Ireland: "Urination Once Again". Much of the pedestrian traffic heads towards the college entrance between Burke and Goldsmith, the most popular meeting place in the city.

Trinity College

ⓦ www.tcd.ie. Free access to visitors. Walking tours from the main gate led by Trinity students mid-May to Sept Mon–Sat 9 daily, Sun 7 daily; 30min; €5, or €10 including admission to the Old Library. An imposing architectural set piece at the heart of the city, Trinity College was founded in 1592 by Queen Elizabeth I to prevent the Irish from being "infected with popery and other ill qualities" at French, Spanish and Italian universities. Catholics were duly admitted until 1637 when restrictions

were imposed that lasted until the Catholic Relief Act of 1793. The Catholic Church, however, banned its flock from studying here until 1970 because of the college's Anglican orientation; today, seventy percent of the students are Catholic. Famous alumni range from politicians Edward Carson and Douglas Hyde, through to philosopher George Berkeley and Nobel-prizewinning physicist Ernest Walton, to writers such as Swift, Wilde and Beckett.

The appealing eighteenth-century symmetry of **Front Square**, flanked by the Chapel and the Examination Hall, gives onto Library Square, which features the oldest surviving building, the Rubrics, a red-brick student dormitory dating from around 1701. In New Square beyond, the School of Engineering occupies the old **Museum Building** (1852), designed in extravagant Venetian Gothic style by Benjamin Woodward under the influence of his friend, John Ruskin, and awash with decorative stone-carving of animals and floral patterns.

The Old Library and the Book of Kells

May–Sept Mon–Sat 9.30am–5pm, Sun 9.30am–4.30pm; Oct–April Mon–Sat 9.30am–5pm, Sun noon–4.30pm (closed for 10 days over Christmas and New Year); €8. Trinity's most compelling tourist attraction – sometimes with half-hour queues from June to August – is the **Book of Kells**, kept in the eighteenth-century Old Library, which is entered from Fellows' Square. As well as the *Book of Kells*, beautiful pages of illuminated manuscripts such as the *Book of Armagh* (both early ninth century) and the *Book of*

▼ CAMPANILE, TRINITY COLLEGE

Mulling (late eighth century) are on display, preceded by the fascinating exhibition "Turning Darkness into Light", which sets Irish illuminated manuscripts in context – ranging from ogham (the earlier, Celtic writing system of lines carved on standing stones) to Ethiopian books of devotions.

Upstairs is the library's magnificent, barrel-vaulted **Long Room**. As a copyright library, Trinity has had the right to claim a free copy of all British and Irish publications since 1801; of its current stock of three million titles, 200,000 of the oldest are stored in the Long Room's oak bookcases. Besides interesting temporary exhibitions of books and prints from the library's collection, the 65-metre Long Room also displays a gnarled fifteenth-century **harp**, the oldest to survive from Ireland, and an extremely rare original printing of the 1916 Proclamation of the Irish Republic, made on Easter Sunday in Liberty Hall.

▲ LONG ROOM, OLD LIBRARY

The Douglas Hyde Gallery

☏ 01/896 1116, ⊛ www.douglashydegallery.com. Mon–Wed & Fri 11am–6pm, Thurs 11am–7pm, Sat 11am–4.45pm; free. Guided tours of the current exhibitions Tues 1.15pm & Sat 2pm; free. In the 1970s Arts Block opposite the Old Library on Fellows' Square, right by the college's Nassau St entrance, the Douglas Hyde is one of Ireland's most important galleries of modern art. Named after Ireland's first president, it hosts top-notch temporary shows by innovative Irish and international artists working in a variety of media.

The Bank of Ireland

College Green. Mon, Tues & Fri 10am–4pm, Wed 10.30am–4pm, Thurs 10am–5pm; guided tours Tues 10.30am, 11.30am & 1.45pm; free. Opposite Trinity, the Neoclassical, granite Bank of Ireland was built in 1729 by Sir Edward Pearce – himself an MP – as the **House of Parliament**.

The Book of Kells

Pre-eminent for the scale, variety and colour of its decoration, the **Book of Kells** probably originated at the monastery on Iona off the west coast of Scotland, which was founded around 561 by the great Irish scholar, bard and ruler St Colum Cille (St Colmcille in English). After a Viking raid in 806, the Columbines moved to the monastery of Kells in County Meath, and around 1653, the manuscript was moved to Dublin for safekeeping during the Cromwellian Wars. The 340 calfskin folios of the *Book of Kells* contain the four New Testament gospels along with preliminary texts, all in Latin. It's thought that three artists created the book's lavish decoration, which shows Pictish, Germanic and Mediterranean, as well as Celtic influences.

▲ HOUSE OF LORDS

An Irish parliament had existed in one limited form or another since the thirteenth century, but achieved its greatest flowering here in 1782 – "Grattan's Parliament" after the prime mover behind the constitutional reform – when it was granted legislative independence from the British Parliament. Catholics were still barred from sitting, but many signs of sovereignty were established during this period, including the foundation of the Bank of Ireland; around this time, the Lords deemed it necessary to build themselves a separate entrance on Westmoreland Street, designed by James Gandon in 1785 in the Corinthian style, to distinguish it from the Ionic colonnade of what is still the main entrance. After the rebellion of 1798, however, the Irish House was persuaded and bribed to vote itself out of existence, and with the 1801 Act of Union, Ireland became part of the United Kingdom, governed from Westminster. The Bank of Ireland bought the building for £40,000 in 1802, and the Commons chamber was demolished to remove

a highly charged symbol of independence.

The barrel-vaulted **House of Lords** was also meant to be knocked down, but survives to this day to host high-level state functions and as the main attraction for visitors. Here you'll find one or two exhibits such as the Lord Chancellor's richly embroidered purse, used to carry the Great Seal of Ireland, and tapestries showing William of Orange's victories over James II and his Catholic supporters, the *Siege of Derry* and the *Battle of the Boyne*. It's also planned to put the mace used in the former House of Commons on display here. Sold on by the descendants of the last Speaker, the mace was bought at Christie's of London by the bank in 1937 for £3100.

The richly stuccoed **Cash Hall** – an elegant spot to do any banking chores you may have – used to be the Parliament's Hall of Requests, where constituents would petition their representatives.

Grafton Street

Running south from College Green to St Stephen's Green,

▼ GRAFTON STREET

pedestrianized Grafton Street starts inauspiciously with "the tart with the cart", a gaggingly kitsch bronze, complete with wheelbarrow of cockles and mussels, of eighteenth-century street trader Molly Malone. For those who hate shopping and crowds, Grafton Street won't get any better; for people-watchers, however, it's a must, noted especially for its **buskers**, who range from string quartets to street poets.

The street's major landmark, **Bewley's Oriental Café**, owes its beautiful mosaic facade to the mania for all things Egyptian that followed the discovery of Tutenkhamun's tomb in 1922. Founded by the Quaker Bewley family as a teetotal bulwark against the demon drink, this famous Dublin institution was forced to close down in 2004 in the face of escalating ground rents that have made Grafton Street one of the world's five most expensive shopping streets on which to trade. Fortunately, the ornate premises have since reopened, incorporating a much-reduced *Bewley's Café*, a branch of *Café-Bar-Deli* (see p.73) and a seafood restaurant, *Mackerel* (see p.74).

Powerscourt Townhouse

Guided tours Sat 11am–1pm & 2–5pm; free. Powerscourt Townhouse is a stylish shopping centre that incorporates the eighteenth-century Palladian mansion of Lord Powerscourt (see p.176). The house's main door, on South William Street, gives straight onto the trompe l'oeil stone floor of the entrance hall and, beyond, the central mahogany staircase, with its flighty rococo plasterwork by James McCullagh and what are thought to be the most elaborately carved balusters

▲ ATRIUM, POWERSCOURT TOWNHOUSE

in Ireland. More geometrical, Neoclassical work by the house's other stuccodore, Michael Stapleton, can be seen in two commercial outlets upstairs, the Solomon Gallery and The Town Bride.

The **café-bar** in the atrium is notable for its location – bathed in light on sunny days – in what was once the mansion's inner courtyard.

Dawson Street

Dawson Street's busy thoroughfare accommodates the city's main bookshops and several other interesting speciality shops, as well as an utterly forgettable row of over-designed "superpubs". It's also flanked by the **Mansion House**, built in 1705 and embellished with a stucco facade and civic coat-of-arms in Victorian times, which has been the residence of Dublin's Lord Mayor since 1715 (not open to the public).

St Ann's Church

Dawson St ☎01/676 7727. Mon–Fri 10am–4pm. The lopsided

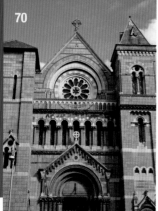

▲ ST ANN'S CHURCH

Romanesque-style facade of St Ann's Church is a curious Victorian landmark at the end of South Anne Street. Its plain, dimly-lit, balconied **interior**, however, is typical of the early eighteenth century. Here, each week, 120 loaves of bread are laid out on shelves behind the altar, according to a bequest for the poor of the city which has persisted since 1723. Parishioners have included the art collector Sir Hugh Lane and Thomas Barnardo, founder of the eponymous children's homes, while Wolfe Tone (1785) and Bram Stoker (1878) were both married here. A **stained-glass window** in the chancel commemorates Felicia Hemans, of 21 Dawson St, who penned "The boy stood on the burning deck" in her poem *Casabianca* of 1828.

It's worth calling for details of the lunchtime and evening concerts of classical music given at St Ann's.

Shopping

Avoca

11 Suffolk St ☎01/677 4215, ⓦwww .avoca.ie. Highly successful small Irish department store, stocking its own clothing ranges for women and children, jewellery, beautiful rugs and throws woven at the original mill in Avoca, Co. Wicklow, plus toys and chic houseware – plenty of potential gifts. There's a splendid deli in the basement, and an equally delightful café on the second floor (see p.72).

Books Upstairs

36 College Green ☎01/679 6687. Particularly strong on Irish literature, literary criticism and biography, as well as many works of general Irish interest. Also a good range of periodicals and gay and lesbian literature, and plenty of discounted books.

Brown Thomas

88–95 Grafton St ☎01/605 6666, ⓦwww.brownthomas.com. The city's flagship department store, Brown Thomas is sophisticated and pricey, featuring a long roll-call of Irish and international designer labels, and complemented by its trendier younger sibling, BT2, opposite.

Cathach Books

10 Duke St ☎01/671 8676, ⓦwww .rarebooks.ie. Closed Sun. The place to come for first editions by Irish writers, rare Irish maps and prints of literary interest.

Celtic Whiskey Shop

27–28 Dawson St ☎01/675 9744, ⓦwww.celticwhiskeyshop.com. Probably the best selection of Irish whiskeys anywhere, including some rare examples from distilleries that have now closed down and familiar names at reasonable prices. The well-informed staff always have bottles open to taste and will ship around the world.

Costume

10 Castle Market ☏01/679 4188. Stylish, upmarket boutique, selling everything from jumpers and coats to evening dresses, by less familiar international designers and its own label.

Design Centre

Top floor, Powerscourt Townhouse Centre ☏01/679 5863, ⓦwww .designcentre.ie. An extensive showcase for Irish designers of women's fashion, such as Louise Kennedy and John Rocha, as well as diverse clothes and accessories by international names.

Designyard

48–9 Nassau St, ⓦwww.designyard .ie. At the time of writing, this Temple Bar stalwart was about to move into new, four-storey premises opposite Trinity. On offer will be the familiar mix of jewellery, vases, sculpture and objets d'art by contemporary, mostly Irish, craft designers.

ESL Jewellery

First floor, Powerscourt Townhouse Centre ☏01/679 1603. Closed Sun. Attractive modern jewellery, much of it made in-house – the plain gold and silver bangles and earrings are particularly striking. Specially commissioned work undertaken.

Hodges Figgis

56–58 Dawson St ☏01/677 4754. A Dublin institution since the eighteenth century, behind an ornate, multi-storeyed Dutch-style facade. Books on Ireland are on the ground floor, with everything covered – from fiction and history to language and travel. Book bargains can be found in the basement.

Kevin & Howlin

31 Nassau St ☏01/677 0257, ⓦwww .kevinandhowlin.com. Closed Sun. Nothing but Donegal tweed, with off-the-peg jackets and suits for men and women – allow about seven weeks for tailor-made – as well as the ubiquitous caps and hats.

Kilkenny

6 Nassau St ☏01/677 7066. A varied collection of fine Irish crafts: Newbridge silver cutlery and jewellery; John Rocha's elegant collection for Waterford Crystal; Jerpoint glassware; and extensive ranges of ceramics and of women's clothes and accessories by contemporary designers.

Louis Mulcahy

46 Dawson St ☏01/670 9311, ⓦwww.louismulcahy.com. Closed Sun. Beautiful household objects, including vases, lights, crockery and even washbasins, by one of Ireland's most famous potters, plus a small selection of scarves and other woollen items.

Magill's

Clarendon St, next to Westbury Mall. Closed Sun. The helpful staff at this traditional deli have all you need to compile a fine picnic: County Mayo smoked salmon, a good selection of Irish cheeses,

▼ LOUIS MULCAHY

▲ MAGILL'S

tubs of *antipasti*, tempting breads and all manner of specialities from around the world.

Sheridan's Cheesemongers

11 South Anne St ☎ 01/679 3143, ⓦ www.sheridanscheesemongers .com. Closed Sun. Fantastic, pungent array of cheeses, mostly by Irish artisan producers, plus cold meats and other deli goods, sold by knowledgeable staff.

Cafés

Avoca Café

11 Suffolk St. On the top floor of this department store (see p.70), the bright, buzzy café is thronged at lunchtimes. Out of the open kitchen comes everything from shepherd's pie to potted crabmeat with watercress and potato salad, as well as a tempting array of desserts and cakes, and a fine choice of wines and soft drinks (notably homemade lemonade), all beautifully presented and courteously served.

Cornucopia

19–21 Wicklow St. Mon–Wed, Fri & Sat 8.30am–8pm, Thurs 8.30am–9pm, Sun noon–7pm. A small, friendly buffet café that's been popular with veggies for many years. On a menu which changes daily and is labelled for special diets, there's an excellent range of breakfasts, salads, soups and main courses such as Thai curry, as well as cakes, breads, juices and organic wine.

Dunne and Crescenzi

14–16 South Frederick St. Mon–Sat 8.30am–11pm, Sun 10am–9pm. A cosy Italian café, deli and wine shop, with croissants and spot-on coffee for breakfast, and, for the rest of the day, all manner of Italian sandwiches and excellent plates of *antipasti*, as well as salads and half a dozen daily special main courses. Packed at lunchtime, with the outside tables at a particular premium in summer.

Fresh

Second floor, Powerscourt Townhouse Centre. Closed Sun. A great setting, overlooking the shopping centre's glassed-in Georgian courtyard, and a marvellous vegetarian and vegan menu, using organic ingredients wherever possible: soups, salads, sandwiches, pasta, veggie tarts, curries and hotpots; various breads, cakes and desserts; and wines, juices and smoothies.

Gotham Café

5 South Anne St. Open daytime & evening. This lively café, with outside tables on a quiet lane just off Grafton Street, does a reasonably priced global menu that includes great pizzas and salads, and dishes such as Louisiana crab cakes and Thai vegetable curry.

La Maison des Gourmets

15 Castle Market. Closed Sun. Chic *salon de thé* above a French patisserie. Perch on the high beige banquettes to tuck into light meals such as smoked salmon and chive cream *tartine* – which will leave just enough room for a delicious cake and coffee.

Lemon

South William St (Mon–Fri 8am–7.30pm, Sat 9am–7.30pm, Sun 10am–6.30pm) & Dawson St (Mon–Wed, Fri & Sat 8am–7.30pm, Thurs 8am–9pm, Sun 8am–6.30pm). Hyperactive modern cafés that dish up great coffee and a huge range of very good, inexpensive savoury and sweet crêpes, to eat in or take away – try the delicious banana maple delight with almonds. The Dawson St branch has more room to breathe than the cramped affair on South William St, but both have heated outdoor tables.

Nude

21 Suffolk St. Mon–Wed 7.30am–9pm, Thurs & Fri 7.30am–midnight, Sat 8am–midnight, Sun 10am–8pm. Funky, canteen-style café with a big open kitchen, serving up hot and cold wraps, panini, salads, pasta, noodles, soups and some weird and wonderful juices and smoothies, to eat in or take away. Organic ingredients are used wherever possible, and there is ample choice for vegetarians.

Restaurants

AYA

48 Clarendon St ☎01/677 1544, ⓦ www.aya.ie. Just behind Brown Thomas department store, the focus here is Dublin's first conveyor-belt sushi bar. There are regular tables, too, for more substantial and expensive Japanese dishes.

Café-Bar-Deli

Grafton St ⓦ www.cafebardeli.ie. A branch of the South Great George's St restaurant (see p.118), employing the same highly successful formula, now occupies part of *Bewley's* old flagship café where, on the ground floor, you can still admire Harry Clarke's *Birds of Paradise* stained-glass windows.

▼ DUNNE AND CRESCENZI

Dunne & Crescenzi

Italian wine & fine food in Dub

Trinity College, Grafton Street and around

▲ TROCADERO

Cedar Tree and Byblos

11 St Andrew's St ☎01/677 2121.
Byblos closed Sun lunchtime,
Cedar Tree open evenings only. In
a lively cellar opposite the
landmark *International Bar*,
the welcoming *Cedar Tree* offers
a delicious and reasonably
priced array of Lebanese meat,
seafood and vegetarian meze
dishes – all the more tempting if
you can get here before 7.30pm
for the early-bird menu. Its
upstairs branch, *Byblos*, serves
up similar but simpler and
cheaper fare.

Cookes

14 South William St ☎01/679 0536.
Chic restaurant with very
good service, where echoing
tiled floors and large windows
facing Powerscourt Townhouse
magnify the buzz. There are
plenty of delicious salads to
start you off, while seafood
features heavily on the main-
course menu, though you'll also
find appealing pasta options
and meaty fare such as roast

partridge with chestnuts and
celeriac purée. Reasonably
priced set lunch and early-bird
menus.

Fitzer's

51 Dawson St ☎01/677 1155,
ⓦwww.fitzers.ie. Part of a reliable
chain of moderately priced
restaurants, offering tempting
standards such as Wicklow lamb
shank and cod with lemon
butter sauce, as well as several
daily specials, plenty of choices
for vegetarians and a cheap
early-bird menu. This branch is
adorned with colourful modern
art, chandeliers and high leather
banquettes, and there are heated
outside tables too.

Imperial

12A Wicklow St ☎01/677 2580. A
thumbs-up from loyal Chinese
customers, who generally rate
it the best restaurant in the
city centre. Specialities include
butterfly prawns with orange
sauce and steamed sea bass
with spring onions and ginger,
among a wide array of seafood.
Excellent dim sum, served
daily until 5.30pm, is especially
popular on Sundays.

Mackerel

Grafton St ☎01/672 7719, ⓦwww
.mackerel.ie. This contemporary
fish restaurant in a bright,
elegant, chandeliered room on
the first floor of the former
Bewley's café is a welcome
addition to the Dublin culinary
scene. Service can be a little
hurried, but the food more than
makes up for it: all manner of
fruits of the sea to start with,
followed by a daily-changing
menu of imaginative and
well-executed fish dishes, such
as seared tuna with chilli and
mango salsa.

Milano

38 Dawson St ☎01/670 7744.
Branch of the long-established
pizza chain (see p.102).

Pasta Fresca

3 Chatham St ☎01/679 2402. Large,
informal, warmly decorated
restaurant with a few tables and
chairs outside, and a good-value
array of varied *antipasti*, fresh
pasta, grills, salads, pizzas and
daily specials. Inexpensive set
menus pre- and post-theatre,
and at lunchtime Mon–Fri.

Salamanca

1 St Andrew's St ☎01/677 4799.
A huge range of good-value
tapas – try the very tasty
and substantial house paella
– enhanced by friendly
service, soft lighting and warm,
simple decor.

The Steps of Rome

1 Chatham Court, Chatham St
☎01/670 5630. Tiny, basic
restaurant, serving very cheap
and excellent pizza, alongside
variations such as *calzone*, as
well as pasta, salads and a few
meat dishes. If you can't get a
table, there's pizza by the slice to
take away.

Trocadero

3 St Andrew's St ☎01/677 5545,
🖳www.trocadero.ie. Evenings only,
closed Sun. A welcoming haven,
done out with plush booths,
signed photos of showbiz visitors
and yards of red velvet. Excellent,
though predictable, international
food, whether à la carte or on
the reasonably priced set menus,
which include a good-value
pre-theatre option (you need to
vacate the table by 7.45pm).

Wagamama

South King St ☎01/478 2152.
Basement branch of the

well-known, good-value chain,
with an open kitchen knocking
out healthy Japanese meat and
vegetarian dishes to punters
sharing long bench tables. Best
for noodle soups, dumplings and
a wide variety of wholesome
juices; takeaway service available.

Pubs and bars

Ba-Mizu

Powerscourt Townhouse Centre.
Large, low-lit modern bar with
comfy leather furniture in the
vaulted stone cellars of Lord
Powerscourt's former mansion.
There's a lengthy cocktail list, a
popular food menu, featuring
dishes such as asparagus and
goat's cheese risotto, and outdoor
tables on South William Street.

The Bank

College Green. Behind its
distinctive Scottish sandstone
facade, the former Belfast Bank
has been sensitively converted
in all its Victorian splendour
in to one of Dublin's most
luxurious bars: mosaic floors,
stained glass ceiling, beautiful
plaster rosettes and porphyry
columns, all best admired from
the projecting mezzanine. More
prosaic sustenance is provided
by a good selection of beers,
wines and cocktails, as well as
salads, sandwiches and main
meals, but who needs the latest
stock market prices flashed
above the bar?

Dakota

9 South William St. Thurs till 2am, Fri &
Sat till 2.30am. A stylish conversion,
in chocolate and brick, of a
fabric warehouse. Table service
at the dark leather booths and
armchairs aims to pull in a late-
twenties and early-thirties crowd,
who duly cram the place at

▲ DAKOTA

weekends. There's a wide array of food, including sharing plates of nibbles to soak up the drink.

Davy Byrne's

21 Duke St. After extensive redecoration as a lounge bar, in a mix of Art Deco and other vaguely modernist styles, you'll have your work cut out to imagine Davy Byrne's "moral pub", where Bloom takes a break for a Gorgonzola sandwich and a glass of Burgundy in *Ulysses*. All the same, it's a good place for a quiet drink and perhaps a plate of oysters, a sandwich, a salad or a plate of shepherd's pie.

Grogan's Castle Lounge

15 South William St. Lively, eccentric traditional pub with quiet outdoor tables, where works for sale by local artists hang on the walls, and budding writers and artists take colourful inspiration from the stained-glass

memorial to famous *Grogan's* regulars.

The International Bar

23 Wicklow St ☎01/677 9250. Sociable, sometimes rowdy, old-fashioned pub that heaves congenially at weekends. The ground floor with its stained glass and ornate woodcarving is particularly sought after, so you may have better luck finding space in the basement bar. Just about every evening sees some form of entertainment on offer: comedy on Mon (improv) and Wed–Sun, singer-songwriters on Mon and jazz most Tuesdays.

Kehoes

9 South Anne St. Characterful meeting place, where Dubliners tend to settle in if they can get a seat, especially in either of the cosy snugs. The low mahogany bar, with its old-fashioned till and drawers, used to double up as a grocery, while upstairs, where the last resident publicans in the city centre formerly lived, still feels like a comfortable sitting room.

McDaid's

3 Harry St. This literary landmark was the home-from-home of novelist and dramatist Brendan Behan, who would spend his days drinking, entertaining, sleeping it off and drinking again here. Despite now selling its own T-shirts, the bright, high-ceilinged pub is still popular with locals, with pleasant overspill seating upstairs for when the crush gets too mighty.

Messrs Maguire

1–2 Burgh Quay. Mon, Tues & Sun till midnight, Wed till 1am, Thurs till 2am, Fri till 2.30am, Sat till 3am. Though not quite as classy as the *Porterhouse* (see p.103), this microbrewery pub overlooking the river, with countless floors and mezzanines off a grand, winding staircase, is well worth trying out. There's a basic food menu featuring dishes such as bangers and mash.

Mulligan's

8 Poolbeg St. A little off the beaten track, this large, no-nonsense pub remains a favoured watering hole for journalists and workers at the nearby *Irish Times*. Vies with *Ryan's* (see p.158) and of course *The Gravity Bar* (see p.125) as home of the best pint in Dublin.

O'Neill's

2 Suffolk St. Huge, disorientating old pub, adorned with acres of oak panelling and green leather, where, despite the throngs of Trinity students, you should be able to find yourself a quiet corner. Renowned for its long and varied food menu, including an all-day carvery.

▼ THE INTERNATIONAL BAR

The Palace Bar

21 Fleet St. Relaxing, sociable Victorian pub famed both for the quality of its pint and for its handsome decor of mirrored screens and ornate woodcarving. The overflow bar upstairs hosts sessions of traditional music on Wed, Thurs & Sun.

South William

52 South William St. Thurs till 1am, Fri & Sat till 3am. New DJ bar that's more informal and lively than its angular, contemporary look might suggest. On top of a wide range of beers and cocktails, it offers the ultimate comfort food – hot pies, with an eclectic choice of fillings.

Clubs and live venues

Doyle's

9 College St ☎01/571 0616. Famed for being the place to spot up-and-coming singer-songwriters at its Ruby Sessions (Tues 9pm), *Doyle's* pub also hosts other live musical events and has a Sunday night comedy show.

Gaiety Theatre

South King St ☎01/677 1717, ⓦwww.gaietytheatre.ie. The *Gaiety* transforms itself each Friday and Saturday night from theatre into a three-level hotbed of dance, trance and, possibly, romance, claiming to be the latest-opening club in the city. With four bars and up to four DJs spinning discs in different rooms, plus a variety of live acts, there's plenty to entice.

Kildare Street and Merrion Square

Ireland's political and cultural Establishments have their power bases in the tight confines of Kildare Street and Merrion Square. Leinster House and its grounds, home of Ireland's parliament, straddles the two locations, surrounded by the unmissable treasures of the National Museum, the National Library and its impressive literary exhibitions, the National Gallery's trove of European art and the civil service HQ, Government Buildings. Former residences of a historical Who's Who of Ireland, from O'Connell to the Wildes, Merrion Square's Georgian terraces are now occupied by such varied organizations as the Arts Council and the Football Association of Ireland, while its quiet, tree-shaded lawns lighten the heavy, stately feel. There are no pubs or restaurants on Merrion Square itself, but Kildare Street supports one or two places to refuel, and most of the cultural institutions have a café.

Leinster House

Kildare St ☎ 01/618 3781, ⊛ www
.oireachtas.ie. Now the seat of
the **Oireachtas** (the Irish
Parliament), Leinster House
was built in 1745 as a mansion
on the edge of town for James
Fitzgerald, Earl of Kildare
(later the Duke of Leinster).
The architect, Richard Castle,
designed the impressive
pedimented frontage to be
viewed along Molesworth
Street, and employed the Swiss
Lafranchini brothers to adorn
the ceilings with Baroque
stucco work. After serving as
the headquarters of the Royal
Dublin Society from 1815,
the house was acquired by
the government of the newly
formed Irish Free State in 1924.

The Oireachtas has
two chambers: elected by
proportional representation,

the **Dáil** (or House of
Representatives, who are known
as *teachtaí Dála* or TDs) sits in
the nineteenth-century former
lecture theatre of the Royal
Dublin Society; members of
the **Seanad** (Senate), who
are either nominated by the
Taoiseach (prime minister) or
elected from various panels or
by the universities, meet in a
semicircular eighteenth-century
room that was the mansion's
picture gallery. Parliament
usually sits from mid-January
to early July (breaking for
Easter), and from October
until Christmas, on Tuesday
afternoons, Wednesdays and
Thursdays.

Overseas visitors wishing to
arrange a free **guided tour**
need to be sponsored by their
embassy in Dublin (see p.208);
visits are possible year-round

(indeed, you're likely to see more of the building itself when the Oireachtas isn't in session), May and June being the busiest months.

The National Museum

Kildare St ☎01/677 7444, ⊛www .museum.ie. Tues–Sat 10am–5pm, Sun 2–5pm; free. Guided tours Tues–Sat 3.30pm, Sun 2.30pm and at other variable times posted up in the entrance rotunda each day; 40min; €2. The National Museum on Kildare Street is the finest of a portfolio of jointly run museums – including the Natural History Museum (see p.83) and Collins Barracks (see p.151), which focuses on the decorative arts – and is a must-see for visitors to Dublin. Undoubted stars of the show here are a stunning hoard of prehistoric gold and a thousand years' worth of ornate ecclesiastical treasures, but the whole collection builds up a fascinating and accessible story of Irish archeology and history. The shop in the beautiful entrance rotunda sells a range

of high-quality crafts inspired by works in the museum, and there's a small café.

Prehistoric gold (*ór*), much of it discovered during peat-cutting, takes pride of place on the ground floor of the main hall. From the Earlier Bronze Age (c. 2500–1500 BC) come *lunulae*, thin sheets of gold formed into crescent-moon collars. After around 1200 BC, when new sources of the metal were apparently found, goldsmiths could be more extravagant, fashioning chunky torcs, the spectacular Gleninsheen collar and the Tumna Hoard of nine large gold balls, which are perforated, suggesting a huge necklace. Further prehistoric material is arrayed around the walls of the main hall, including the fifteen-metre-long Lurgan Logboat, dating from around 2500 BC, which was unearthed in a Galway bog in 1902.

The adjacent Treasury holds most of the museum's better-known **ecclesiastical exhibits**, notably the ornate, eighth-century Ardagh Chalice and the Tara Brooch, decorated with beautiful knot designs. Also on the ground floor is the museum's most recent exhibit, **"Kingship and Sacrifice"**, showcasing the leathery bodies of four Iron Age noblemen that were preserved and discovered in various bogs around Ireland.

Upstairs, **"Viking-age Ireland"** (c. 800–1150) features models of a house and the layout of Dublin's Fishamble Street, while an adjoining room displays some famous Christian objects from the same period, notably the beautiful Crozier of St Tola and the Cross of Cong, created to enshrine a fragment of the True Cross given to the king of Connacht by the pope in 1123.

The next exhibit moves on to **medieval Ireland** (1150–1550), to cover the first English colonists, their withdrawal to the fortified area around Dublin known as "the Pale" after 1300, and the hybrid culture that developed across the period – you can listen to recordings of poetry written in Ireland in Middle Irish, Middle

English and Norman French. Unmissable here is a host of small, ornate **shrines**, made to hold holy relics or texts, such as the Shrine of the Cathach, containing a manuscript written by St Columba (St Colmcille) of Iona, legendary bard, scholar, ruler and evangelizer of Scotland.

The National Library

Kildare St ⊛ www.nli.ie. Mon–Wed 10am–9pm, Thurs & Fri 10am–5pm, Sat 10am–1pm; free. The National Library was opened in 1890, shortly after the National Museum, whose design it mirrors across the courtyard of Leinster House. Its main draw are the long-term temporary **exhibitions**, on subjects such as W.B. Yeats, that are mounted in a beautiful, high-tech space on the lower ground floor. Visitors are also allowed up to the hushed, domed **Reading Room** on the first floor, decorated with ornate bookcases and an incongruously playful frieze of cherubs. It is in the office here that Stephen Daedalus engages the librarians – who appear under their real names – in literary talk

▼ READING ROOM, NATIONAL LIBRARY

▲ MONKEYS PLAYING BILLIARDS, HERALDIC MUSEUM

in the "Scylla and Charybdis" episode of *Ulysses*. On the way up, on the mezzanine landing, look out for the curious stone plaques representing, from left to right, Asia, Europe, America and Africa. In the **Genealogy Room** (Mon–Fri 10am–4.45pm, Sat 10am–12.30pm; free), professional genealogists can give advice to anyone researching their family history on how to access the records here and elsewhere in Dublin, as well as in Belfast.

The library's ground floor shelters a very attractive **café** and a small bookshop.

The Heraldic Museum

2–3 Kildare St ⓦwww.nli.ie. Mon–Wed 10am–8.30pm, Thurs & Fri 10am–4.30pm, Sat 10am–12.30pm; free. A few doors down from the National Library, by which it is administered, the Heraldic Museum contains such items as Sir Roger Casement's Order of St Michael and George, the Lord Chancellor's purse, and the mantle and insignia of the Order of St Patrick. And if your mantelpiece just isn't complete without an Irish coat-of-arms, the attached Office of the Chief Herald is the place to come – it'll cost you around €3000 and take up to a year

to complete. These august establishments occupy a mid-nineteenth-century brick edifice in Venetian style that used to house the deeply conservative, Anglo-Irish Kildare Street Club, which novelist George Moore – himself a leisured member of the landed class – lambasted in *Parnell and His Island* in 1887: "a sort of oyster-bed into which all the eldest sons of the landed gentry fall as a matter of course . . . drinking sherry and cursing Gladstone in a sort of dialect, a dead language which the larva-like stupidity of the club has preserved". The O'Shea brothers, who executed the whimsical **stone carving** on the facade, may well have shared Moore's view – look out for the three monkeys playing billiards on one of the ground-floor windows.

The National Gallery

Access from Merrion Square West or from Clare St via Millennium Wing. ⓣ01/661 5133, ⓦwww .nationalgallery.ie. Mon–Sat 9.30am–5.30pm, Thurs till 8.30pm, Sun noon–5.30pm; free (€3 donation suggested). Free guided tours Sat 3pm, Sun 2pm, 3pm & 4pm; meet in the Shaw Room (Dargan Wing Level 1, near Merrion Square entrance). The National Gallery hosts

▲ THE NATIONAL GALLERY

a fine collection of Western European art dating from the Middle Ages to the twentieth century. The gallery's old building, divided into Beit, Milltown and Dargan wings, has now been joined by the Millennium Wing, which hosts temporary exhibitions around its striking atrium. The resulting layout of the gallery, however, can be confusing, so the first thing to do when you go in is to pick up a floor plan leaflet (free). As well as a shop, café and restaurant (see p.85), the gallery offers classical and contemporary concerts, lectures and workshops (detailed in the monthly *Gallery News*, available in the foyer).

Level 1 is chiefly given over to Irish art from the seventeenth century onwards, including a large gallery in the Millennium Wing devoted to the twentieth century. The real stand-out in the Irish collection, however, is the Yeats Museum (below the National Portrait Gallery), which traces the development of Jack B. Yeats (1871–1957), younger brother of the writer W.B., from an unsentimental

illustrator of everyday scenes to an expressive painter in abstract, unmixed colours.

Highlights of **Level 2** include a fine selection of works from the Early Renaissance; Caravaggio's dynamic *The Taking of Christ*, and nearby, a characteristic Vermeer, *Woman Writing a Letter*, one of only 35 accepted works by the artist; outstanding works by Velázquez, Rubens and Mantegna; a fascinating room devoted to art in eighteenth-century Rome; and an excellent survey of French art from Poussin to the Cubists. In the mezzanine **Print Gallery**, as well as temporary exhibitions throughout the year, watercolours by Turner are exhibited every January, when the light is low enough for these delicate works.

Merrion Square

Begun in 1762, Merrion Square represents **Georgian town-planning** at its grandest. Its long, graceful terraces of red-brown brick sport elaborate doors, knockers and fanlights, as well as wrought-iron balconies (added in the early nineteenth century) and tall windows on the first floor, where the main reception rooms would have been. The north side of the square was built first and displays the widest variety of design.

The broad, manicured lawns of the square's **gardens** themselves are a joy, quieter than St Stephen's Green, and especially agreeable for picnics on fine weekends. Revolutionary politician Michael Collins is commemorated with a bronze bust on the gardens' south side, near a slightly hapless stone bust of Henry Grattan (see p.63 & p.68), while writer, artist and mystic George Russell ("AE") stands gravely near the southwest corner and his former home at no. 74. But the square's most remarkable and controversial statue is at the northwest corner: here, opposite his childhood home at no. 1 (now the American College Dublin), **Oscar Wilde** reclines on a rock in a wry, languid

▼ OSCAR WILDE STATUE, MERRION SQUARE

pose that has earned the figure the nickname "the fag on the crag". In front of him, a male torso and his wife Constance, pregnant with their second child, stand on plinths inscribed with Wildean witticisms: "This suspense is terrible. I hope it will last"; "I drink to keep body and soul apart". Nearby on the railings around the square's gardens, dozens of artists hang their paintings for sale every Sunday (and some Saturdays, depending on the weather).

The **Merrion Square South** terrace, which has the greatest concentration of famous former residents, gives a particularly vivid sense of the history of the place. Politician Daniel O'Connell bought no. 58 in 1809, the Nobel Prize-winning Austrian physicist Erwin Schrödinger occupied no. 65 and Gothic novelist Joseph Sheridan Le Fanu died at no. 70, which is now the Arts Council building. At no. 39 stood the British Embassy, burnt down by a crowd protesting against the Bloody Sunday massacre in Derry in 1972.

The Natural History Museum

Merrion Square West ☎ 01/677 7444, ⓦ www.museum.ie. Unfortunately, the museum has recently closed for several years, due to severe structural problems. Billing itself as "a museum of a museum", the Natural History Museum has evolved remarkably little since its inauguration in 1856. The tone is set on the lawn outside, by a heroic bronze of Surgeon-Major T.H. Parke with his foot on an animal skull and a rifle in his hands – born in Roscommon, Parke went with Stanley on his 1887 expedition to the Congo River and was the first

Irishman to cross Africa. The museum boasts around ten thousand **animal displays**, out of a holding of two million specimens –impressive in any age. Guarding the ground-floor **Irish Room** stand three skeletons of giant Irish deer which, despite intimidating rivals and impressing females with the largest antler span – three metres – of any deer ever, became extinct around 9000 BC.

Upstairs, the **World Collection** concentrates on the zoology of Africa and Asia, but includes the Barrington collection of birds, many of which were hapless enough to crash into Irish lighthouses. The lower gallery here, the last resting place of a dodo skeleton, is the best spot to view the skeletons of two whales stranded on Irish shores, one of them a twenty-metre fin whale. The upper gallery deals with invertebrates, including the **Blaschka Collection**, beautiful, nineteenth-century glass models of marine creatures; look out also for a pair of cosy golden gloves, knitted from threads secreted by the fan mussel.

Government Buildings

Merrion St Upper ⓦ www.taoiseach .gov.ie. Guided tours Sat 10.30am, 11.30am, 12.30pm & 1.30pm; free tickets from the National Gallery (Merrion Square entrance) on the day. Tours may be cancelled at short notice due to government business – call ⓣ 01/619 4116 to check. Next to the Natural History Museum rises the Neoclassical pile of Government Buildings, headquarters of the civil service and their ministers. Erected between 1904 and 1922 as the Royal College of Science, this was the last great building

work by the British – and was promptly commandeered by the ministers of the Free State as a secure base during the Civil War of 1922–23.

Tours of the stylishly refurbished complex will take you into the Cabinet room, decorated with portraits of Irish heroes, and the Taoiseach's office, which has its own lift to the rooftop helipad. On the ceremonial staircase look out for Evie Hone's *My Four Green Fields*, a striking modernist representation of the four provinces of Ireland in stained glass.

The Yeats House

82 Merrion Square ⓣ 01/676 1173. Mon–Fri 9.30am–1pm & 2–5pm, plus some Saturdays in summer noon–4pm; free. The grandiosely proportioned residence of W.B. from 1922 to 1928 will appeal mostly to Yeats buffs. It was restored from a ruin in the late 1990s, using gorgeous marble fireplaces and chandeliers rescued from similar houses on Merrion Square. Still the most imposing room is the former **drawing room**, decorated with richly coloured cornices, where Yeats would entertain and host plays. As the rooms are now working offices, it's better, though not essential, to phone ahead.

No. 29 Fitzwilliam Street Lower

ⓦ www.esb.ie/no29. Tues–Sat 10am–5pm, Sun 1–5pm, closed last three weeks of Dec; €5. This townhouse at the southeast corner of Merrion Square has been carefully reconstructed in the style of a middle-class **Georgian home** of the period 1790–1820 by the Electricity Supply Board, using furniture from the National Museum's collection. The ESB may sound like a strange curator for such a venture, but the house was rebuilt as an act of homage after the Board had knocked down 26 Georgian houses here to build its adjoining offices in the 1960s.

Entertaining guided **tours** bring to life the details of bourgeois Georgian life, both below stairs and in the elegant living rooms upstairs, which benefited from such gadgets as a lead-lined wine cooler and a belly-warmer for soothing gastric complaints. From this corner of the square there's a fine view down Mount Street Upper of the "peppercanister" church of St Stephen's, a Greek Revival work dating from 1824.

Shopping

Cleo

18 Kildare St ☎ 01/676 1421, ⓦ www .cleo-ltd.com. Closed Sun. Small clothes shop specializing in traditional Irish designs and natural fibres, including hand-knitted sweaters, linen shirts and woollen coats, scarves and other accessories.

Cafés and restaurants

Fitzer's

Millennium Wing, National Gallery, Clare St entrance. ⓦ www.fitzers.ie. Restaurant Mon–Fri noon–3pm, Sat &
Sun noon–4pm, café same hours as gallery (see p.81). In a gorgeous, contemporary setting, flooded with light from the new wing's glass roof, *Fitzer's* is a well-presented self-service restaurant, offering dishes such as chicken stuffed with emmental, ham and rocket, at very reasonable prices. The café upstairs stretches to lasagne, quiches, soups, salads and sandwiches, as well as tempting cakes, scones and cookies.

Patrick Guilbaud

Merrion Hotel, 21 Merrion St Upper ☎ 01/676 4192, ⓦ www .restaurantpatrickgilbaud.ie. Closed Sun & Mon. One of Dublin's finest and most expensive, a classic French restaurant that makes the most of Irish seasonal produce. Formal and showy in the evenings, "Paddy Giblets" loosens his collar just a little at lunchtime, when the €35 set menu (two courses plus coffee and petits fours) represents very good value.

Town Bar & Grill

21 Kildare St ☎ 01/662 4724, ⓦ www .townbarandgrill.com. Cavernous, bustling cellar, decorated simply and elegantly, where the very high standards of cooking – with a strong Italian influence – match the complex menu and extensive wine list. Pricey, but there's a good-value set menu at lunchtimes.

St Stephen's Green to the Grand Canal

As well as being a major landmark and transport hub, St Stephen's Green is central Dublin's largest and most varied park, whose statuary provides a vivid history lesson in stone, wood and bronze. Among diverse minor attractions in the vicinity, the main sightseeing draws date from the Georgian period: the splendid stucco work of Newman House and the elegant streets and squares to the east of the Green, which are also home to some fine upmarket eateries. Two nightlife strips that run off the Green are worth making time for: the hallowed Baggot Street crawl of traditional pubs to the east; and the vibrant, studenty trail of DJ bars and live venues down Camden and Wexford streets, culminating in the stylish and varied offerings of the old Harcourt Street Station.

St Stephen's Green

Mon–Sat 8am–dusk, Sun 10am–dusk.

The largest of central Dublin's squares, St Stephen's Green preserves its distinctive Victorian character, with a small lake, bandstand, arboretum and well-tended flower displays. It was originally open common land, a notoriously dirty and dangerous spot and the site of public hangings until the eighteenth century. In 1880, however, it was turned into a public park with funding from the brewer Lord Ardilaun (Sir Arthur Guinness), who now boasts the grandest of the

▼ ST STEPHEN'S GREEN

A monumental tour of St Stephen's Green

A short stroll around the monuments of St Stephen's Green gives you a vivid sense of the city's history, of diverse episodes and characters that are each firmly rooted in their location; maps at the main entrances will help you find your way. Probably the most striking of the Green's statues is a piercing bronze bust of **James Joyce**, gazing intently over his bony hand towards his alma mater, Newman House, just across the road on St Stephen's Green South. At the southeast corner, the **Three Fates fountain** was presented to Dublin by the German government in recognition of the help given to refugee children after World War II.

An uninspiring bust on the south side of the central floral display does scant justice to the remarkable **Countess Markiewicz**, dynamic socialist and feminist, who was second-in-command of the insurgents at St Stephen's Green during the Easter Rising of 1916. On the west side of the flower display, a tiny plaque inlaid in a wooden park bench commemorates the so-called "fallen women" – mostly unmarried mothers or abused girls – who were forced to live and work in severe conditions in Ireland's **Magdalen laundries**; the last of them, in Dublin, wasn't closed down until 1996. Just beyond, on a small rise, *Knife Edge*, a bronze memorial by Henry Moore to **W.B. Yeats,** is more spiritually uplifting. On the far west side of the Green, an animated bronze of **Robert Emmet**, leader of the 1803 Rebellion, looks proudly across towards the site of his birthplace, now demolished.

Facing Grafton Street from the northwest corner, **Fusiliers' Arch**, which remembers Royal Dublin Fusiliers killed in the Boer War, is still known to some as "Traitors' Gate". Humour resurfaces at the northeast corner, where a row of granite monoliths in honour of eighteenth-century nationalist **Wolfe Tone** is nicknamed "Tonehenge". Behind it stands a moving commemoration of the **Great Famine**.

Green's many **statues** (see also above), seated at his leisure on the far western side. Over-anxious locals make exaggerated complaints that drunks and ne'er-do-wells are returning the Green to its former unsavoury nature, but it's actually a pleasant, popular spot to take a break in the very heart of the city centre. From the Green's northwestern corner, by the top of Grafton Street, you can hire a **horse and carriage**, either as a grandiose taxi or for a tour of the sights, which will typically set you back €50 for thirty minutes.

St Stephen's Green North

Known as the "Beau Walk" in the eighteenth century, St Stephen's Green North is still the most fashionable side of the square. The **Shelbourne Hotel** here (see p.191) claims to have been the best address in Dublin since its establishment in 1824. Beyond the hotel at the start of Merrion Row, the tiny, tree-shaded **Huguenot Cemetery** was opened in 1693 for Protestant refugees fleeing religious persecution in France, many of whom settled in The Liberties (see p.122). A large plaque inside the gates

▼ THE SHELBOURNE HOTEL

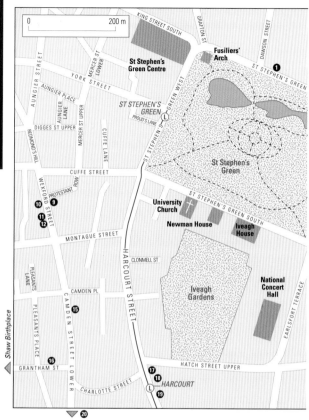

gives a roll-call of Huguenot Dubliners, among whom the most famous have been writers Dion Boucicault and Sheridan Le Fanu.

At weekends, local artists hang their paintings for sale on the railings along the north side of St Stephen's Green.

Newman House

85–86 St Stephen's Green South
☎01/716 7422. Guided tours only: June–Aug Tues–Fri 2pm, 3pm & 4pm; €5. Newman House boasts some of the finest Georgian interiors in Dublin, noted especially for their decorative plasterwork. The house is named after **John Henry Newman**, the famous British convert from Anglicanism, who was invited to found the Catholic University of Ireland here in 1854, as an alternative to Anglican Trinity College and the then recently established "godless" Queen's Colleges in Belfast, Cork and Galway. James Joyce and Éamon de Valera were educated here at what became University College Dublin (UCD), now relocated to a large campus in the southern suburbs.

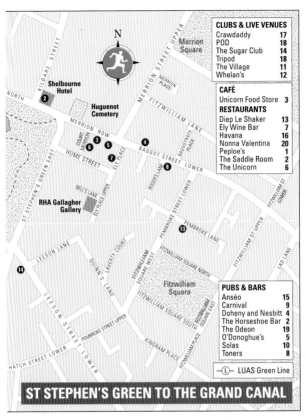

CLUBS & LIVE VENUES

Crawdaddy	17
POD	18
The Sugar Club	14
Tripod	18
The Village	11
Whelan's	12

CAFÉ

Unicorn Food Store	3

RESTAURANTS

Diep Le Shaker	13
Ely Wine Bar	7
Havana	16
Nonna Valentina	20
Peploe's	1
The Saddle Room	2
The Unicorn	6

PUBS & BARS

Anséo	15
Carnival	9
Doheny and Nesbitt	4
The Horseshoe Bar	2
The Odeon	19
O'Donoghue's	5
Solas	10
Toners	8

–Ⓛ– LUAS Green Line

ST STEPHEN'S GREEN TO THE GRAND CANAL

Newman House began life as two houses: no. 85 is a Palladian mansion built by Richard Castle in 1738 and adorned with superb Baroque **stucco work** by the Swiss Lafranchini brothers, while the much larger no. 86 was added in 1765. On the top floor of the latter are a lecture room, done out as in Joyce's student days (1899–1902) and the bedroom of the English poet **Gerard Manley Hopkins**. Having converted from Anglicanism, Hopkins became a Jesuit priest and then Professor of Classics here in 1884; after five wretched years in Dublin, he died of typhoid and was buried in an unmarked grave in Glasnevin Cemetery.

The University Church and Iveagh House

Next to Newman House stands the Byzantine-style curiosity of the 1850s **University Church**, complete with ornately carved capitals and extravagant painting and gilding. It got a hostile reception when it was first built, in the style of an eleventh-century Italian basilica, but is now a fashionable venue for

▲ THE UNIVERSITY CHURCH

weddings. Along the street stands **Iveagh House**, the first building Richard Castle designed in Dublin (1730) but now much altered as the home of the Department of Foreign Affairs.

Iveagh Gardens

Mon–Sat 8am–6pm, Sun 10am–6pm, closes at dusk in winter. Accessible through a gate behind the National Concert Hall (see p.205) on Earlsfort Terrace, or from Clonmell Street (off Harcourt Street), the little-known Iveagh Gardens are a perfect place to recharge your batteries in the heart of the city. Designed as a pleasure ground in 1863, this secret garden unveils a grotto, a cascade, fountains, a maze and a rosarium.

The Shaw Birthplace

33 Synge St ☎01/475 0854, ⊛www .visitdublin.com. May–Sept Mon, Tues, Thurs & Fri 10am–1pm & 2–5pm, Sat, Sun & public holidays 2–5pm; €7, or €12 Dublin Tourism combined ticket with either the Dublin Writers' Museum or the James Joyce Museum in Sandycove, or a choice of other sights (see p.203). The acclaimed playwright and man of letters George Bernard Shaw was born in this unpretentious terraced house in July 1856. His family, having fallen on hard times, stayed here for ten years before moving to Harcourt Street.

The self-guided tour of the house, which has been kitted out with appropriate period furniture, decor and plenty of Shaw memorabilia, begins in the basement **kitchen** where the young GBS often sought solace away from the "loveless" atmosphere of his parents'

▼ IVEAGH GARDENS

upstairs domain. On this floor too is the starkly plain maid's room and a small but neat garden replete with an austere outside privy.

Upstairs are the family **bedrooms** – Shaw's is tiny – and a remarkably claustrophobic parlour, all chintz and red velvet. On the top floor is the more expansive **reception room** equipped with a period pianoforte. It was here that Shaw's mother held her musical soirées and that the young Shaw gained his first musical insights – he was later to become a critic.

Fitzwilliam Square and around

The area to the east of St Stephen's Green is the most rewarding in the city for a Georgian architectural tour: an aimless wander will reveal plenty of wrought-iron balconies and much-photographed doorways sporting elegant knockers and fanlights. At its centre lie the still-private lawns of the small but well-preserved Fitzwilliam Square (1825). **W.B. Yeats** lived here, at no. 42, from 1928 to 1932, while his brother, the painter Jack B., had a house and studio round the corner at no. 18 Fitzwilliam Place. Together with its continuation Fitzwilliam Street, this forms a – now much-interrupted – kilometre-long terrace of **Georgian houses**, marching off towards the magnificent backdrop of the Wicklow Mountains.

The RHA Gallagher Gallery

Ely Place ☎01/661 2558, ⊛www .royalhibernianacademy.com. Tues–Sat 11am–5pm, Thurs till 8pm, Sun 2–5pm; free. Guided tours (45min) of the current exhibition Wed 1.15pm; free. Hosting major temporary shows by Irish and international

▲ GEORGIAN DOOR KNOCKER

artists, the Royal Hibernian Academy of Arts' Gallagher Gallery is one of the country's leading **contemporary art** venues. This discreet, red-brick 1970s building stands at the end of a quiet Georgian cul-de-sac, where once stood the home of Oliver St John Gogarty, wit, writer and the model for Buck Mulligan in *Ulysses*. Its well-designed viewing spaces are home to the RHA Annual Exhibition, usually in May and June, and include the ground-floor **Ashford Gallery**, devoted to introducing the work of emerging, mostly Irish artists.

Cafés

Unicorn Food Store

Merrion Row. Closed Sun. Smart deli-café offering delicious, mostly Italian food to eat in or take away. It's all very user-friendly – for sandwiches, you choose your own bread and fillings from a huge selection, while pastas and salads come in three sizes – and there's great coffee and cakes to follow.

Restaurants

Diep le Shaker

55 Pembroke Lane, off Pembroke St Lower ☎01/661 1829, ⊛www .diep.net. Closed Sat lunchtime & Sun. Dublin's best and most expensive Thai restaurant. The decor is bright and swanky, and the menu, strong on fish and seafood, offers imaginative takes on thoroughly authentic dishes: try the pomelo salad with tiger prawns, the scallops with asparagus and sugar snaps, or the chargrilled beef sirloin with fish sauce, chilli and lime dressing.

Ely Wine Bar

22 Ely Place ☎01/676 8986, ⊛www .elywinebar.ie. Closed Sun. Popular, congenial and moderately priced wine bar that offers wholesome food, using carefully sourced, mostly organic Irish ingredients – some from the family farm in County Clare – to accompany over ninety wines by the glass. Choose either a simple dish such as a cheese platter, or something more substantial like cod with sautéed potatoes and crispy chorizo.

Havana

3 Camden Market, Grantham St ☎01/476 0046, ⊛www.havana .ie. Closed Sun. Congenial, laid-back bar-restaurant where, surrounded by eccentric decor and cool Cuban sounds, you can graze on tasty and cheap tapas such as paella or lentil and chorizo stew.

Nonna Valentina

1 Portobello Rd ☎01/454 9866, ⊛www.dunneandcrescenzi.com. In an attractive house by the Grand Canal, this recently opened Italian restaurant looks set to be as successful as its stable-mate *Dunne & Crescenzi*. Excellent, authentic dishes include shellfish pasta with a tomato and chilli sauce, and fillet steak in bilberry sauce, all complemented by attentive service. It's expensive but there are reasonably priced lunch and early-bird menus from Monday to Friday.

Peploe's

16 St Stephen's Green North ☎01/676 3144, ⊛www.peploes.com. Styling itself a "wine bistro", this chic basement restaurant and wine bar offers well-prepared dishes, from linguini with clams in white wine to venison with cauliflower purée and raspberry jus, served by affable, smartly dressed staff.

The Saddle Room

Shelbourne Hotel, 27 St Stephen's Green ☎01/663 4500. Sprawling, upmarket restaurant with a lively mix of traditional and modern decor: dark oak walls and shiny gold padded booths, an oyster bar and an open kitchen. The culinary emphasis is on steak and seafood, carefully sourced and meticulously prepared, followed by some creative desserts.

The Unicorn

12B Merrion Court, off Merrion Row ☎01/662 4757. Closed Sun. Characterful, upmarket Italian trattoria, buzzing with politicians and media types tucking into authentic fare from the varied antipasti buffet, or main courses such as *saltimbocca alla Romana* – veal stuffed Parma ham and sage. In summer, the buzz tends to move from the stylish interior to the tables set in the secluded alley outside.

Pubs and bars

Anséo

18 Camden St.
Unpretentious venue with plenty of velour banquettes to chill out on, and one of the bars of the moment for its easy-going atmosphere and nightly roster of DJs. The upstairs room hosts jazz on Wednesdays, and more live music is planned.

Carnival

11 Wexford St.
Popular, grungy DJ bar – hung with a desultory few Venetian masks to justify the name – with mellow lighting and a few simple booths, specializing in funk and jazz.

Doheny and Nesbitt

5 Baggot St Lower. Don't be dismayed if the tiny front bar of this famous old pub, all dark wood and cut-glass partitions, is packed: there's a spacious back bar – a good place to catch TV sport – where the interior courtyard for smokers is almost as coveted these days as the atmospheric snug.

The Horseshoe Bar

Shelbourne Hotel, 27 St Stephen's Green. In this renovated luxury hotel, the Horseshoe's deep-red leather banquettes and white marble counter maintain a cosy pub feel. The recent cleaning of the cautionary, satirical

▲ THE ODEON

prints by Hogarth above the bar has not deterred the city's politicos and journos, who still gather here to drink, swap tall tales and set the world to rights.

The Odeon

Old Harcourt Street Station, Harcourt St. Late opening with DJ Thurs (till 1.30am), Fri (till 2.30am) & Sat (till 2.30am, cover charge after 10pm). Palatial and sophisticated bar in the old railway station, sporting Art Deco fittings, comfy armchairs and an ornamental bar salvaged from a South African bank. One of Dublin's few gastropubs, serving good, modern food such as salmon steak with a casserole of mustard lentils and mussels. Heaving most nights, it's chilled out on Saturday and Sunday for brunch. The outdoor seats

▲ O'DONAGHUE'S

under the station portico now fittingly overlook the new LUAS stop.

O'Donoghue's

15 Merrion Row. The centre of the folk and traditional music revival that began in the late 1950s, *O'Donoghue's* will forever be associated with groundbreaking balladeers The Dubliners. Nightly sessions from about 9pm draw a considerable crowd, partly because the pub is a notable landmark on the tourist trail. Earlier in the day, however, the simple, flagstoned bar and sizeable heated yard are good spots to appreciate a quiet pint of Guinness.

Solas

31 Wexford St. Handy for *The Village* and *Whelan's* (see opposite), this loud and lively bar offers bright, comfy booths, good DJs every night of the week, and an appealing outdoor terrace on the first floor. The global-influenced food menu ranges from snacks to salads and hot meals.

Toners

139 Baggot St Lower. The sign outside, "TONERS – A PUB", says it all: plain, stone floors, a cosy snug and mirrored partitions, where despite the crowds you'll never have to wait too long for a pint.

Clubs and live venues

Crawdaddy

Old Harcourt Street Station, Harcourt St ☎01/478 0166, ⊛www.pod.ie. Named after a famed London blues club, this compact live venue offers an imaginative programme of mainly indie and alternative bands, but occasionally branches out into jazz, reggae and world music.

POD

Old Harcourt Street Station, Harcourt St ☎01/478 0166, ⊛www.pod.ie. Housed in the station's vaults, *POD* ("Place of Dance") has enjoyed many a makeover during its more than decade-long existence. It's currently sporting black granite walls, overhead amoebic inflatables and rich mandarin booths – all guaranteed to enhance the lighting, whose vibrancy matches the intense rhythms supplied by resident and international guest DJs. Major draws are the Antics indie night (Wed), plus Backbeat (Thurs) and Stereotonic (Fri) for hardcore dance fans.

The Sugar Club

8 Leeson St Lower ☏01/679 7188, ⓦ www.thesugarclub.com. A lush and plush Southside venue just off St Stephen's Green, *The Sugar Club* hosts a diverse and often left-field variety of entertainment (bands, torch-singers, comedy, cabaret) – some divine, others innately terrible – but the atmosphere is always unquestionably on the button.

Tripod

Old Harcourt Street Station, Harcourt St ☏01/478 0166, ⓦ www.pod.ie. A combination of live venue (one of the city's largest, with a 1300 capacity), bar and club, staging an eclectic range of genre-crossing gigs (from Hayseed Dixie to Lee 'Scratch' Perry) and regular club nights such as the often-packed Heat (Wed).

The Village

26 Wexford St ☏01/475 8555, ⓦ www.thevillagevenue.com. Startlingly successful since its arrival a couple of years back, *Whelan's* bigger sister has double the capacity (around 750) and consequently books bigger names, while following its sibling's eclectic booking policy. DJs spin sounds in the hyper-cool bar nightly (into the early hours Thurs–Sat).

Whelan's

25 Wexford St ☏01/478 0766, ⓦ www.whelanslive.com. Featuring a popular front bar too, *Whelan's* has recently celebrated fifteen years as one of the city's most successful live venues, thanks to an extensive programme of the old and the new – a blend of traditional music, renowned folk acts, emerging talent and occasional one-off performances by major names.

Temple Bar

Sandwiched between the busy thoroughfare of Dame Street and the Liffey, Temple Bar is marketed, with a fair dose of artistic licence, as Dublin's "Left Bank" (inconveniently, it's on the right bank as you face downstream). Its transformation into the city's main cultural and entertainment district came about after a 1960s plan for a new central bus terminal here was abandoned after much procrastination. Instead, the area's narrow cobbled streets and old warehouses, by now occupied by short-lease studios, workshops and boutiques, began to be sensitively redeveloped as an artistic quarter in the 1980s. Nowadays, as well as more galleries and arts centres than you can shake a paintbrush at, Temple Bar shelters a huge number of restaurants, pubs and clubs, engendering a notoriously raucous nightlife scene that attracts more outsiders than Dubliners.

Graphic Studio Gallery

Cope Street ☎01/679 8021, ⓦwww .graphicstudiodublin.com. Mon–Fri 10am–5.30pm, Sat 11am–5pm. In an attractive converted warehouse down a small alley, announced by the word "ART" emblazoned in red neon, this commercial gallery hosts monthly exhibitions by contemporary, mostly Irish, printmakers, including those who have been invited to work at its nearby print studio.

Temple Bar Gallery and Studios

5–9 Temple Bar ☎01/671 0073, ⓦwww.templebargallery.com. Tues–Sat 11am–6pm, Thurs till 7pm. Free. This publicly funded gallery, purpose-built in the 1990s with thirty artists' studios attached, exhibits cutting-edge Irish and international artists working in a wide range of media.

Original Print Gallery

4 Temple Bar ☎01/677 3657, ⓦwww.originalprint.ie. Mon–Fri 10.30am–5.30pm, Sat 11am–5pm, Sun 2–6pm. A commercial gallery where you can catch changing exhibitions of contemporary prints by both up-and-coming and established Irish and international artists.

▼ TEMPLE BAR

TEMPLE BAR

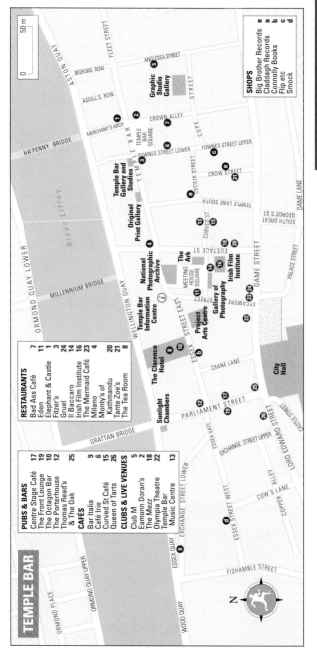

0 50 m

RESTAURANTS

Bad Ass Café	7
Eden	11
Elephant & Castle	1
Fitzer's	3
Gruel	24
Il Baccaro	14
Irish Film Institute	16
The Mermaid Café	23
Milano	4
Monty's of Kathmandu	20
Tante Zoe's	21
The Tea Room	8

PUBS & BARS

Centre Stage Café	17
The Front Lounge	19
The Octagon Bar	10
The Porterhouse	12
Thomas Read's & The Oak	25

CAFÉS

Bar Italia	9
Café Irie	6
Curved St Café	15
Queen of Tarts	26

CLUBS & LIVE VENUES

Club M	5
Eamonn Doran's	2
The Mezz	18
Olympia Theatre	22
Temple Bar Music Centre	13

SHOPS

Big Brother Records	e
Claddagh Records	a
Connolly Books	b
Flip etc	c
Smock	d

Temple Bar information

Temple Bar has its own, friendly information centre on Essex Street East (Mon–Fri 9am–5.30pm, Sat 10am–5.30/6pm, Sun noon–3pm; ☎01/677 2255, ⓦwww .templebar.ie).

The Ark

11A Eustace St ☎01/670 7788, ⓦwww.ark.ie. The Ark is Europe's first custom-built cultural centre for children (aged 3–14), housing theatres, galleries and a workshop. Get in touch for details of its plays, exhibitions, workshops, festivals, concerts, readings, opera, dance and multimedia programmes.

Irish Film Institute

6 Eustace St ☎01/679 3477, ⓦwww.irishfilm.ie. In a converted eighteenth-century Quaker meeting house, the IFI, though principally an art-house cinema (with a good film bookshop), has evolved into a stylish and sociable all-round venue, whose bar-restaurant (see p.101) is a fashionable meeting-place.

Gallery of Photography

Meeting House Square ☎01/671 4654, ⓦwww.irish-photography.com. Tues–Sat 11am–6pm, Sun 1–6pm. Free. It's well worth checking out what's on at this gallery, which stages some great exhibitions of contemporary photographs from Ireland and around the world, in smart, well-lit rooms above a good photographic bookshop.

National Photographic Archive

Meeting House Square ☎01/603 0374, ⓦwww.nli.ie. Mon–Fri 10am–5pm, Sat 10am–2pm. Free. From the photographic collections of the National Library – around 600,000 photographs, mostly on Irish historical subjects, from political events to early tourist snaps – the archive mounts a series of often fascinating temporary exhibitions. The attached shop sells popular postcards and prints from the collections.

Project Arts Centre

39 Essex St East ☎01/881 9613 or 881 9614, ⓦwww.project.ie. The bright-blue flagship of the Dublin contemporary arts scene – which began life as an art project in the foyer of the Gate Theatre – Project hosts theatre, dance, film, comedy and live music as well as challenging visual and performance art.

Sunlight Chambers

At the bottom of Parliament Street, which runs up from

▼ SUNLIGHT CHAMBERS

Grattan Bridge to the Neoclassical portico of City Hall, stand the Sunlight Chambers, whose curious facade merits a short detour. Built in the early twentieth century in the style of an Italian Renaissance palace by the Sunlight soap company, the Chambers sport colourful ceramic **friezes** on their exterior on the theme of hygiene; underneath the soot you can make out farmers and builders getting their clothes dirty on the upper tier, and women washing them below.

▲ TEMPLE BAR SQUARE

Shopping

Big Brother Records

4 Crow St ☎01/672 9355, ⓦwww .bigbrotherrecords.com. Closed Sun. Basement trove of vinyl and CDs, focusing on hip-hop, funk, soul, electronica and deep house; check out the noticeboard's fliers for the latest on the city's club nights.

Claddagh Records

2 Cecilia St ☎01/677 0262, ⓦwww.claddaghrecords.com. Unquestionably the finest traditional music emporium in Dublin. You can find just about every currently available recording here and, if you're not sure what you're looking for, the helpful and knowledgeable staff can point you in the right direction. Also stocks contemporary Irish music, Scottish and English folk, world music, country and blues.

Connolly Books

43 Essex St East ☎01/670 8707, ⓦwww.connollybooks.ie. Closed Sun. Vibrant socialist bookshop that covers labour and Irish history, philosophy, politics and biography, as well as stocking Irish-language, children's and second-hand books and left-wing newspapers, pamphlets and magazines. Events, meetings and talks are also held here, and a progressive film club is planned.

Cow's Lane Market

Sat 10am–5.30pm, closed Jan & Feb. This small market on a pedestrianized alley concentrates on contemporary women's clothes, bags and jewellery by Ireland's up-and-coming designers – who are generally out in all weathers staffing the stalls themselves.

Flip, Helter Skelter and Sharp's Ville

4–6 Fownes St Upper ☎01/671 4299. Trio of small shops, selling second-hand and new street clothes, notably T-shirts and combat gear, as well as caps, bags and other accessories.

Smock

20–22 Essex St West ☎01/613 9000. Closed Sun. Sophisticated party and smart fashions for a slightly older market by international designers such as Martin Margiela.

Temple Bar Food Market

Meeting House Square. Sat 10am–5pm. A magnet for Dublin's foodies, but also one of your best bets to grab Saturday lunch. As well as organic meat, fruit and veg, stalls sell tapas, Mexican food, hot dogs, burgers, breads, cakes and a huge variety of cheeses, and there's a West Clare oyster bar.

Cafés

Bar Italia

Essex Quay. Closed Sun. Small, Italian-run café in a good corner location with outdoor tables on the tiny piazza in front. Croissants, cakes and very good coffee for breakfast; tasty panini,

▼ IL BACCARO

soups, antipasti, salads and a daily pasta special such as wild boar *pappardelle* for lunch.

Café Irie

11 Fownes St Lower. Daily 9am–9pm. Alternative, rootsy café offering cheap sandwiches, bagels, panini and wraps with a tempting variety of copious fillings – "build your own" (one meat, one cheese, one veg) gives the flavour of it. Salads are available if that all sounds too starchy.

Curved Street Café

Filmbase, Curved St. Mon & Tues 9.30am–6pm, Wed 9.30am–8.30pm, Thurs 9.30am–7.30pm, Sat noon–5.30pm. This friendly spot in the first-floor atrium of a film-making centre sources ingredients, especially cheese, from small Irish producers and transforms them into tasty soups and sandwiches, such as ham, sundried tomato and Dijon mayonnaise on artisan bread. The cakes are scrummy, the coffee excellent and there are views of the bustling alley below from the full-length windows.

Queen of Tarts

4 Cork Hill, Lord Edward St. Small, laid-back patisserie-cum-café offering bagels, veggie and meaty fry-ups and granola for breakfast; chicken, spinach and cheese tarts, Greek salad and sandwiches for lunch; and cakes baked fresh on the premises to keep you going between times.

Restaurants

Bad Ass Café

9–11 Crown Alley ☎01/671 2596, ⓦwww.badasscafe.com. Popular, cheery restaurant – where Sinéad O'Connor once worked

as a waitress – serving pizzas, burgers, salads and pasta, with a varied children's menu, at reasonable prices.

Eden

Sycamore St/Meeting House Square ☎01/670 5372, ⓦwww .edenrestaurant.ie. Stylish, upmarket but convivial restaurant, with much-coveted tables out on the square in summer. Excellent modern Irish cuisine with a global twist, in dishes such as Castletownbere scallops with warm potato and bacon salad. Cheaper menus at lunchtime (brunch on Sat & Sun) and in the early evening (Sun–Thurs).

Elephant & Castle

18 Temple Bar. Ever-popular, cosy, pine-furnished diner that opens for breakfast on weekdays and much-sought-after brunches on weekends. Later in the day, the choice stretches from omelettes, gourmet burgers, salads and sandwiches to mains such as venison with chestnut purée and wild mushrooms in a gin sauce. No bookings.

Fitzer's

Temple Bar Square ☎01/679 0440, ⓦwww.fitzers.ie. Landmark branch, with modern minimalist decor, of the reliable chain of restaurants – see p.74.

Gruel

67 Dame St. Wholesome, inexpensive food from an open kitchen, including simple "gruel awakening" breakfasts on weekdays. At lunchtime, roast meat rolls, soups, salads and pizza are prepared to eat in or take away. In the evening, it's a very good-value, no-frills restaurant (no bookings and just one house wine), doling out dishes such as merguez sausage with apricot

▲ THE MERMAID CAFÉ

chutney and couscous, as well as plenty of veggie options.

Il Baccaro

Meeting House Square ☎01/671 4597. Closed lunchtimes (except Sat). Friendly, reasonably priced trattoria, serving up a tempting range of antipasti, good versions of Italian standards, and wine from the barrel, in an atmospheric cellar.

Irish Film Institute

6 Eustace St. Great for an inexpensive lunch or dinner before the show, or just a drink, whether in the cosy bar or the echoing atrium. Simple meals range from burgers, fish and chips and lasagne to fish cakes and goat's cheese salad, with lots of vegetarian options.

The Mermaid Café

69–70 Dame St ☎01/670 8236, ⓦwww.mermaid.ie. Chic restaurant with unfussy modern decor, where the emphasis is on helpful service and great global-influenced food, with an equally well-travelled wine list. The short menu always includes their signature New England crab cakes with piquant mayonnaise, but otherwise changes every few days. Though expensive, it's more manageable at lunchtime when there are set menus Mon–Sat, and brunch on Sun.

Milano

19 Temple Bar ☎01/670 3384. British visitors will be on familiar ground in this Dublin chain, the Irish version of *Pizza Express*: the tried-and-trusted formula of well-prepared pizzas, salads and pastas in a smart-casual setting.

Monty's of Kathmandu

28 Eustace St ☎01/670 4911, ⓦwww .montys.ie. Closed Sun lunchtime. Excellent, authentic Nepalese restaurant where bright, simple decor complements some deliciously refreshing starters and main courses such as succulent tandoori jumbo prawns and spicy chicken gorkhali, cooked with yoghurt, chilli, coriander and ginger. If you get your act together, order the momo dumplings stuffed with chicken or vegetables 24 hours in advance. Good-value early-bird (Mon–Thurs) and lunch set menus.

Tante Zoe's

1 Crow St ☎01/679 4407, ⓦwww.tantezoes.com. Dublin's only Cajun-Creole restaurant, a lively place dishing up shrimp in spicy tomato sauce and other authentic New Orleans favourites in smart, seductive surroundings. Prices are on the high side, but there are cheaper menus at lunchtime (including brunch with live jazz on Sun) and in the early evening.

The Tea Room

The Clarence Hotel, 6–8 Wellington Quay ☎01/670 7766, ⓦwww .theclarence.ie. In Dublin's most stylish hotel, *The Tea Room* is one of the city's most elegant restaurants, with a spectacular balcony bar. The menu features Irish produce in season, given Continental treatment in dishes like John Dory with grilled fennel, goat's cheese and pine nuts. One to save up your cents for, though the early-bird menu and especially the lunch menu represent good value.

▼ THE CLARENCE HOTEL

Pubs and bars

Centre Stage Café
6 Parliament St. Open Thurs–Sat evenings. Tiny, low-key gay bar opposite *The Front Lounge*, theatrically decorated with chandeliers and glitterballs, serving a wide range of drinks and snacks.

The Front Lounge
33 Parliament St ☎ 01/670 4112. Open till 2.30am Fri & Sat, 1am Sun. Behind an Art-Deco frontage, a sophisticated interior of polished wood floors and comfy red armchairs and sofas, with contemporary art exhibitions on the walls. A big hit with both gay and straight Dubliners, not least for its range of entertainment, including karaoke on Tuesdays, cabaret on Wednesdays and DJs at the weekend. Good cocktails and cappuccinos.

The Octagon Bar
The Clarence Hotel, 6–8 Wellington Quay. The octagonal bar of *The Clarence* (see p.191), bathed in artificial daylight and panelled with light oak, is one of Dublin's coolest hangouts, though by no means feels exclusive. The unusual snug – like an enclosed church pew – is perfect for making and breaking confidences, while the open fire draws small crowds in winter.

The Porterhouse
16 Parliament St ☎ www .porterhousebrewco.com. Open till 2am Thurs, 2.30am Fri & Sat. Excellent microbrewery-bar, sporting huge brass vats in its rambling but cosy interior. For €5 you can sample three stouts, including the oyster stout – not a joke, and tastes a lot better than it sounds. Live music every night, including traditional sessions on Sunday, and good food.

Thomas Read's and The Oak
1 Parliament St. Open till 1am Thurs, 2.30am Fri & Sat. Two contrasting, interconnected bars. *Thomas Read's* is a high-ceilinged café-bar, packed with a youngish crowd at weekends; quieter by day, it's perfectly located for people-watching, on the corner of Dame Street just opposite the beautifully refurbished City Hall. *The Oak* next door is a more introverted spot, cosy and traditional, with much of its dark panelling filched from deconsecrated churches.

Clubs and live venues

Club M
Bloom's Hotel, 6 Anglesea St ☎ 01/671 5622, ☎ www.blooms.ie. Closed Sun. Very much one for the younger and more boisterous set, *Club M* features three floors, five bars and a laser lightshow. Nights such as Cosmopolitan (Fri) and Therapy (Mon) feature stalwart local DJs blending dance, chart and R'n'B sounds.

Eamonn Doran's
3A Crown Alley ☎ 01/679 9114. Doran's cemented its reputation as the place to catch both hopeless wannabes and potential contenders a long time ago, and its basement continues to host an eclectic range of bands and singers, plus regular club nights.

The Mezz
23 Eustace St, ☎ www.thehubmezz .com. Raucous, grungy bar that lays on a very popular and eclectic nightly roster of live music and DJs. From

▲ THE MEZZ

Olympia Theatre

Dame St ☎01/677 7744, ⓦwww.mcd.ie/venues/ ?c=olympiatheatre. An old and much esteemed venue, the *Olympia* continues to stage a variety of musical events, featuring major Irish names such as Paul Brady and Luka Bloom, as well as international stars. For much of the summer it turns over to the Ragus traditional music and dance show.

Temple Bar Music Centre

Curved St ☎01/670 9202, ⓦwww.tbmc.ie. Brash and determinedly modernist, *TBMC*'s booking policy is decidedly left-field, focusing mainly on art-house and indie bands. The bar area is often used for free concerts showcasing emerging acts and the place transforms itself into a late club (until 3am) at weekends – with a wide variety of themed events.

Tuesday (sometimes Wed) to Sunday you can go on to *The Hub* nightclub downstairs, which usually has a live band – anything from traditional Irish to punk – then a DJ.

Dublin Castle and around

On a ridge above the Liffey, where previously the Vikings had established themselves, the Anglo-Norman invaders rebuilt Dublin in the thirteenth century around a doughty castle. Several other remnants of British hegemony are still dotted around the castle: the beautifully restored rotunda of City Hall; Christ Church Cathedral, with its huge crypt and photogenic covered bridge; and St Patrick's Cathedral, sheltering an intriguing array of memorials. It's possible to tour the lavish State Apartments inside Dublin Castle, but they're now decidedly outshone by the Chester Beatty Library, a world-class collection of books and objets d'art from around the globe. On the castle's east side, South Great George's Street is a vibrant strip of restaurants and bars, flanked by the clothes, book and record stalls of the Market Arcade.

Dublin Castle

Entrances on Dame St, Castle St and Ship St. You're free to walk around the **courtyards** of Dublin Castle, an architectural mish-mash that's home to police and tax offices, as well as various tribunals set up to investigate political corruption over the last ten years. The castle was the seat of British power in Ireland for seven hundred years, after its establishment by the Anglo-Normans in the early thirteenth century as the main element of their walled city, and successfully withstood all attempts to take it by force. It did, however, succumb to a major fire in 1684 and was rebuilt during the eighteenth century as a complex of residential and administrative buildings over two quadrangles, giving it a sedate, collegiate appearance.

Looming over the Lower Yard, the **Record Tower** was built in 1258 but heavily renovated and Gothicized in the early nineteenth century; it was originally a prison and now, fittingly but not at all compellingly, hosts the **Garda Síochána Museum**, stuffed with musty memorabilia of

▼ DUBLIN CASTLE

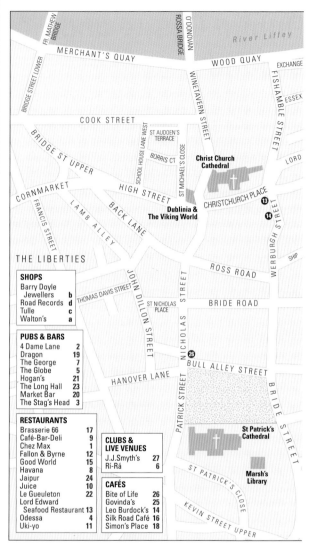

SHOPS

Barry Doyle Jewellers	**b**
Road Records	**d**
Tulle	**c**
Walton's	**a**

PUBS & BARS

4 Dame Lane	2
Dragon	19
The George	7
The Globe	5
Hogan's	21
The Long Hall	23
Market Bar	20
The Stag's Head	3

RESTAURANTS

Brasserie 66	17
Café-Bar-Deli	9
Chez Max	1
Fallon & Byrne	12
Good World	15
Havana	8
Jaipur	24
Juice	10
Le Gueuleton	22
Lord Edward Seafood Restaurant	13
Odessa	4
Uki-yo	11

CLUBS & LIVE VENUES

| J.J.Smyth's | 27 |
| Rí-Rá | 6 |

CAFÉS

Bite of Life	26
Govinda's	25
Leo Burdock's	14
Silk Road Café	16
Simon's Place	18

the Irish police force. If it's open (at the time of writing, it was closed for repairs due to subsidence), it's well worth looking in on the adjacent **Chapel Royal**, an ornate Gothic Revival gem; note especially the viceroys' coats of arms carved on the balcony rail and around the altar. Behind the tower and chapel, overlooked by the Chester Beatty Library, lies the pretty castle **garden**: now adorned with a swirling

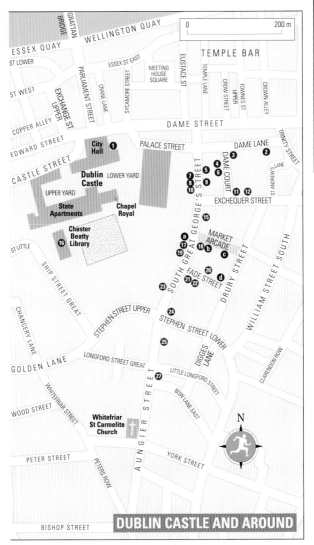

DUBLIN CASTLE AND AROUND

motif taken from the passage grave at Newgrange (see p.181), it marks the site of the "black pool" (*dubh linn*) which gave the city its English name. The Upper Yard follows the outline of the medieval castle. Above

its original main gate, the Cork Hill State Entrance, stands a **statue of Justice**, wearing no blindfold and turning her back on the city – a fitting symbol of British rule, locals reckon.

The State Apartments and Undercroft

Dublin Castle ☎01/645 8813, ⓦwww.dublincastle.ie. Guided tours only Mon–Fri 10am–4.45pm, Sat & Sun 2–4.45pm; 50min; €4.50; Heritage Card. It's advisable to ring ahead, as the State Apartments are sometimes closed for state occasions, when a tour of the Undercroft and the Chapel Royal or courtyards may be substituted. Places on the timed tours are allocated on a first-come, first-served basis, so it's worth arriving early and, if necessary, booking a place for later in the day. Built as the residence of the English viceroy and entered from the castle's Upper Yard, the State Apartments now host major Irish state occasions – including the signing of the ground-breaking Anglo-Irish Agreement by Taoiseach Garrett Fitzgerald and Prime Minister Margaret Thatcher in 1985. The Grand Staircase leads up to the east wing of **bedrooms** and drawing rooms, which had to be refurbished after a major fire in 1941, and were restored to their original eighteenth- and nineteenth-century style. The bedrooms served as a Red Cross hospital during World War I, and here the wounded James Connolly, one of the leaders of the 1916 Easter Rising, was treated before being carted off to a firing squad at Kilmainham Gaol. The tour's artistic highlight is *The Countess of Southampton* by van Dyck, a keenly wrought, restrained – apart from the shimmering dress – portrait of the 17-year-old Elizabeth Leigh, painted for her wedding.

The brass chandelier in the **Throne Room**, with its shamrock, rose and thistle emblems, commemorates the 1801 Act of Union, while the **Picture Gallery** beyond is lined with viceroys, including – hiding ignominiously behind the door – the first Marquis of Cornwallis, who not only lost the American colonies, but also faced rebellions as viceroy first of India, then of Ireland (1798). **St Patrick's Hall**, formerly a ballroom which hosted investitures of the Knights of St Patrick, is now used for the inaugurations and funerals of Irish presidents. Its overblown, late-eighteenth-century ceiling paintings show St Patrick converting the Irish, Henry II receiving the submission of the Irish chieftains and George III's coronation.

The tour finishes at the excavations of the **Undercroft** beneath the Lower Yard, which have revealed the base of the gunpowder tower of the medieval castle and steps leading down to the moat, fed by the old River Poddle on its way down to the Liffey, as well as part of the original Viking ramparts.

The Chester Beatty Library

Dublin Castle ☎01/407 0750, ⓦwww.cbl.ie. Tues–Fri 10am–5pm, Sat 11am–5pm, Sun 1–5pm, plus

▼ CHESTER BEATTY LIBRARY

▲ CITY HALL

May–Sept Mon 10am–5pm; free. Guided tours Wed 1pm & Sun 3pm & 4pm; free. Housed in the eighteenth-century Clock Tower Building at the back of Dublin Castle, the Chester Beatty Library preserves a dazzling collection of books, manuscripts, prints and *objets d'art* from around the world. Superlatives come thick and fast here: as well as an **Islamic collection** that's one of the finest in existence, containing some of the earliest manuscripts from the ninth and tenth centuries, the library holds important **biblical papyri**, including the earliest surviving examples in any language of Mark's and Luke's Gospels, St Paul's Letters and the Book of Revelations. Elegantly displayed in high-tech galleries, the artefacts tell the story of religious and artistic traditions across the world with great ingenuity, a formula which justifiably won the CBL the European Museum of the Year award in 2002.

The collection was put together by the remarkable **Sir Alfred Chester Beatty**, an American mining magnate who moved himself and his works to Dublin in the early 1950s, after cutting a deal with the Irish government on import taxes and estate duties. In 1957 he was made the first honorary citizen of Ireland, and when he died in 1968, he bequeathed his collection to the state and was given a state funeral.

Most of the CBL's vast holding is accessible only to scholars via the reference library, with less than two percent on show in the public galleries at any one time – though that's more than enough to keep you occupied for a few hours. It makes sense to start with the second-floor gallery, which covers Sacred Traditions, while the first floor deals with Artistic Traditions (alongside a space for fascinating temporary exhibitions), with each divided into Western, Islamic and Eastern sections; exhibits range from sixteenth-century biblical engravings by Albrecht Dürer to books carved in jade for the Chinese emperors, and from gorgeously illustrated collections of Persian poetry to serene Burmese statues of the Buddha.

City Hall

Dame St ⓦ www.dublincity.ie/cityhall. Mon–Sat 10am–5.15pm, Sun 2–5pm; free. Under the gleamingly restored rotunda of City Hall, creamy Portland stone columns, interspersed with statues of **Daniel O'Connell** (the city's first Catholic Lord Mayor) and other notables, bathe in wonderful natural light from the dome. The sumptuous Neoclassical building was constructed between 1769 and 1779 as the Royal Exchange, but fell into disuse after the Act of Union of 1801 passed governance of Ireland back to London; Dublin Corporation bought it in 1851, and it's still

▲ DUBLIN COAT OF ARMS, CITY HALL

the venue for city council meetings.

Among the Arts and Crafts **murals** under the dome that trace Dublin's history, look out for Lambert Simnel – 10-year-old pretender to Henry VII's throne – being carried through the streets after his mock coronation in Christ Church Cathedral in 1487; the ill-starred Simnel ended up enslaved as the king's kitchen-scullion. The colourful floor **mosaic** shows the civic coat of arms, three castles topped by flames, which apparently represent the zeal of the citizens to defend Dublin – reinforced by the city motto *Obedientia Civium Urbis Felicitas* ("Happy the City whose Citizens Obey").

The Story of the Capital

Dame St Mon–Sat 10am–5.15pm, Sun 2–5pm; €4. The vaults beneath City Hall now shelter this fascinating multimedia journey through Dublin's history and politics – with occasional hints of self-promotion for the exhibition's sponsors, the city council. The story is told through exhaustive display panels, slick interactive databases and a series of videos, complemented by an entertaining audioguide narrated by Irish actress Sinéad Cusack with snippets from leading historians.

Dublin and the Messiah

Opposite the cathedral on Fishamble Street once stood Neal's Music Hall, where Handel conducted the combined choirs of Christ Church and St Patrick's cathedrals in the first performance of his *Messiah* in 1742. As the takings were going to charity, ladies were requested not to wear hoops in their crinolines, to get more bums on seats. Jonathan Swift's verdict was, "Oh, a German, a genius, a prodigy". In a private garden on the site, the composer's reward is a statue of himself conducting in the nude, perched on a set of organ pipes. Every April 13, on the anniversary of the first performance, Our Lady's Choral Society gives a singalong performance of excerpts from the *Messiah* here.

There are few exhibits as such, a notable exception being the intricate **city seal** and its strongbox, which, instituted after the seal was stolen in 1305, required the presence of all six keyholders. To make up for the lack of hard evidence on show, however, the enterprising curators have commissioned a series of **artworks**, including *Utopian Column*: a stack of glass plates engraved with historical scenes and flooded with light.

Christ Church Cathedral

☎01/677 8099, ⊛www.cccdub .ie. June–Aug daily 9am–6pm; Jan–May & Sept–Dec 9.45am–5/6pm; €5, discounted to €3.95 with ticket for Dublinia (see p.112). Choral Evensong Wed & Thurs 6pm, Sat 5pm, Sun 3.30pm, Sung Eucharist Sun 11am.

Hemmed in by buildings and traffic, Anglican Christ Church appears as an unexceptional Neogothic hulk, but its interior reveals its long history as the seat of the Archbishop of Dublin. In about 1030, the Viking king of Dublin, Sitric Silkenbeard, built a wooden cathedral here, which was replaced by the Normans between 1186 and 1240 with a magnificent stone structure. Of this, the crypt (see "Treasures of Christ Church" below), the **transept**, which retains some eroded Romanesque carvings, and the remarkable leaning **north wall** can still be seen – as the church was built over a bog, the roof and south wall collapsed in 1562 and the north side was pulled half a metre out of the perpendicular.

In the 1870s, distiller Henry Roe lavished the equivalent of €30 million on the heavy-handed restoration you can see today, and bankrupted himself.

Near the entrance, you'll find the **tomb of Strongbow**, the Norman leader who captured Dublin in 1170. The original tomb, around which Dublin's landlords had gathered to collect rents, was destroyed by the roof collapse, and had to be replaced with an effigy of the Earl of Drogheda so that business could proceed as usual. The half-figure alongside is probably a fragment of the original tomb, though legend maintains that it's an effigy of Strongbow's son, hacked in two by his own father for cowardice in battle.

▼ STRONGBOW'S TOMB, CHRIST CHURCH CATHEDRAL

The **chapels** off the choir show the Anglo-Normans celebrating their dual nationality. To the left stands the Chapel of St Edmund, the ninth-century king of East Anglia who was martyred by the Vikings, while on the right is the Chapel of St Laud, the sixth-century bishop of Coutances in Normandy. The floor tiles here are original – they were replicated throughout the cathedral in the 1870s – while on the wall you can see an iron box containing the embalmed heart of twelfth-century St Laurence O'Toole, Dublin's only canonized archbishop.

Treasures of Christ Church

Christ Church Cathedral. Same ticket and hours as the rest of the cathedral, except that in winter on Sun it closes after Choral Evensong. If you descend the stairs by the south transept of Christ Church, you'll reach the **crypt**, the least changed remnant of the twelfth-century cathedral; formerly a storehouse for the trade in alcohol and tobacco, it's one of the largest crypts in Britain and Ireland, extending under the entire cathedral for over fifty metres. Here you'll find the **Treasures of Christ Church exhibition**, which includes an interesting twenty-minute audiovisual presentation on the history of the cathedral, as well as a miscellany of manuscripts and church crockery. Look out for a ropey-looking tabernacle and pair of candlesticks made for James II on his flight from England in 1689, when, for three months only, Latin Mass was again celebrated at Christ Church (the existing cathedral paraphernalia was hidden by quick-thinking Anglican officials under a bishop's coffin). In extravagant contrast is a chunky silver-gilt plate, around a metre wide, presented by King William III in thanksgiving for his victory at the Battle of the Boyne in 1690.

Dublinia & The Viking World

High St ☏ 01/679 4611, ⊛ www .dublinia.ie. April–Sept daily 10am–5pm; Oct–March Mon–Fri 11am–4pm, Sat & Sun 10am–4pm; €6.25, children €3.75, family ticket €17. Housed in the former Synod Hall of the Church of Ireland, Dublinia & The Viking World provides a lively, hands-on portrait of Viking and medieval Dublin that's especially good fun for kids (phone for details of special activities during the summer months). On the ground floor, themes such as the medieval fair and the plague are explored via walk-through tableaux of streets and houses, with sound effects and lots of fun, interactive possibilities, such as throwing balls at a criminal in the stocks.

The first floor's centrepiece is a fascinating **model of**

▼ DUBLINIA

▲ BRIDGE OF SIGHS, CHRIST CHURCH

Dublin in about 1500, showing the walled city dominated by Christ Church, while neighbouring rooms explore the excavations of the Viking and medieval settlements at nearby Wood Quay. On the second floor, the Great Hall, where the Anglican bishops met until 1982, is now the home of **The Viking World**, which features a near-life-size ship, audiovisuals on the sagas and the chance to try on slave chains.

Before crossing the graceful, much-photographed **bridge** over to Christ Church Cathedral, it's worth climbing **St Michael's Tower**, a remnant of the seventeenth-century Church of St Michael and All Angels, for fine views over the city.

St Patrick's Cathedral

℡01/475 4817, ⓦwww
.stpatrickscathedral.ie. March–Oct daily 9am–6pm; Nov–Feb Mon–Fri 9am–6pm, Sat 9am–5pm, Sun 9am–3pm; €5. Visitors not admitted, except for worship, during services, which include Choral Matins Mon–Fri 9.40am (during school terms); Choral Evensong Mon–Fri 5.45pm (except Wed in July & Aug), Sun 3.15pm; Choral Eucharist/Matins Sun 11.15am.
St Patrick's history is remarkably similar to that of its fellow Anglican rival Christ Church: it was built between 1220 and 1270 in Gothic style, but its roof collapsed in 1544, leading to a decline that included its ignominious use as a stable by Cromwell's army in 1649. Its Victorian restoration, however, by Sir Benjamin Guinness in the 1860s, was more sensitive than Christ Church's, and it has a more appealing, lived-in feel, thanks largely to its clutter of quirky **funerary monuments**. To the right of the entrance in the harmoniously proportioned nave are various memorials to **Jonathan Swift**, the cathedral's dean for 32 years, including his and Stella's graves, his pulpit and table, and a cast of his skull – both his and Stella's bodies were dug up by Victorian phrenologists, studying the skulls of the famous. In the south transept, look out for the marble monument to Archbishop Marsh, (see p.114) the finest work by sculptor Grinling Gibbons in Ireland. The Door of Reconciliation, by the north transept, recalls a quarrel between the earls of Kildare and Ormond in 1492. Ormond sought sanctuary in the cathedral's chapterhouse, but Kildare cut a hole in the door and stretched his arm through to shake Ormond's hands – so giving us the phrase "chancing your arm".

Jonathan Swift

"Here is laid the body of Jonathan Swift . . . where fierce indignation can no longer rend the heart. Go, traveller, and imitate if you can this earnest and dedicated champion of liberty."

Swift's epitaph in St Patrick's Cathedral, penned by himself and translated here from the Latin, conveys not only his appetite for political satire and campaigning, but also perhaps a certain prescience about the longevity of his fame. Born in Dublin in 1667 and educated at Trinity College, Swift went to England in 1689 to work as secretary to the retired diplomat Sir William Temple. Here he met Esther Johnson, nicknamed **Stella**, the daughter of Temple's housekeeper, who became his close companion – whether platonic or sexual, no one knows – until her death in 1728.

Swift was ordained in the Church of Ireland in 1695, and anonymously wrote his first major work, **A Tale of a Tub**, in 1704, satirizing the official churches and the unscrupulous "modern" writers of his day. Sent to London to lobby the government for the relief of church taxes, from 1710 he was at the centre of England's political and literary life, a friend of Tory ministers as well as of Alexander Pope and John Gay. When the Tories fell, however, instead of the English bishopric he had hoped for, he was made Dean of St Patrick's Cathedral, in 1713. Here he turned his caustic wit on Irish injustices, writing a series of pamphlets in the 1720s and 1730s including **A Modest Proposal**, one of the most admired works of irony in the English language, which suggests that the Irish poor sell off their children to the rich as "a most delicious, nourishing and wholesome food". At this time too, he wrote his most famous work, the gloriously imaginative satirical novel, **Gulliver's Travels** (1726).

Swift's later years were blighted by a progressive mental illness causing dizziness, and when he died in 1745, he left his estate to build St Patrick's on James's Street, the first psychiatric hospital in Ireland.

In the northwest corner of the nave stands a slab carved with a Celtic cross that once marked the site of a well next to the cathedral, where St Patrick baptized converts in the fifth century. Back near the entrance, you can't miss the extravagant **Boyle monument**, which Richard Boyle, Earl of Cork, erected in 1632 in memory of his wife, Katherine, who had borne him fifteen children, including the famous physicist Robert Boyle (shown in the bottom centre niche). Viceroy Wentworth, objecting to being forced to kneel before a Corkman, had the monument moved here from beside the altar, but Boyle exacted revenge in later years by engineering Wentworth's execution.

Marsh's Library

St Patrick's Close, ⓦwww .marshlibrary.ie. Mon & Wed–Fri 10am– 1pm & 2–5pm, Sat 10.30am–1pm; €2.50. The oldest public library in Ireland, Marsh's Library has remained delightfully untouched since it was built by Sir William Robinson, the architect of Kilmainham Hospital, in 1701, and still functions as a research and conservation library. Its founder, **Archbishop Narcissus Marsh**, was particularly interested in science, mathematics and music, and oversaw the first translation of the Old Testament into Irish.

▲ MARSH'S LIBRARY

His books form one of the library's four main collections, totalling 25,000 works relating to the sixteenth, seventeenth and early eighteenth centuries. They're housed in beautiful rows of dark-oak bookcases, each with a carved and lettered gable (for cataloguing purposes) topped by a bishop's mitre, and three screened alcoves, or "cages", where readers were locked in with rare books.

The library mounts regular **exhibitions** from its collections on subjects such as astronomy, and displays a death mask of its former governor, Jonathan Swift (see opposite), as well as a cast of Stella's skull.

Whitefriar Street Carmelite Church

Aungier Street ⓦ www.carmelites.ie. Re-established in 1827 on the site of a dissolved Carmelite priory, Whitefriar Street Carmelite Church caters to a wide cross-section of Catholic worshippers with a panoply of shrines and statues. **Our Lady of Dublin**, a fifteenth-century carved-oak Madonna and Child, takes pride of place by the entrance, the only

wooden image to have survived the dissolution of Ireland's monasteries. Used as a pig trough after the Reformation, it was rescued in the 1820s by Father Spratt, the priest who re-founded the church, from a pawn shop near St Mary's Abbey, where the statue had probably originally stood. There was no sign, however, of the image's silver crown, which was said to have been used for the mock coronation of the

▼ ST VALENTINE, WHITEFRIAR STREET CARMELITE CHURCH

pretender Lambert Simnel in Christ Church Cathedral in 1487 (see p.110).

Whitefriar Street is also the scene of many romantic pledges, as a casket on the north side of the church supposedly enshrines the remains of **St Valentine**, the third-century Roman martyr, donated by Pope Gregory XVI in 1835.

Shopping

Barry Doyle Jewellers

Upstairs, 30 Market Arcade, South Great George's St ☎01/671 2838, ⓦwww.barrydoyledesign.com. Closed Sun. Stylish contemporary designs, including many sophisticated silver necklaces, in all price ranges. Commissions undertaken.

The Market Arcade

Between South Great George's St and Drury St. Some shops open Sun. Laid-back indoor market with an alternative edge, offering second-hand books and records,

▲ TULLE

upmarket and street clothing, jewellery and speciality foods. The excellent *Simon's Place* café (see opposite) is also here.

Road Records

16B Fade St ☎01/671 7340, ⓦwww .roadrecs.com. Tucked away off South Great George's Street, Road is the ultimate indie, electronica and alternative country specialist, stocking vinyl and CDs. The best place to find new releases, it also offers an extensive range of left-field Irish recordings.

Tulle

28 Market Arcade, South Great George's St ☎01/679 9115. Closed Sun. This hip boutique stocks everything from denim to evening dresses and one-off designs for special occasions, by small international designers such as Malene Birger.

Walton's

69 South Great George's St ☎01/475 0661. Music school ☎01/478 1884, ⓦwww.newschool.ie. Music school closed Sun. Dublin's leading music shop sells the full range

▼ THE MARKET ARCADE

of Irish traditional instruments from tin whistles to harps, as well as teaching aids, sheet music and CDs of Irish artists. The attached music school offers two-hour crash courses (minimum five students) for absolute beginners in the tin whistle or bodhrán, the two most popular – and easiest to learn – instruments of Irish music.

Cafés

Bite of Life

55 Patrick St. A small, welcoming café with fresh flowers on the tables and newspapers to peruse, *Bite of Life* serves up cheap, excellent food, including fresh ciabatta rolls with imaginative fillings, salads, homemade soups and cakes – the chocolate biscuit cake is particularly feted.

Govinda's

4 Aungier St ⓦ www.govindas.ie. Mon–Sat noon–9pm. Excellent Hare Krishna-run vegetarian café, serving cheap and filling samosas, salads, pizzas and burgers, as well as daily specials such as pasta and vegetables au gratin. They also offer great juices and lassis, as well as cakes and other desserts.

Leo Burdock's

2 Werburgh St. Daily noon–midnight. Dublin's most famous fish-and-chipper (takeaway only, but the garden of Christ Church Cathedral is just over the road) is all gleaming surfaces and friendly service. The multi-award-winning menu now stretches to lemon sole goujons, but otherwise there are no surprises. Expect to queue lunchtimes and evenings.

Silk Road Café

Chester Beatty Library, Dublin Castle. Same hours as museum (see p.125). This stylish and good-value museum café, spilling over into the Library's sky-lit atrium, is well worth a visit in its own right. The chef (who's from Jerusalem, one of Chester Beatty's favoured hunting grounds) rustles up mostly Middle Eastern food – lamb moussaka, falafels, spinach and feta filo pie and plenty of other veggie options – as well as very good salads and creative panini. To round off, there's great coffee and titbits such as Turkish delight and baklava.

Simon's Place

Market Arcade, South Great George's St. Closed Sun. Funky, unpretentious spot with plain wooden furniture that's popular for its basic soups, salads, filling sandwiches and fine coffee. A good to place to check out what's on in the city, as it's scattered with fliers and posters.

Restaurants

Brasserie 66

66 South Great George's St ☏01/400 5878, ⓦwww .brasseriesixty6.com. The epitome of the modern international bistro, with unobtrusive

▼ SILK ROAD CAFÉ

decor and a self-conscious lack of frills (tea towels for napkins, carve your own hunk of bread). All this to focus attention on the food, of course, which is unpretentious and well-executed, using carefully sourced ingredients, inexpensive but excellent dishes such as breaded veal escalope with rocket salad. There's a wide choice of wines by the glass, and breakfast is served on weekdays, brunch at weekends.

Café-Bar-Deli

12–13 South Great George's St, ⓦ www.cafebardeli.ie. A former *Bewley's Café* that's been smartly updated without losing its character: comfy red booths, bentwood furniture, brass rails and a white marble bar. The reasonably priced menu of simple food is a winner, too, with some interesting starters; pastas such as rigatoni with gorgonzola, spinach and cream; Mediterranean salads; thin, crispy pizzas; and mouthwatering desserts. No bookings.

Chez Max

1 Palace St ☎ 01/633 7215. Archetypal French bistro, decorated with nostalgic posters, offering an evening menu of classic French dishes such as *boeuf bourguignon*, supplemented by *porc aligot* (confit of pork belly with garlic and cheese mash) and other specialities from the owner's home region of Lozères in southwest France. Lunch consists of salads and simpler main courses, including a good-value *plat du jour*, while cold meat and cheese platters are available all day long. Simple French breakfast is available Mon–Fri, an inexpensive early-bird menu Sun–Thurs.

Fallon and Byrne

11–17 Exchequer St ☎ 01/472 1000, ⓦ www.fallonandbyrne.com. Foodie heaven in a converted telephone exchange: there's a smart grocery store on the ground floor, a seductive, Parisian-style brasserie upstairs – offering everything from burgers to oysters to French-influenced dishes such as lamb rump with Puy lentils – and a shop and wine bar in the basement, which serves cheaper food, such as cheese and charcuterie boards, though in much less appealing surroundings.

Good World

18 South Great George's St ☎ 01/677 5373. Open daily until 3am. Daytime dim sum (12.30–6pm) is especially popular on Sundays, while in the evenings regular customers – sometimes raucous after pub closing – come for a varied, inexpensive menu that specializes in seafood and sizzling dishes.

Havana

South Great George's St ☎ 01/400 5990, ⓦ www.havana.ie. Closed Sun lunchtime. Recently opened branch of the Camden Street favourite (see p.92), replicating the successful formula in terms of menu, decor and soundtrack. Live salsa and merengue Saturday till 2am.

Jaipur

41 South Great George's St ☎ 01/677 0999, ⓦ www.jaipur.ie. Evenings only. Colourful modern decor is the setting for a wide range of richly flavoured, fairly pricey Indian food, notably a delicious Goan seafood curry and plenty of dishes for vegetarians, backed up by considerate service and a decent wine list. Set menus range from an early-bird cheapie to a €50 tasting menu.

Juice

73–83 South Great George's St ☏01/475 7856. Stylish, moderately priced vegetarian and vegan restaurant. The chef is more creative in the evenings, rustling up dishes such as stir fries, mushroom Wellington and aduki bean Juiceburgers; simpler and cheaper lunchtime dishes might include tabouleh and scrambled tofu. The early-bird menu (Mon–Fri) is great value.

Le Gueuleton

1 Fade St. Closed Sun. A recent instant hit on Dublin's restaurant scene, serving great French bistro food from an open kitchen at reasonable prices. Well-executed dishes such as mackerel with spring onions, new potatoes and aioli, accompanied by good-value French wine, are followed by some novel desserts. No booking by phone, but if you turn up in person, you can put your name down for a table later in the evening.

Lord Edward Seafood Restaurant

23 Christchurch Place ☏01/454 2420. Closed Sat lunchtime & Sun. Established in 1890, and apparently little changed since, the *Lord Edward* offers an old-fashioned combination of fresh and simple seafood dishes – fish stew a speciality – traditional hospitality from bow-tied waiters and manageable prices, from its second-floor perch with fine views of Christ Church Cathedral. The congenial bar and lounge of the eponymous

▲ ODESSA

pub below also serve decent food (Mon–Fri lunchtimes).

Odessa

13–14 Dame Court, off Dame St ☏01/670 7634, ⊛www.odessa.ie. Friendly service and cool sounds and decor, whether you sink into the velour bench seats on the ground floor or the leather armchairs downstairs. The wide-ranging menu features dishes such as spinach, ricotta and almond filo parcels, as well as a fish of the day; brunch is offered at weekends and there's a good-value, early-bird menu Sun–Thurs.

Uki-yo

7–9 Exchequer St ☏01/633 4071, ⊛www.ukiyobar.com. Open till 2.30am Thurs, Fri & Sat. Chic Korean and Japanese bar-restaurant with a novel take on the Dublin snug: karaoke boxes out the back for €25 per hour. Out front,

▲ UKI-YO

you can graze at the bar on appetizers such as tasty prawn and pork dumplings, or tuck into something more substantial at the sturdy, dark-wood tables, such as salmon teriyaki and chicken curry; cheap early-bird menu available. To wash it down, there's a wide selection of wine and sake.

Pubs and bars

4 Dame Lane

4 Dame Lane ☎01/679 0291. Open till 1.30am Mon–Thurs & Sun, 3am Fri & Sat. Announced by burning braziers just along the lane from *The Stag's Head*, this airy, minimalist bar-club probably has the stylistic edge over its bare-brickwork-and-wood rivals. Good tunes, too: anything from techno to funk, with a DJ every night in the ground-floor

bar, Friday & Saturday in the upstairs room.

Dragon

64 South Great George's St ☎01/478 1590. Open till 2.30am Mon & Thurs–Sat. Expansive gay bar in a former bank, extravagantly done out in plush purples, reds and blues and decked out with botanical prints, Buddhas and dragons. As well as a dance floor, there are cosy booths and a large, first-floor terrace. Popular drag show Mon, DJs Thurs–Sat.

The George

89 South Great George's St ☎01/478 2983. Open till 2.30am Wed–Sun. Ireland's longest-established gay bar still draws huge crowds at weekends. The outside is painted a gaudy purple with a neon-lit sign offering "Bona Polari" (gay-adopted Romany slang meaning "good

chat"), while the inside, full of character, is spread across two distinct sections: a lavishly decorated main venue on two floors, and a quieter, more traditional pub to the right. Entertainment includes cabaret, quiz nights, DJs and Sunday-night bingo with drag queen, Shirley Temple-Bar.

The Globe
11 South Great George's St. Lively watering-hole that's much favoured by students and twenty-somethings, perhaps for its lack of a design concept: just long, wooden tables, exposed bricks and low lighting. Live jazz Sunday evenings.

Hogan's
35 South Great George's St. Open till 1am Thurs, 2.30am Fri & Sat. Another favourite of the cheery, beery under-thirties, especially hectic during weekend late opening. It's a rambling, easy-going bar, with huge picture windows onto the street, an eclectic range of music and a tempting assortment of sofas and armchairs.

The Long Hall
51 South Great George's St. Old-time classic, sporting ornate plasterwork, mirrors and dark-wood panelling, a suitably long bar, friendly staff and a good pint of Guinness.

The Market Bar
Fade St. Closed Sun lunchtime. Civilized "superpub" with a no-music policy, in a huge, simply furnished red-brick space (a former abattoir) that's particularly appealing during the day thanks to its glass roof. Good for a drink, though its food menu, which attempts global tapas, is less successful.

The Stag's Head
1 Dame Court. Pretty Victorian bar, all dark wood and stuffed, tiled and stained-glassed stags, that attracts a hugely varied crowd. You'll have to come early to grab a seat in the snug, but later in the evening you might be lucky under the large windows upstairs. The menu (Mon–Sat lunchtimes), offers cheap, unpretentious pub grub: fish and chips, boiled bacon and cabbage, soup and sandwiches.

Clubs and live venues

Rí-Rá
13 Dame Court ☎01/677 4835, ⓦwww.rira.ie. Though nowadays more institution than innovator, there's still plenty to thrill at split-level *Rí-Rá*, especially when the redoubtable Dandelion is unleashing the beat at Monday's long-standing "Strictly Handbag" – great sounds and a unique atmosphere. Friday night features guest DJs, often including major international names.

J.J. Smyth's
12 Aungier St ☎01/475 2565. The best place on the Southside to catch blues and jazz-fusion bands (to whom Sunday and often Thursday nights are devoted), this pub's intimate upstairs room rocks most nights to the sound of the city's finest 12-bar and "let's try that again in 7/4 time" merchants.

The Liberties and Kilmainham

While the impact of Ireland's recent economic boom is clearly visible in other areas of the city, the predominantly working-class Liberties district remains for the most part decidedly untouched. Its main appeal lies in wandering its bustling streets and markets, perhaps picking up a bargain among the antiques shops of Francis Street. The area takes its name from the various freedoms, such as low rents and freedom of passage, granted by charter to the residents of its several separate districts. After the arrival of the Huguenots in the seventeenth century, it became a thriving mercantile area, largely dependent upon textiles, but as trade fell away in the nineteenth century, decline set in and the area's name became synonymous with poverty. Such conditions formed a hotbed for republicanism and, later, trades unionism. On its eastern fringe lies the historic church of St Audoen's while, to the west of the Liberties, the Guinness Brewery, one of Ireland's most profitable enterprises, is celebrated in its towering Storehouse museum. Further west still, the district of Kilmainham is home to the innovative Irish Museum of Modern Art and Kilmainham Gaol, a former prison indelibly associated with the struggle for Irish freedom.

St Audoen's

Church of Ireland St Audoen's, Cornmarket, High St ☎01/677 0088, ⓦ www.heritageireland.ie. June–Sept daily 9.30am–5.30pm,

last admission 4.45pm. Free. Just west of Christchurch Cathedral, two contrasting churches are dedicated to **St Audoen** (in French, Ouen), seventh-century

The Guinness story

Founded by Arthur Guinness in 1759, the **Guinness Brewery** initially manufactured ale, but in the 1770s started making porter, a drink that had become popular with the porters of London's markets and soon found a market in Ireland. Arthur's new brew, whose distinctive black colouring derived from the addition of roasted barley to the brewing process, found such favour that by 1796 it was being exported to London, and three years later ale production ceased altogether. From that point, Guinness and succeeding members of his family never looked back and, at its peak in the mid-twentieth century, their brewery produced some 2,500,000 pints of their now eponymous product a day. Although demand has since declined, Guinness remains the average Dubliner's favourite tipple.

bishop of Rouen and the patron saint of Normandy. The forbidding edifice of Catholic St Audoen's was raised in 1846, while the Church of Ireland version, built by the Anglo-Normans around 1190, is now an intriguing tourist site, though there are still services every Sunday – the church has been continuously used for worship longer than any other in Dublin.

The appeal of St Audoen's lies in the fascinating physical evidence showing how its fortunes waxed and waned over the centuries. As it prospered through association with the city's guilds, the original church, with its deeply moulded Romanesque doorway, was augmented by a chancel and St Anne's Guild Chapel, making a two-aisled **nave**. The latter is now the main exhibition area, with interesting displays on the parish, the guilds and the church's architecture. By the fifteenth century, St Audoen's was the top parish church among Dublin's leading families, and the addition in 1455 of the Portlester Chapel marked the zenith of its fortune. After the Reformation, however, many members of the Guild of St Anne refused to become Protestant, and by the nineteenth century St Audoen's had retreated to its original single nave. You can now poke around the roofless chancel and **Portlester Chapel** where, before the building was declared a national monument, locals would hang their washing out to dry.

It's worth going down the steps behind the Protestant church to Cook Street to see the thirteenth-century **St Audoen's Arch** and a heavily restored two-hundred-yard stretch of the Norman city walls.

Francis Street

Currently undergoing piecemeal rejuvenation, Francis Street is a major centre for Dublin's **antiques** trade and home to some cosy local pubs. The street takes its name from the Franciscan abbey, founded in 1235, whose site is now occupied by the Neoclassical church of St Nicholas of Myra, constructed in 1830 to celebrate Catholic Emancipation in Ireland. Just to the north stands the **Iveagh Market Hall**, financed by the then Lord Iveagh, Edward Cecil Guinness. The building has been closed for some years, but its facade is still adorned with a number of carved heads of Moorish and oriental traders. The rather cheeky-looking, bearded one is said to be E.C. Guinness himself.

Maternity Hospital Gateway

On The Coombe, one of the city's oldest thoroughfares, stands the only vestige of the old Coombe Maternity Hospital. Founded in 1826 by a Mrs Boyle in response to the fate of a young woman who died in childbirth trying to reach

▼ MATERNITY HOSPITAL GATEWAY

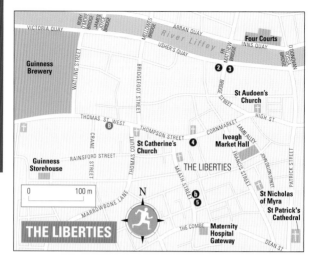

the Rotunda Hospital across the river, the hospital moved to Dolphin's Barn several decades ago. However, its **gateway** offers testament to a number of Dublin eccentrics whose nicknames have been etched into the stone. While Nancy Needle Balls was presumably keen on knitting, it's harder to fathom what Stab the Rasher or Johnny Wet Bread were up to.

Guinness Storehouse

Off Belleview ☎01/408 4800, ⊛www .guinness-storehouse.com. Daily: July & Aug 9.30am–7pm, Sept–June 9.30am–5pm. €14. The seven-storey Guinness Storehouse occupies a mere fraction of the 64-acre St James's Gate Brewery, a complex so massive that at one time it ran its own railway system, surviving tracks of which are still visible in the surrounding streets. You'll

▼ GUINNESS STOREHOUSE

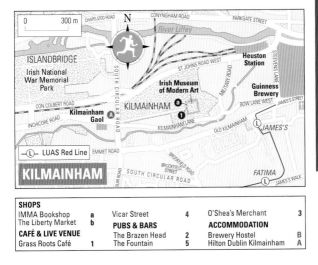

SHOPS				
IMMA Bookshop	a	Vicar Street	4	O'Shea's Merchant	3
The Liberty Market	b	**PUBS & BARS**		**ACCOMMODATION**	
CAFÉ & LIVE VENUE		The Brazen Head	2	Brewery Hostel	B
Grass Roots Café	1	The Fountain	5	Hilton Dublin Kilmainham	A

certainly get a whiff of the brewing process as you approach.

The Storehouse's self-guided **tour** is an exploration of the first three floors of this high-tech temple to the black stuff. Things start off with an explanation of the brewing process – a whirl of water (not from the Liffey, despite the myth) and a reek of barley, hops and malt – before progressing to the storage and transportation areas, the latter featuring a surviving railway engine. A huge barrel dominates the section on the lost art of coopering.

The remainder of the tour consists of a staggering array of marketing memorabilia, supported by plenty of facts and figures about the Guinness empire. There's a gallery devoted to John Gilroy, an esteemed painter also employed as a commercial artist for the company, who was responsible for the original Guinness insignia – a pelican, until changed by another employee, the novelist Dorothy L. Sayers.

Right at the top of the tower is the tour's highlight, where you can savour your complimentary pint of perhaps the best Guinness in Dublin while absorbing the superb **views** of the city and the countryside beyond.

Irish Museum of Modern Art

Royal Hospital, Military Rd ☎01/612 9900, ⓦwww.imma.ie. Tues–Sat 10am–5.30pm, Sun & public holidays noon–5.30pm. Guided tours of the exhibitions Wed, Fri & Sun 2.30pm; free. Guided tours of the Royal Hospital hourly July to mid-Sept Mon–Sat 11am–4pm, Sun 1–4pm; free; to book places call ☎01/612 9967.

Occupying the former Royal Hospital, the Irish Museum of Modern Art (IMMA) has a well-earned reputation for its imaginative **exhibitions**, which include selections from its own permanent collection as well as loaned works. All shows are temporary and can range from retrospectives of major international artists to displays of new works by

▲ IRISH MUSEUM OF MODERN ART

The Liberties and Kilmainham · PLACES

exhibition next to IMMA's reception in the south wing is devoted to the Hospital's history.

Kilmainham Gaol

Inchicore Rd ☎ 01/453 5984, ⓦ www .heritageireland.ie. April–Sept daily 9.30am–5pm; Oct–March Mon–Sat 9.30am–4pm, Sun 10am–5pm. Guided tours every 45min until 1hr 15min before closing; €5.30; Heritage Card. Kilmainham Gaol has an iconic place in the history of Ireland's struggle for independence and, during its latter years, came to symbolize both Irish political martyrdom and British oppression. Opened in 1796, the gaol became the place of incarceration for captured revolutionaries, including the leaders of the 1916 **Easter Rising**, who were executed here. Even after the War of Independence, Republicans were imprisoned here, though it closed in July 1924 after the release of its last inmate, Éamon de Valera – later to become Ireland's Taoiseach and president.

Guided **tours** of the prison provide a chilling impression of the prisoners' living conditions and the gaol's Spartan regime. Its single cells ensured that prisoners were forced into solitary contemplation, and since the building was constructed on top of limestone, their health was often sorely affected by damp and severe cold in winter.

Before embarking on the tour, it's well worth visiting the **exhibition galleries**. The ground floor's display includes a mock-up of a cell and an early mug-shot camera. Here too is a small side gallery containing paintings by Civil War internees and a huge and very self-indulgent self-portrait of Constance Gore-Booth (better known as the Countess

modern Irish painters and sculptors. Some of IMMA's most exciting exhibitions draw upon the museum's **Outsider Art** collection – works, largely paintings, by unschooled artists that explore the complexity of the psyche – as well as the Madden Arnholz collection of **Old Master prints**, with works by Goya, Rembrandt and Hogarth, among others.

The **Royal Hospital** itself was built between 1680 and 1684 by William Robinson (also responsible for the restoration of Dublin Castle) at the behest of the Duke of Ormonde, who had been inspired by Louis XIV's Les Invalides in Paris. Set around a courtyard, the Hospital is externally a model of grey stone symmetry, while its **interior** includes an impressive banqueting hall featuring seventeenth- and eighteenth-century portraits, and a Baroque chapel with a reconstructed papier-mâché ceiling and woodcarvings by the Huguenot James Tarbaret. A small heritage

Markiewicz, see p.87) as the "Good Shepherd". The upstairs gallery provides an enthralling account of the struggle for independence with numerous mementoes, old cinematic footage of Michael Collins (see p.167), the death mask of revolutionary Robert Emmet (1778–1803) and the letter ordering the release of Charles Stewart Parnell.

Irish National War Memorial Park

Con Colbert Rd, Islandbridge ⓦ www .heritageireland.ie. Mon–Fri 8am–dusk, Sat & Sun 10am–dusk. Free. Designed by Sir Edwin Lutyens and opened in 1939, a date that subsequent events would prove poignant, the park's pavilions, monuments, fountains and pools pay tribute to the 50,000 Irishmen who

PLACES

The Liberties and Kilmainham

▼ KILMAINHAM GATE

died on the fields of Belgium and Northern France fighting for the British army during World War I. Their names are inscribed on granite **memorial books** kept in the pair of pavilions found at each end of the park. A tranquil place, with views across the Liffey to Phoenix Park, the gardens are also a horticultural pleasure, particularly in spring.

Shopping

Francis Street
The antiques shops here are a great place to explore, with bargains to be found on furniture, cast iron fireplaces, old lamps, stained glass and any number of knick-knacks and *objets d'art*.

IMMA Bookshop
Royal Hospital, Kilmainham. The best place to head not only for books on modern art and paraphernalia related to the museum's exhibits, but also for its extensive collection of titles on modern architecture too.

The Liberty Market
Meath St. Thurs–Sat 10am–5pm. A higgledy-piggledy indoor maze of stalls retailing everything from cheap clothes and footwear to Westlife posters and replica football gear.

Cafés

Grass Roots Café
IMMA, Royal Hospital, Kilmainham. Serving everything from snacks to reasonably priced full lunches, IMMA's basement café also offers a potent cup of coffee.

Pubs and bars

The Brazen Head
20 Bridge St Lower ☎01/679 5186. Established in 1189 and laying claim to the title of Ireland's oldest pub, *The Brazen Head's* many rooms – featuring all manner of music-related memorabilia on the walls – ramble round a large courtyard. Traditional musicians play every night (as well as Sun 1.30–4.30pm), though the quality of the sessions can be extremely variable.

The Fountain
63–64 Meath St. A typical old-fashioned locals' bar, popular with local traders.

O'Shea's Merchant
12 Bridge St Lower ☎01/679 3797. Opposite the more famous *Brazen Head*, the *Merchant* nurtures the atmosphere of a homely, good-natured country pub in the centre of the city, providing sanctuary for "culchies" from any county, but especially Kerrymen. Traditional sessions are hosted every night in high season from around 10pm, including set dancing on Mondays and Wednesdays, and it's a good place to watch a GAA game.

Live venues

Vicar Street
58–59 Thomas St West ☎01/454 5533, ⓦ www.vicarstreet.com. Arguably the city's premier small live music venue, this 300-seater has an estimable programme of live music, comedy and other events, featuring major names.

Around O'Connell Street

Running due north from O'Connell Bridge, broader than it is long, to Parnell Square, O'Connell Street is the main artery of Dublin's Northside. Lined with numerous impressive memorials and the remarkable 120-metre high stainless steel "Spike" sculpture, this bustling thoroughfare was originally laid out in the fashion of the grand Parisian boulevards. Poorly redeveloped since the damage caused by the 1916 Easter Rising, nowadays the street is very much a mishmash of modern shop frontages, though glancing at the upper storeys reveals some of its former glory. The streets around, however, represent a consumer's paradise and, particularly on Liffey Street Lower and in the burgeoning Italian quarter centred on Bloom Lane (the result of a local developer's fascination with all things Tuscan), you'll find plenty of stylish bars and cafés. Notable cultural landmarks east of O'Connell Street include the Abbey Theatre, hub of the twentieth-century revival in Irish theatre, and, along the Quays, the impressively opulent eighteenth-century Custom House.

Ha'penny Bridge

Dublin's most renowned crossing, the cast-iron Ha'penny Bridge is the oldest of the pedestrian river crossings, with great views of the river along the Quays in both directions. It began life in 1816 as the Wellington Bridge but soon acquired its nickname thanks to a halfpenny toll, levied until 1919.

O'Connell Street

O'Connell Street has a remarkable number of **monuments**, mostly

▲ TRAMS ON O'CONNELL STREET

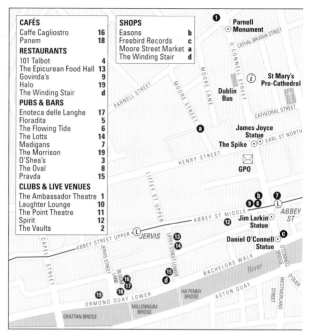

CAFÉS	
Caffe Cagliostro	16
Panem	18
RESTAURANTS	
101 Talbot	4
The Epicurean Food Hall	13
Govinda's	9
Halo	19
The Winding Stair	d
PUBS & BARS	
Enoteca delle Langhe	17
Floradita	5
The Flowing Tide	6
The Lotts	14
Madigans	7
The Morrison	19
O'Shea's	3
The Oval	8
Pravda	15
CLUBS & LIVE VENUES	
The Ambassador Theatre	1
Laughter Lounge	10
The Point Theatre	11
Spirit	12
The Vaults	2

SHOPS	
Easons	b
Freebird Records	c
Moore Street Market	a
The Winding Stair	d

positioned in its broad central reservation. Crossing O'Connell Bridge you'll first encounter the imposing figure of **Daniel O'Connell**, "The Liberator", who played a major role in nineteenth-century

▼ STATUE OF JIM LARKIN, O'CONNELL STREET

political campaigns to secure independence. The winged figures by his side represent O'Connell's bravery, patriotism, fidelity and eloquence while the smaller female figure nearby symbolizes Ireland unchained. At the Abbey Street junction stands Oisín Kelly's statue of **Jim Larkin**, a key trades union activist during the first half of the twentieth century, caught in the act of addressing a crowd.

Further up, by the junction with Earl Street North, the city's most striking landmark stands on the spot occupied by Nelson's Pillar until it was blown up in 1966 – the frankly astonishing Dublin Spire, or "**Spike**" as it's colloquially known, which was constructed to celebrate the city's entry into the new millennium (though

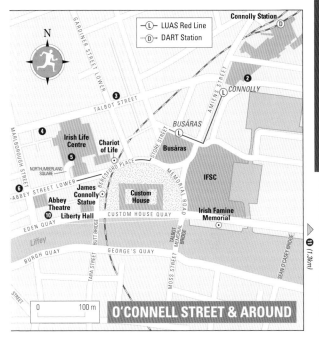

O'CONNELL STREET & AROUND

0 — 100 m

was not completed until 2003). Designed by Ian Ritchie, the 120-metre high stainless-steel needle, surmounted by a beacon, is easily the tallest structure in the city centre. Just three metres wide at its base, it tapers to a mere 15cm at its summit. In the early morning or at dusk, its surface takes on an ethereal blue colour while at night it seems to loom ominously over the city. What the ghost of the author **James Joyce**, whose adjacent, somewhat rakish statue stands just down Earl Street North, would make of it all is open to question.

Near the very top of O'Connell Street stands a monument to **Charles Stewart Parnell**, one of the major figures in Ireland's nineteenth-century Home Rule movement.

General Post Office

O'Connell St Lower. Mon–Sat 8am–8pm; free. The General Post Office is a building of crucial significance in Ireland's political history. On Easter Monday, April 1916, **Pádraig Pearse** (see p.159) strode from its doors to read a proclamation on behalf of the Provisional Government of the Irish Republic declaring Ireland's independence from Britain. The rebels held on to the GPO for six days, one of several buildings seized that day, during which much of the surrounding area was badly damaged by the fighting. Eventually, however, the weight of British Army artillery fire proved too much to withstand and the insurgents set the GPO ablaze before fleeing. Most, however – including Pearse himself

▲ GENERAL POST OFFICE

– were either captured or gave themselves up in nearby streets.

Initial public reaction to the "**Easter Rising**" was profoundly hostile. Much of central Dublin was in ruins and more than 1300 people had been killed or seriously wounded. Nevertheless, Britain's execution of all the Rising's leaders (barring Éamon de Valera, who was not of Irish birth) proved utterly miscalculated and sparked increasing demands for Home Rule.

The GPO itself, which dated back to 1818, did not survive the Rising, except for its Ionic **portico** which still bears the marks of gunfire. Inside, the most enthralling sight is Oliver Sheppard's intricately wrought bronze statue **The Death of Cúchulainn**, representing a key moment in the Irish legend *Táin Bó Cúailnge*.

The Abbey Theatre

26 Abbey St Lower ☎01/878 7222, ⓦwww.abbeytheatre.ie. Backstage tours Tues & Thurs 2.30pm; €6; call ☎01/887 2223 to book. Ultimately the focal point for Ireland's twentieth-century cultural revival, the Abbey Theatre first opened its doors in December 1904 to present three plays, two by the poet and dramatist **W.B. Yeats** and the other by his patron **Lady Gregory**. The theatre's company turned professional in 1906 and Yeats and Gregory, along with J.M. Synge, became its first directors. The staging of Synge's tragi-comic *Playboy of the Western World* the following year, with its frank language and suggestion that Irish peasants would condone a murder, provoked riots on its opening night. Later, in 1926, Seán O'Casey's *The Plough and the Stars* incited bitter outrage, the audience regarding its view of the Easter Rising as derisive, not least because the theatre had begun to receive state funding the previous year.

The original Abbey burnt to the ground in 1951 and its more modern, outwardly grim replacement opened in 1966. Informative guided **tours** – a must for anyone interested in the link between Ireland's

▼ THE DEATH OF CÚCHULAINN

culture and politics – take in both back- and front-stage areas and recount key moments in the Abbey's history. The theatre's **programme** continues to include a range of drama, blending revivals of Irish classics with new works by established writers such as Hugh Leonard and Brian Friel, while the much smaller **Peacock Theatre** in the basement is devoted to new experimental works.

In 2005, financial mismanagement almost caused the Abbey's closure, but a subsequent government grant secured its future and resulted in recent redevelopment of its interior. However, there are plans to relocate the theatre into a newly built development in the docklands.

St Mary's Pro-Cathedral

Marlborough St ☎01/874 5441, ⓦwww.procathedral.ie. Mon–Fri 7.30am–6.45pm, Sat 7.30am–7.15pm, Sun 9am–1.45pm & 5.30–7.45pm, public holidays 10am–1.30pm; free.

Featuring a six-columned facade modelled on the Temple of Theseus in Athens, St Mary's is the city's principal Catholic church. Its side-street position resulted from Protestant opposition to plans to locate the building on Sackville Street (now O'Connell Street), a site which instead became occupied by the General Post Office. St Mary's opened in 1825 but did not adopt its full title as Pro-Cathedral until the end of the nineteenth century, when its status "standing in" for a Catholic cathedral (which the city had lacked since the Reformation) was sanctioned by the then archbishop of Dublin, Dr Walsh. The current archbishop continues to serve as the church's parish priest.

Despite its impressive frontage, there's little of attraction inside, and the Pro-Cathedral is best known nowadays for its male **Palestrina Choir**, founded in 1903 and named after the sixteenth-century Italian composer. The choir can be heard singing Latin Mass every Sunday at 11am, though during July and August its place is taken by visiting choirs.

Custom House

Custom House Quay. Opened in 1791, the imposing Custom House is one of several notable Dublin landmarks designed by the English architect **James Gandon** (others include the Four Courts and the O'Connell Bridge). Constructed on a submerged mudflat that required covering with a layer of solid pine planks, and showing off Gandon's fabulously intricate architectural detail, the Custom House cost the then unearthly sum of £500,000 sterling, a figure that proved even more extravagant when the Act of

▼ LIFFEY STREET LOWER

Union transferred customs and excise to London in 1800.

The building's grandiose Neoclassical **exterior**, around one hundred metres in length, features sculptures by Gandon's contemporary Edward Smyth, with cattle heads symbolizing Ireland's beef trade, and others representing Ireland's rivers, including the Liffey above the main entrance. Its 35-metre-high dome was modelled upon Christopher Wren's Greenwich Hospital.

After 1801, the Custom House became the administrative centre for the city's work on public hygiene and Poor Law relief. The building suffered a major fire in 1833 and was completely gutted in 1921 after being set alight by the IRA. Subsequently restored, though with significant changes to its internal structure and facade, it housed various government departments; some of its more illustrious employees included Brian O'Nolan, better known as the comic novelist Flann O'Brien, and the songwriter Percy French.

▼ CUSTOM HOUSE DOME

Around the Custom House

Just around the corner from the Custom House on Beresford Place, and facing Liberty Hall, the headquarters of SIPTU, Ireland's largest trade union, stands, appropriately, a **statue of James Connolly** – socialist theorist, trade union activist and one of the leaders of the Easter Rising. Nearby, at the junction with Abbey Street Lower, Oisín Kelly's remarkable **Chariot of Life sculpture** shows a charioteer struggling to control his horses, meant to represent the conflict between passion and reason. The mammoth forty-acre site of the International Financial Services Centre dominates the eastern edge of Memorial Road, a symbol of the "Celtic Tiger" boom of the 1990s.

Irish Famine Memorial

Custom House Quay. Set between the looming presence of the IFSC and the Liffey, these six **life-size bronzes** were designed and cast by the Dublin sculptor Rowan Gillespie to mark the 150th anniversary of the worst year of the **Great Famine** (1845–49), or Black '47 as it is sometimes known. Over the course of the famine more than a million people died of starvation and another million and a half emigrated, while the British government adopted a laissez-faire approach and continued to export food from Ireland around the world. That these stark, beseeching figures are staring eastwards is not coincidental.

Shopping

Eason's

40 O'Connell St Lower. Open late Thurs until 8.45pm, Fri until 7.45pm. The largest branch of the Irish chain

▲ JAMES CONNOLLY STATUE

The Winding Stair

40 Ormond Quay Lower. Closed Sun. The ground floor of this bookshop and restaurant (see below) is chock-full of second-hand titles, with particularly good sections on Irish literature and biography.

Cafés

Caffe Cagliostro

Bloom Lane. A splendid, tiny Italian café serving arguably the Northside's best coffees and delicious pastries, with newspapers for perusal. There are tables outside in fine weather.

Panem

21 Ormond Quay Lower. Petite but perfectly formed, *Panem* dishes up a worthy range of good-value snacks and savouries, including freshly-made soups, a strikingly good homemade focaccia – a variety of pasta dishes and the richest hot chocolate you'll find in Ireland.

store offers an extensive range of books, as well as stocking a vast selection of newspapers and magazines. There's a branch of Tower Records on the first floor and a café on the second.

Freebird Records

Downstairs, 1 Eden Quay. Open late Thurs until 7.30pm; closed Sun. Freebird crams an astonishing range of new and second-hand CDs into its racks, covering every genre from rock to hip-hop, via reggae, jazz, blues and folk, with an extensive section on Irish indie bands and singers.

Moore Street Market

Moore St. Mon–Sat 10am–6pm. This lively street market – a long-standing Dublin institution – and its adjacent shops reflect the city's changing ethnicity. The traditional butchers, fishmongers and greengrocers are still present, though you're bound to see price tags in Cantonese too, and there are also a number of Afro-Caribbean stalls.

Restaurants

101 Talbot

100–101 Talbot St ☎01/874 5011, ⓦwww.101talbot.com. Closed all day Sun & Mon and lunchtime Tues–Sat. Wise diners make advance bookings at this upstairs establishment. The imaginative starters, including Vietnamese-style warm squid salad, are but a prelude to the delightful Mediterranean-influenced dishes, such as crispy lamb with Moroccan spices or roasted red peppers stuffed with a blend of pistachio nuts and vegetables, presented with style and served with élan. A three-course early bird menu (€21.50) is served until 8pm.

The Epicurean Food Hall

13–14 Liffey St Lower. This dedicated food mall will leave you spoilt for choice, wondering which of the dozen or so eateries (and a bar) to plump for. Options include *Leo Burdock's* fish and chips, tempting Chinese street food, *Christophe's* superb-value *boeuf bourguignon* and wonderful coffee and *bruschette* from *La Corte* café.

Govinda's

84 Abbey St Middle. Open till 9pm Mon–Sat; closed Sun. This bright, breezy and inexpensive south Indian vegetarian restaurant has added some culinary variety to the Northside. The menu includes a range of tasty soups and dishes such as cauliflower, potato and carrot curry, served with fresh dill yoghurt, dhal and rice – in generous helpings. Treat yourself to the *malpoora* (small fried doughnuts), and don't miss the mango lassi.

Halo

Morrison Hotel, Ormond Quay Lower ☎01/887 2421, ⓦwww .morrisonhotel.ie. Brilliantly designed modern decor married to faultlessly presented cuisine makes *Halo* a gourmet's dream. The menu combines Irish ingredients with a cosmopolitan range of herbs, spices and delicacies. Starters include seared scallops with polenta served in pomegranate sauce; main courses cover fish and meat dishes, such as pan-fried pike fillet in a truffle sauce, or loin of venison in a tangy anis and cinnamon jus. Expect to pay around €50 (plus wine) for a three-course meal.

The Winding Stair

40 Ormond Quay Lower ☎01/872 7230. Many lamented the passing of the old upstairs café above The Winding Stair bookshop (see p.135), but others have been won around by its replacement restaurant's basic ambience and good cheer and, not least, the often stunningly good food, including a tasty range of fresh seafood and dishes sourced from Irish producers – plus there are still the views of Ha'penny Bridge and the Liffey to gaze at.

▼ THE FLOWING TIDE

Pubs and bars

Enoteca delle Langhe

Bloom Lane. A focal point of
Dublin's recently established
Italian quarter, the *Enoteca*
brings all the flavours of a
Neapolitan bar to the city,
serving up an extensive range
of wines and a small, but still
intriguing, menu of antipasti and
main courses.

Floradita

Irish Life Mall, Abbey Street Lower
℡ 01/878 1032, ⓦ www.floradita
.co.uk/dublin. The latest branch of
a chain which has branches in
London, Madrid and Moscow is
a swish, split-level affair with an
upstairs restaurant offering tasty
– if somewhat pricey – Cuban
and Latin-American cuisine,
with occasional live bands, while
the ground floor bar specializes
in an outlandish range of Cuban
cocktails.

The Flowing Tide

9 Abbey St Lower. Long connected
with the Abbey Theatre
opposite, this pub features
tasteful stained-glass windows, a
mural celebrating the theatre's
history and a horseshoe-shaped
bar. A good spot for a decent
pint and a a filling lunchtime
sandwich.

The Lotts

9 Liffey St Lower. It's often
standing room only at this
friendly corner bar, which lays
claim to being the Northside's
smallest. It offers a tasty
selection of Mediterranean-
inspired meals in its fashionable
café-bar next door.

Madigans

4 Abbey St Lower. A straightforward,
pleasant, wood-panelled

▲ THE MORRISON

bar serving well-kept stout,
Madigans never seems to get
crowded, despite its proximity to
O'Connell Street.

The Morrison

Morrison Hotel, Ormond Quay Lower.
Chic and stylishly modern, with
good views of the river, this
hotel bar is one of the city's
mellowest places to pass the
time. Don't be deterred by the
apparently ultra-hip exterior –
inside you'll find a broad mix of
locals and hotel guests enjoying
their pints or sampling the range
of tempting cocktails.

O'Shea's

19 Talbot St ℡ 01/836 5670. Hugely
popular, thanks to its first-rate
service and very reasonably
priced meals, including probably
the ultimate Irish breakfast
(served all day), *O'Shea's* also
hosts occasional traditional-
music sessions and gigs.

The Oval

78 Abbey St Middle. In former days
this calm, friendly, atmospheric
bar was often packed with

newshounds from the adjacent *Irish Independent*. The paper has since moved its HQ, though the bar's international clocks remain in place.

Pravda

Liffey Street Lower. Open late: Thurs until 1.30am, Fri & Sat until 2.30am. A real oddity, this Soviet-influenced theme bar sports revolutionary murals in the "noble worker" style and, appropriately, serves Russian and Polish lagers in addition to the standard pint. Standard fare such as burgers and spicy chicken wings is served during the day.

Clubs and live venues

The Ambassador Theatre

O'Connell Street Upper ☎0818/719 300, ⓦ www.mcd.ie. An old but well-regarded venue at the very northern end of O'Connell Street, the *Ambassador*'s programme is decidedly eclectic, focusing very much on middle-ranking, left-field indie and rock bands.

Laughter Lounge

4–8 Eden Quay ☎1800/266339, ⓦ www.laughterlounge.com. Thurs–Sat from 8.30pm. Dublin's only venue devoted entirely to comedy features an ever-changing line-up of top Irish stand-ups and occasional international guests.

The Point Theatre

East Link Bridge Rd, North Wall Quay ☎0818/719 391, ⓦ www.thepoint. ie. Once a railway depot, the cavernous *Point*, 1.5km east of O'Connell Bridge, is Ireland's largest dedicated music venue with a capacity of 7500 (half of this for seated gigs). Unsurprisingly, it hosts major international names, with high prices to boot.

Spirit

57 Abbey St Middle ☎01/877 9999, ⓦ www.spiritdublin.com. Wed–Sun 10.30pm–5am. One of the city's largest clubbing venues, *Spirit*'s three floors are devoted to a variety of club nights, including the popular Revelation (Fri) and Carnavale (Sat). Entry prices can be steep at weekends (around €20 if international guest DJs are spinning the tables).

The Vaults

Harbourmaster Place ☎01/605 4700, ⓦ www.thevaults.ie. Fri & Sat 11pm–3am. Tucked away under Connolly Station, this spacious cellar bar hosts popular club nights at weekends, with a house and funk focus.

North from Parnell Square

Situated at the northern end of O'Connell Street, Parnell Square might lack the subtle allure of its Georgian equivalents on the Southside, but still possesses a certain charm. Three sides of the square are busy thoroughfares, the southern part dominated by the prominent cupola of the eighteenth-century Rotunda Maternity Hospital, while just around its eastern corner is the prestigious Gate Theatre. The peaceful northern side of the square, is worth a visit in its own right; here you'll find the Garden of Remembrance, devoted to the memory of those who died in the struggle for Ireland's independence, while other highlights include one of Dublin's premier art galleries, the Hugh Lane, and the Dublin Writers Museum, an excellent place to learn more about the city's literary history. Away from Parnell Square, nearby attractions include an information centre devoted to the works of James Joyce and to the northeast, across the Royal Canal, stands Croke Park, a major sports arena and home to the innovative GAA Museum.

The Gate Theatre

1 Cavendish Row, Parnell Square East ☎01/874 4045 or 01/874 6042, ⊛www.gate-theatre.ie. The Gate Theatre has been a hub of quality dramatic productions since it was founded in 1928 by two Englishmen, life-long lovers Hilton Edwards and Micheál Mac Liammoir. In a strong tradition continuing today, the theatre showcased modern European and American theatre, as well as classic and new Irish works, and its enduringly powerful programme saw it quickly become a contender to the Abbey's crown (see p.132). Both Orson Welles and James Mason began their careers here.

Garden of Remembrance

Parnell Square East. April–Sept 8.30am–6pm, Oct–March 9.30am–4pm; free. A tranquil

▼ ROTUNDA MATERNITY HOSPITAL, PARNELL SQUARE

PLACES

North from Parnell Square

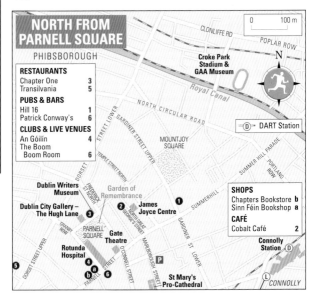

NORTH FROM PARNELL SQUARE

PHIBSBOROUGH

0	100 m

N

RESTAURANTS
Chapter One   3
Transilvania   5

PUBS & BARS
Hill 16   1
Patrick Conway's   6

CLUBS & LIVE VENUES
An Góilín   4
The Boom
  Boom Room   6

Croke Park
Stadium &
GAA Museum

CLONLIFFE RD

POPLAR ROW

Royal Canal

NORTH CIRCULAR ROAD

🚉 DART Station

MOUNTJOY
SQUARE

Dublin Writers
Museum

Garden of
Remembrance

Dublin City Gallery –
The Hugh Lane

James
Joyce Centre ❶

❸

❷

Gate
Theatre

Rotunda
Hospital

PARNELL
SQUARE

❺

❹
a
❻

St Mary's
Pro-Cathedral

SHOPS
Chapters Bookstore   b
Sinn Féin Bookshop   a

CAFÉ
Cobalt Café   2

Connolly
Station 🚉

CONNOLLY

spot, the Garden of Remembrance was created in 1966 on the fiftieth anniversary of the Easter Rising, and commemorates those who

▼ *CHILDREN OF LIR*, GARDEN OF REMEMBRANCE

died in the cause of Irish independence. The garden's **railings** are replete with Celtic and Christian symbols, including a cruciform-shaped pond. At its western end stands Oisín Kelly's arresting **Children of Lir statue**, based on the complex legend of the lord of the sea whose children by his first wife were transformed into swans by her resentful sister, whom Lir had subsequently married. The statue portrays Lir's anguish at the moment of metamorphosis.

Dublin City Gallery – The Hugh Lane

Parnell Square North ☎01/222 5550, ⊛www.hughlane.ie. Tues–Thurs 10am–6pm, Fri & Sat 10am–5pm, Sun 11am–5pm; free, but €2 donation suggested. The elegant, Georgian, stone-clad Charlemont House, with its curved walls and Neoclassical interior has provided a permanent

▲ THE HUGH LANE GALLERY

home for the Hugh Lane Gallery since 1933. Sir Hugh, a nephew of Lady Gregory (see p.132), wanted Dublin to house a major gallery of Irish and international art. He amassed a considerable collection by persuading native artists to contribute their work and purchasing many other paintings himself, particularly from the **French Impressionist** school.

The gallery holds around half of the Lane collection (the rest is in London's National Gallery) and only a fraction is on display here at any one time. You're likely to see works by Renoir, Monet and Degas, as well as Pissarro and the Irish painters Jack B. Yeats, Roderic O'Connor and Louis de Brocquy, and stained glass pieces by Evie Hone and Harry Clarke. There are also usually temporary exhibitions of more modern artworks.

Part of the gallery is devoted to a recreation of Dublin-born painter **Francis Bacon's studio**, transported from its original location at Reece Mews in South Kensington, London, where the artist lived and worked for the last thirty years of his life. After his death in 1992, his studio was donated to the gallery by his heir, John Edwards, and reconstructed here with astonishing precision – more than seven thousand individual items were meticulously catalogued and placed here. The studio can only be viewed through the window glass but among the apparent debris are an old Bush record player, empty champagne boxes and huge tins of the type of matt vinyl favoured by Bacon, the fumes of which exacerbated his asthma. The surrounding rooms hold displays of memorabilia, such as photographs and correspondence, as well as a detailed database of every item found in the studio (accessible via touchscreen consoles) and large canvases from the painter's last years.

The Gallery runs guided **tours** of the exhibits (Tues 11am & Sun 1.30pm), a programme of lectures and films related to its current shows (Sun 3pm) and very popular classical music concerts (Sun noon) – and all of these events are free.

▲ DUBLIN WRITERS MUSEUM

Dublin Writers Museum

18 Parnell Square North ☎ 01/872 2077, ⓦ www.writersmuseum.com. Mon–Sat 10am–5pm (July & Aug Mon–Fri until 6pm), Sun & public holidays 11am–5pm; €7; €12 Dublin Tourism Combined Ticket (see p.203). For anyone wanting to learn more about Dublin's rich literary history, this museum makes the ideal starting point. With a wealth of anecdotes and information, the audio-guide (available from reception, and included in the admission price)

Bloomsday

Perhaps no other writer has so encapsulated the life, lore and mores of his native city as **James Joyce** so successfully achieved in his remarkable novels, most notably **Ulysses** (1922). So precise are the author's descriptions of the locales visited by the book's protagonists on the date of the book's setting, June 16, that it is possible to follow literally in their footsteps. This annual pilgrimage undertaken by Joyce aficionados across the city has become known as **Bloomsday**. Though you can undertake to cover the Bloomsday route independently (a *Ulysses* map is available from the Dublin Tourism Centre), guided walks and other associated events are organized by the James Joyce Centre (see opposite).

Strangely, for someone who documented his native city's life with such pride, Joyce came to loathe Dublin, once describing the place in a letter as a "city of failure, of rancour and of unhappiness", and concluding "I long to be out of it".

Though his early works, such as the short-story collection **Dubliners** and the semi-autobiographical novel **A Portrait of the Artist as a Young Man**, draw heavily upon his upbringing, Catholic education and Dublin experiences, by the time of the latter's publication in 1916, Joyce had long abandoned Ireland. Not long after meeting a Connemara-born chambermaid, **Nora Barnacle**, having first taken her out on June 16, 1904, the pair eloped to Europe. Other than two brief visits to Ireland, Joyce spent the rest of his life in exile living in cities across Europe, most notably Paris, where *Ulysses* was published in 1922 and where he finally wed Nora in 1931. Joyce's only subsequent published work was the convoluted *Finnegans Wake* (1939). When he died in 1941, *Ulysses* was still unavailable in Ireland, and was not published in the country until the 1960s.

helps to illuminate literature's pivotal role in Irish society, particularly in terms of politics and national identity. The displays cover not only such giants as Wilde, Shaw, Joyce and Beckett, but also lesser-known figures like Sheridan Le Fanu and Oliver St John Gogarty (see p.91 and p.162).

The **ground floor** of the museum contains a plethora of displays on particular writers and literary schools, covering first or early editions, playbills, programmes and memorabilia. A varied and changing selection of modern paintings of writers hangs in the hall, which leads to a pleasant outdoor Zen garden where you can contemplate works purchased in the museum's well-stocked ground-floor bookshop, or head for the **café** at the rear.

On the first floor is the **Gallery of Writers**, an elegant salon featuring decorative plasterwork by Michael Stapleton – renowned as the finest stuccodore of the Georgian era – James Joyce's piano, and more paintings, of which the most impressive is a portrait of the author George Moore by John B. Yeats, father of the poet and dramatist William B. and the painter Jack B. Yeats. The **Gorham Library**, next door, harbours numerous rare editions.

The James Joyce Centre

35 North Great George's St ☎ 01/878 8547, ⓦ www.jamesjoyce.ie. Tues–Sat 10am–5pm; €5. Walking tours: Sat 11am and 2pm; 1hr; €10. The James Joyce Centre aims to illuminate the work of perhaps Ireland's most imaginative yet most complex writer, who spent part of his life living in the inner Northside, and drew upon his experiences in the creation of his characters and the settings for his works. The centre occupies a grand eighteenth-century town house, restored in the 1980s, that boasts decorative stucco mouldings by Michael Stapleton. The ground floor houses a small shop full of Joyceiana such as books and prints, and an airy **courtyard** which features the actual period door of 7 Eccles Street, fictional home of Leopold and Molly Bloom, two of the main protagonists in *Ulysses*, as well as a somewhat enigmatic Joyce-inspired sculpture of a cow.

The building's **upper floors** hold a recreation of the tiny room occupied by Joyce in Trieste, featuring various books, pianola music rolls and a splendid collection of hats, as well as photographs of people and places associated with *Ulysses*, and touch screen consoles tracing the development of the novel's plot and its variety of characters.

▼ FRONT DOOR, 7 ECCLES STREET, JAMES JOYCE CENTRE

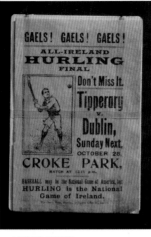

GAELS! GAELS! GAELS!

ALL-IRELAND

HURLING
FINAL

Don't Miss It.

Tipperary
v.
Dublin,
Sunday Next,
OCTOBER 28.

CROKE PARK.
MATCH AT 12:15 p.m.

BASEBALL may be the National Game of America, but
HURLING is the National
Game of Ireland.

▲ THE GAA MUSEUM

Three short documentary films on the writer's life can also be viewed. The centre's **walking tour**, which begins here, is well worth taking if you want to learn more about Joycean connections with the surrounding area.

The GAA Museum

Croke Park, St Joseph's Ave ☎01/819 2323, ⓦ www.museum.gaa.ie. Mon–Sat 9.30am–5pm (July & Aug until 6pm), Sun & public holidays noon–5pm (only open to Cusack Stand ticket holders on match days). Stadium tours on the hour: Mon–Sat 10am–4pm, Sun 1pm–4pm; Sept–June last tour 3pm; no tours on match days; call to check availability. Museum only €5.50; museum and stadium tour €9.50. Bus #123 from O'Connell St. Croke Park is the home of the **Gaelic Athletic Association** (GAA). It's a magnificent and – after much redevelopment – very modern stadium, its capacity of 82,000-plus putting it among the largest in Europe.

Inside the stadium, under the Cusack Stand, is the GAA Museum, one of the finest in Dublin. The **creative exhibits** and imaginative multimedia displays provide a fascinating account of the sports of hurling and Gaelic football, as well as lesser-known games such as handball and camogie (the women's variant on hurling). Upstairs you can have a go at whacking a hurling ball or test your balance and reactions via various simulations.

Historical and political contexts are explored too, in a thoroughly engaging manner – since its foundation in 1884, the GAA has been irrevocably linked with Irish Nationalism. Thus the museum does not shirk from recounting key politically sensitive events such as **Bloody Sunday**, when British troops fired on the crowd attending a match in 1920, killing twelve people in the process.

Taking the stadium **tour** is highly recommended, not just to view this remarkable arena at first hand, but also to learn more about key events in its history – including the momentous decision in April 2005 to suspend the GAA's constitution to allow professional Rugby Union and Association Football international matches to take place here while Lansdowne Road stadium undergoes redevelopment – previously only games of Irish origin, played by amateurs, could be staged here.

Shopping

Chapters Bookstore

Parnell St. Closed Sun. Claiming to be Dublin's largest bookshop (and it's probably true), Chapters' ground floor features a massive range of fiction and fact, including impressive sections on Irish literature and history. Upstairs is devoted to the secondhand section, which also includes bargain-priced CDs and DVDs.

Sinn Féin Bookshop

58 Parnell Square West. Closed Sun. The Republican party's literature outlet stocks a compact range of historical and political tomes, including some you're unlikely to find anywhere else in Dublin, as well as CDs (including some hard-to-find Christy Moore releases), videos and DVDs.

Cafés

Cobalt Café

16 North Great George's St. Closed Sun. A relaxing haven in an area with a dearth of cafés, the *Cobalt* offers a range of coffees as well as light snacks and soups, which can be enjoyed while admiring the original artworks displayed on its walls.

Restaurants

Chapter One

18–19 Parnell Square North ☎01/873 2266, ⓦwww.chapteroner-estaurant .com. Closed all day Sun & Mon and Sat lunchtime. Housed in the cellars of the Dublin Writers Museum, this recently Michelin-starred Northside culinary gem specializes in French-inspired modern Irish food using an imaginative blend of herbs, spices and fruit to enhance a variety of fish and meat dishes. Carnivores can also opt for selections from the charcuterie trolley, and there's a selection of taste bud-titillating desserts. The restaurant offers a pre-theatre special dinner (6–7pm, €35 for three courses); otherwise, expect to pay €65 per head plus wine.

Transilvania

7A Henrietta Place ☎01/873 4375. Closed all day Mon and Tues–Fri lunchtimes. Probably Ireland's only Romanian restaurant, the reasonably priced menu here includes an intriguing range of traditional soups, as well as main courses featuring dishes such as *tocitura* – various meats in a red wine sauce – and *sarmale* – pork, beef and rice wrapped in a cabbage leaf – and delicious rustic cheeses. A cosy place, the atmosphere is sometimes enlivened by Romanian musicians.

Pubs and bars

Hill 16

Gardiner St Middle. Named after Croke Park's most popular stand, the bar is a magnet for GAA devotees, particularly those who follow the fortunes of Dublin's Gaelic football team. Naturally, it's busiest on match-days, though service remains impeccable, when the chance to share the *craic* and banter with fans is the main draw. Reasonably priced lunches are also served during the week.

Patrick Conway's

70 Parnell St. Running since 1745 (when it was known as *Doyle's*), *Conway's* is the oldest pub on the Northside. Its fame is also due to the fact that Pádraig Pearse surrendered to the British on the corner outside

after the Easter Rising. As well as its historical associations, the pub offers filling bar meals (massive baguettes served with chips and salad, soups, roasts and stews), and a live music venue – *The Boom Boom Room* – upstairs (see below).

Club and live venues

An Góilín

Teacher's Club, 36 Parnell Square West ☎086/815 0946, ⊛www.goilin.com. The city's longest-standing traditional singers' club opens its doors every Friday from 9.30pm (though is closed during July and August). For the ridiculously cheap minimum contribution of €2, you can hear some of Dublin's finest, singing unaccompanied, at the regular club nights, or catch guests from across Ireland. Sometimes the latter include *sean-nós* ("old-style") singers from Irish-speaking areas such as Connemara.

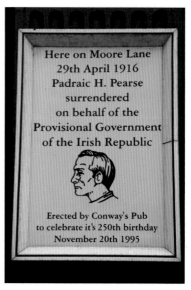

Here on Moore Lane
29th April 1916
Padraic H. Pearse
surrendered
on behalf of the
Provisional Government
of the Irish Republic

Erected by Conway's Pub
to celebrate it's 250th birthday
November 20th 1995

▲ EASTER RISING PLAQUE, *PATRICK CONWAY'S* PUB

The Boom Boom Room

Patrick Conway's, 70 Parnell St ☎01/873 2687, ⊛www .theboomboomroom.tv. The *Boom Boom* hosts a diverse range of live gigs, on various nights of the week (usually Wed–Sun), and features all manner of left-field and experimental local bands and singers, as well as occasional international acts.

From Capel Street to Collins Barracks

Much redeveloped in recent years, the traditionally working-class area west along the Quays from Capel Street is a focus for Dublin's nightlife, with two of the city's finest traditional music establishments and several more modern, fashionable bars. From Grattan Bridge, at Capel Street's southern end, views west along the river are dominated by the arresting Four Courts. Northwest of here, the renovated Smithfield area, home to the Old Jameson Distillery, is renowned for its 300-year-old monthly horse fair, while the crypt of the Northside's oldest church, St Michan's, holds the ghoulish attraction of several mummified bodies from as long ago as the Crusades. To the west, the striking Collins Barracks houses the delights of the National Museum Decorative Arts Collection.

The Four Courts

Inns Quay. Public court galleries Mon–Fri 11am–1pm & 2–4pm (closed Aug & Sept); free. Fronted by Corinthian columns and surmounted by an impressive **dome**, this imposing riverside structure has seen many a legal hearing since it first opened its doors in 1802. Like the Custom House (see p.133), the building was designed by **James Gandon**, and took some sixteen years to complete at a cost of £200,000 sterling. The **four courts** of its name were those of the Chancery, Common Pleas, Exchequer and Kings Bench, though

▼ JAMES JOYCE BRIDGE

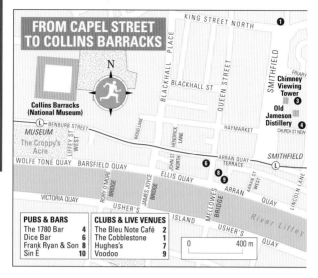

FROM CAPEL STREET TO COLLINS BARRACKS

KING STREET NORTH

BLACKHALL PLACE
BLACKHALL ST
QUEEN STREET
SMITHFIELD
FRIARY
Chimney Viewing Tower

Collins Barracks (National Museum)

Old Jameson Distillery
CHURCH ST NEW

BENBURB STREET
MUSEUM
The Croppy's Acre
LIFFEY ST WEST
WOODLANE
HENDRICK LANE
HAYMARKET
SMITHFIELD

WOLFE TONE QUAY BARSFIELD QUAY
RORY O'MORE BRIDGE
JAMES JOYCE BRIDGE
JOHN ST NORTH
ELLIS QUAY
ARRAN QUAY TERRACE
ARRAN ST WEST
LINCOLN LANE

VICTORIA QUAY
USHER'S
MELLOWES BRIDGE
ARRAN QUAY
River Liffey

USHER'S QUAY
ISLAND

PUBS & BARS		CLUBS & LIVE VENUES	
The 1780 Bar	4	The Bleu Note Café	2
Dice Bar	6	The Cobblestone	1
Frank Ryan & Son	8	Hughes's	7
Sin É	10	Voodoo	9

0 ———— 400 m

somehow a fifth, the Judicature, was forgotten when naming the building. The building was seized by Republicans opposed to the Anglo-Irish Treaty in 1921, and heavily bombarded by Free State forces during the subsequent Civil War using, ironically, howitzers borrowed from the British. Before the siege came to its inevitable end, however, the rebels accidentally set off explosives inside the building, destroying the Public Records Office and innumerable irreplaceable historic documents.

After rebuilding, the Four Courts reopened in 1931 and nowadays houses the **High Court of Justice**. A better – and often more entertaining – bet, though, is to take a seat in the District Court, entered via Chancery Place, which deals with less salubrious local matters.

St Michan's Church

Church St ☎01/872 4154. Tours of the crypt: March–Oct Mon–Fri 10am–12.45pm & 2–4.45pm, Sat 10am–12.45pm; Nov–Feb Mon–Fri 12.30–3.30pm, Sat 10am–12.45pm; €3.50. Dating from 1095, St Michan's was constructed by the Vikings in honour of a Danish bishop. The church was substantially rebuilt some six hundred years later and its interior has subsequently undergone much refurbishment. Next to the church organ, reputedly once played by Handel, is the unusual **Penitents' Pew**, in which parishioners knelt facing the

▲ THE FOUR COURTS

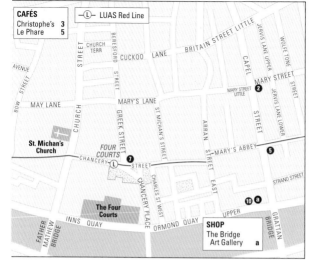

CAFÉS
Christophe's **3**
Le Phare **5**

—Ⓛ— LUAS Red Line

SHOP
The Bridge
Art Gallery **a**

congregation to confess their errant ways.

It's the church's **vaults** that hold the most fascination, however. Guided tours descend an almost sheer staircase to view the contents of tiny crypts, including, most notably, a dozen bodies, some dating back seven hundred years. These have been mummified, a process caused by two factors: the vaults' limestone walls, which absorb the air's natural moisture, and the methane produced by vegetation rotting below the floor. One of the **mummies** is believed to have been a Crusader, another a nun and a third, which lacks a hand, may have been a repentant thief. Another crypt contains John and Henry Sheares, executed for their role in the 1798 Rebellion, as well as the **death mask** of one of the Rebellion's leaders, Wolfe Tone. Two other rebels, Oliver Bond and the Reverend William Jackson, are buried in the church's graveyard, and

some reckon an unmarked grave to the rear houses the body of **Robert Emmet**, leader of the 1803 rising.

Smithfield and Dublin Horse Fair

Horse Fair first Sun of each month 9am–noon. Less an identifiable community than an ongoing process of redevelopment, the centrepiece of this modern "village" is the old, broad, cobbled Smithfield itself, the city's largest civic open space. Surrounded by blocks

▼ MUMMIES, ST MICHAN'S CRYPTS

of executive flats, hotels and shops, Smithfield still manages to host one of Dublin's major sights. The **Dublin Horse Fair** draws numerous traders and other horse-lovers keen to spot a bargain, and onlookers geeing up teenagers willing to race bareback around the surrounding streets. From early November until mid-January, Smithfield also hosts a massive **open-air ice-rink** (see Ⓦ www .smithfieldonice.ie for details).

The Old Jameson Distillery

Bow St, Smithfield ☎ 01/807 2355, Ⓦ www.jamesonwhiskey.com. Daily 9.30am–6pm; last tour 5.30pm; €9.75. The buildings where John Jameson set up his whiskey company have long been turned over to a somewhat touristy shrine to "the hard stuff" – indeed, Jameson's has been distilled in Midleton, Co. Cork for some years.

▼ THE OLD JAMESON DISTILLERY

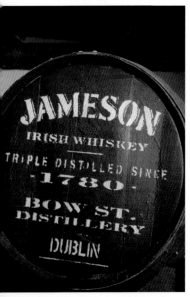

Following a short video on the history of Irish whiskey production, guided **tours** take visitors through the process, covering factors such as milling and mashing – the "washback" mashing barrel was once cleaned by the hazardous means of lowering a worker into its innards, using a candle first to test for carbon dioxide – to the utterly essential distillation element. The production of *uisce beatha* (Irish for "water of life", anglicized to "whiskey") involves a three-stage process. The resulting liquid, known as "young whiskey", is diluted to 62 percent alcohol via the addition of water, and then left in imported oak casks, formerly used for sherry, port or brandy.

Typically, maturation lasts for five to seven years, though some rare whiskeys are left for 25 years before bottling – two percent of the alcohol disappears in the interim, known as the "angel's share". The tour ends with a **tasting** exercise in which three testers are requested to sample four brands of whiskey, plus one each of bourbon and Scotch before plumping for their favourite – if you want to take part, make sure to volunteer at the beginning of the tour, otherwise you'll only receive a complimentary glass of Jameson's from the bar.

The Chimney Viewing Tower

Smithfield Village ☎ 01/817 3838. June–Aug Mon–Sat 10am–5.30pm, Sun 11am–5.30pm; rest of the year call for times; €5; tickets from the adjacent *Park Inn* hotel. The former chimney of the Jameson Distillery stands somewhat distant from Smithfield's modern development. A lift attached to the chimney's side whisks passengers up the tower's

▲ THE CHIMNEY VIEWING TOWER, SMITHFIELD

185 feet to an enclosed viewing platform at the summit. The panoramic views from here are markedly different to the vistas from the Guinness Storehouse's Gravity Bar (see p.125), and vividly present the city of Dublin in action.

National Museum of Ireland: Decorative Arts and History

Collins Barracks, Benburb St ☎01/677 7444, ⓦwww.museum.ie. Tues–Sat 10am–5pm, Sun 2–5pm; free. Guided tours daily 3.30pm; €2. LUAS stop Museum. This excellent museum gets far fewer visitors than its first-class exhibitions deserve. On entering through the main archway, you'll discover what was once Europe's largest regimental drilling square, one hundred paces broad and long. The buildings set around this quadrangle contain a wonderful series of galleries devoted to the fine arts of Ireland, as well as selections from abroad. Unquestionably, the best of these is "**Curator's Choice**", on the first floor of the west block, with pieces selected by museum curators from all over

Ireland. Among its draws are a medieval oak carving of St Molaise; the extravagant cabinet presented by Oliver Cromwell to his daughter Bridget in 1652; and the fourteenth-century Chinese porcelain Fonthill Vase.

The "**Out of Storage**" section is another highlight, with an eclectic collection that ranges from decorative glassware to a seventeenth-century suit of Samurai armour, while others focus on Celtic art, coinage, silverware, period furniture, costumes and scientific instruments; there are usually plenty of temporary exhibits too.

A recent addition on the ground floor is the chain of thematically interconnected galleries, "**Soldiers and Chiefs**", devoted to almost five hundred years of Irish military history. As well as an array of helmets and weaponry, there's the remarkable Stokes tapestry, created by a British soldier who devoted his spare time to the depiction of contemporary garrison life.

Other exhibits include the 200-year-old **Bantry Boat**, captured from the French

▼ EGYPTIAN LAMP, NATIONAL MUSEUM OF IRELAND

frigate *La Résolue* during the abortive invasion of 1796, while displays also recount the Irish involvement in the US Civil War. Added to this are tanks from World War I and a Havilland Vampire fighter plane from more recent times.

The Croppy's Acre

Wolfe Tone Quay. Many of those executed for their part in the **1798 Rebellion** are buried in The Croppy's Acre, an enclosed area just south of Collins Barracks. A Wicklow granite monument marks the precise location of their graves. The origins of the term "Croppy" have been much debated, though it is commonly believed to have been ascribed to Republicans who wore their hair closely cropped at the back, in the style of French revolutionaries. One of the most famous songs of the 1798 Rebellion was *The Croppy Boy*, which Loyalists countered with their own *Croppies Lie Down*.

Shopping

The Bridge Art Gallery

6 Ormond Quay Upper ☎01/872 9702. Closed Sun. Contemporary arts and crafts ranging from ceramics and sculpture to paintings and prints, often at prices that won't see you digging too deep into your pockets. The gallery at the rear also hosts exhibitions of innovative work.

Cafés

Christophe's

Duck Lane. Closed Sun. Next to the Old Jameson Distillery, large, swish *Christophe's* provides everything from excellent coffee and bagels to full breakfasts, roasts and salads, plus a wide range of veggie options.

Le Phare

20 Capel St. Closed Sun. Excellent and good-value café in an area with a dearth of decent eating establishments, offering breakfasts, soups, wraps and lunch specials, including a wonderfully herb-rich Irish stew.

Pubs and bars

The 1780 Bar

Corner of Bow St/Church St New. A cheery, airy bar, the *1780* serves a reliable pint and has a popular lunchtime menu of delicious soups (carrot and ginger is a particular favourite), as well as a range of paninis and club sandwiches. Newspapers for browsing are also to hand.

Dice Bar

78 Queen St. Late opening Fri & Sat (until 2.30am). Low-lit and compact, the *Dice Bar* is an ultra-cool New York-style joint that remains atmospheric without ever feeling too cramped. Most of the ales come from the Dublin Brewing Company, and DJs play nightly, the music ranging from Johnny Cash to French hip-hop, via the most recent indie bands, blues and ska.

Frank Ryan & Son

5 Queen St. Definitely a place for respite from the city's hurly-burly, this sociable, old-fashioned bar is cosiness incarnate. The friendly staff serve a grand pint of stout several cents cheaper than many city-centre alternatives.

▲ HUGHES'S

Sin É

14–15 Ormond Quay Upper. Owned by the same team as *The Cobblestone*, this candlelit bar appeals to a lively, cosmopolitan crowd thanks to its wide selection of brews – including draught wheat beers and bottled Leffe and Chimay – and an eclectic choice of musical entertainment (sometimes live gigs, but mostly DJs).

Clubs and live venues

The Bleu Note Café

61–63 Capel Street. The Northside's hippest place to catch live jazz and blues acts, featuring an attractive street-level bar and two music rooms – upstairs is usually free and operates Thurs–Sun, while downstairs has admission prices for its Friday and Saturday night gigs.

The Cobblestone

77 King St North ☎01/821 1799. Arguably the best traditional-music venue in Dublin, this

dark, cosy bar is also a fine place to sample the hoppy products of the nearby Dublin Brewery Company. High-quality sessions take place nightly from around 9pm (from 7pm Thurs), and on Sunday afternoons, while the Back Room hosts a variety of gigs.

Hughes's

19 Chancery St ☎01/872 6540. Tucked away behind The Four Courts, *Hughes's* attracts the cream of the city's traditional musicians to its nightly sessions (from around 10pm until closing time). Fridays can draw a large crowd, so arrive early to grab a seat.

Voodoo

39 Arran Quay ☎01/873 6013. Much larger than its exterior might suggest, *Voodoo* is the bigger sister to the *Dice Bar* (see opposite) and packs a similarly powerful punch, with nightly gigs showcasing the best of the local indie-band scene.

Phoenix Park

Europe's largest urban walled park, Phoenix Park's undulating landscape sprawls across some 1750 acres. Much of the park is open space, sparsely dotted with trees, shrubs and wild flowers, though there are also areas of woodland and hawthorn, ponds and a lake. Overall, it's an ideal place to escape the city's bustle, offering plenty of pleasant spots for a picnic, as well as being a popular venue for sports, with cricket, football, hurling and even polo played regularly on its numerous pitches. Developed as a deer park for Charles II (a small herd still ranges across its fields), the park takes its name from Phoenix House, the original residence of the British viceroys, a space now occupied by the tumble-down Magazine Fort, though the area's name stems from the Irish fionn uisce ("clear water"). As well as its greenery, there are some notable monuments to explore, including the Phoenix Monument, dating from 1747, the 30-metre-high stainless steel Papal Cross, marking the place where the late Pope John Paul II celebrated Mass in 1979, and the impressive Wellington Monument.

Just beyond the park's northwestern fringes lies the Farmleigh estate, a favourite spot for woodland and lakeside strolls and home to the gorgeous Farmleigh mansion itself.

Other than open-top tour buses, no public transport runs inside the park, so be prepared to burn some shoe-leather, and bring your own refreshments, as food and drink establishments are few and far between.

▼ PAPAL CROSS

Dublin Zoo

☎01/474 8900, ⊛ www.dublinzoo.ie. Mon–Sat 9.30am–6.30pm, Sun 10.30am–6.30pm (Oct–Feb closes at dusk); €14 adults, €9.50 children under 16, children under 3 free. The second-oldest zoo in Europe once bred the lion that used to growl ferociously at the beginning of films produced by Hollywood's MGM studios. Nowadays, the zoo focuses firmly on breeding threatened species, such as Amur tigers and the Waldrapp ibis, for future release into the wild.

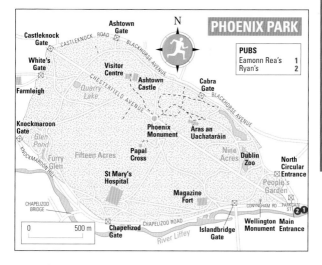

Spread over sixty acres, the zoo's attractions include the **African Plains**, featuring giraffes, rhinos and hippos, and another area devoted to South American creatures such as tamarins and toucans. As well as aviaries and reptile houses, there are also areas for polar bears and gorillas, and the wonderfully sociable meerkats. Regular newborn arrivals draw the crowds and provide photo opportunities, and there's a **City Farm** to keep younger children happy.

Áras an Uachtaráin

🕾01/677 7129, 🌐www.president.ie. Sat 10.30am–4.30pm (Sept–April until 3.30pm). Entry by guided tour only; times depend upon demand; tickets from the Phoenix Park Visitor Centre (see p.156) on the day; free. The home of Britain's viceroys from the 1780s until Ireland's independence, this impressive Palladian abode, graced by a broad frontage and a four-pillared entrance, has been the official residence of the **president of Ireland** ever since Douglas Hyde, the first incumbent, took up office in 1938.

▼ DUBLIN ZOO

▲ ÁRAS AN UACHTARÁIN

Tours of the building – which only take place when the current president is not in residence – start from the Phoenix Park Visitor Centre (minibus transport is provided). A small exhibition centre by the residence's entrance is devoted to the building's history and visitors are whisked through just part of the grandiosely decorated house, including the State Reception Rooms and the Presidential Office. Look out for some impressive stuccowork by the renowned Lafranchini brothers.

Phoenix Park Visitor Centre and Ashtown Castle

☎01/677 0095, ⊛www .heritageireland.ie. Mid- to end of March and Oct: daily 10am–5.30pm, April–Sept: daily 10am–6pm, Nov to mid-March: Sat–Wed 10am–5pm; €2.90 (includes tour of Ashtown Castle); Heritage Card. Accessed via a lane just north of the Phoenix Monument, the visitor centre recounts the story of the park through the ages, focusing on its **wildlife and flora**. As well as the chair in which the late Pope John Paul II sat to celebrate Mass in the park in 1979, you can view the rejected designs for the Wellington Monument, some of which are frankly bizarre, as well as a reconstruction of a Megalithic stone-lined cist grave, thought to date from the fourth century BC, whose original was discovered in the park in 1838. An enjoyable interactive section for children encourages an understanding of forest life, and there are often temporary exhibitions too.

Next door to the centre is **Ashtown Castle**, an early seventeenth-century tower house whose existence was only uncovered when the former residence of the Papal Nuncio, which had been constructed around it, was demolished in 1978. Guided **tours** reveal some of the tower's integral defensive features. The visitor centre also has a small, but extremely popular, adjacent café.

▼ ASHTOWN CASTLE

▲ FARMLEIGH

Farmleigh

☎01/815 5981, ⊛www.farmleigh.ie.
House: early March–Dec Thurs–Sun
& bank holidays 10.30am–5pm. Entry
– by guided tour only – may not be
possible if a visiting delegation is in
residence; call in advance to check.
Grounds: daily 10am–6pm (gates
close 4.45pm); free. Bus #37 from
Hawkins St to Castleknock Gate.
White's Gate on the park's
northwestern fringe provides
access to the splendid Georgian-
Victorian Farmleigh, one of
the most striking buildings in
the city, famed for its gorgeous
interiors. The house is set in
equally impressive eighty-acre
wooded **grounds**, which feature
an attractive ornamental lake,
sunken garden and a 35-metre
clocktower which houses the
estate's water-tank.

Farmleigh was constructed
in 1752 for the Trench family
and later purchased by Edward
Cecil Guinness, the first Earl
of Iveagh, as a rustic residence
offering easy access to his
brewery. Extensions took
place during the 1880s, and
the Guinnesses remained in
residence until the death of the
third earl in 1992. Farmleigh
was then purchased by the
Irish government for use as a
state guesthouse.

Tours commence in the
dining room, whose unusual
decorations include statues
of Bacchus either side of the
fireplace and a clock inlaid
in its centre, all set off by
seventeenth-century Italian
silk tapestries. The **hall** features
Bohemian chandeliers made

from Waterford crystal and a pair of debtors' chairs in which the pauper's legs would be trapped until agreeing to pay their debts. The **library** contains four thousand works on loan from the Iveagh Collection, including a first edition of *Ulysses* and books dating back to the twelfth century. The Blue Room, dedicated to Ireland's Nobel Prize winners, has another strange fireplace, this one situated below a window and looking out towards a fountain, in a manner reminiscent of Magritte.

The real treat, however, is the **ballroom**, decorated with ornate plasterwork in the style of Louis XVI, and featuring an Irish oak floor constructed of wood originally intended for Guinness barrels. From here, delicate linen portières fringe doors leading you to a massive, plant-stocked conservatory. There's a **tearoom** in the stable block behind the house.

The People's Garden

The People's Garden, by the park's main entrance on Parkgate Street, dates from 1864 and, in its neat and systematic design, retains much of the original horticultural style of the Victorian era. Bounded by hedges, yet only a stone's throw from a major thoroughfare, this is a relatively peaceful spot in which to enjoy the sweet scent of the variety of blooms in the parterres. There's also a statue of Seán Heuston, who was executed for his part in the 1916 Easter Rising.

Wellington Monument

The Wellington Monument took some 44 years to complete before it was finally unveiled in 1861. The obelisk – the tallest of its kind in the British Isles at some sixty metres – features bas-reliefs using bronze from cannons captured at Waterloo, depicting scenes from the successful military campaigns of the "Iron Duke".

Magazine Fort

Alongside Military Road is the Magazine Fort, dating from 1734, and built on the site of the original Phoenix House. The fort once housed the munitions of the British garrison based in Dublin, but now lies in dereliction. It's an easy enough climb up the hill to have a wander around its walls and take in some fine views of the park and surrounding area.

Pubs

Eamonn Rea's

25 Parkgate St. A comfortable and homely alternative to *Ryan's*, *Rea's* is very definitely a locals' pub, serving a more-than-decent pint (one of the city's cheapest) and hosting impromptu quizzes. The walls exhibit hurling memorabilia.

Ryan's

28 Parkgate St. Ryan's is the long-time challenger to the reputation of *Mulligan's* (see p.77) for serving the best pint of Guinness in the city, owing to its proximity to the brewery just across the river. At one time it was just a plain bar with two pumps for stout and one for lager (the latter allegedly for eccentrics and country visitors). Nowadays it's a pleasantly refurbished place – the Guinness is still grand and the bar meals reasonably priced. The upstairs restaurant dishes up fine seafood in the evening.

The southern outskirts

The diffuse southern outskirts of Dublin, which extend as far as the Wicklow Mountains, hold two focuses of attention for the visitor. In the green, almost village-like suburb of Rathfarnham, you'll find a much-redeveloped sixteenth-century castle and the Irish-language school founded by revolutionary Pádraig Pearse, now a museum. Along the coast, southeast of the city, lie Sandycove's James Joyce Museum and the charming, historic neighbourhood of Dalkey. The DART train ride here is a scenic attraction in itself, displaying the great sweep of Dublin Bay before dramatically skirting Dalkey and Killiney hills and arrowing off towards Bray and Greystones (see p.173).

Pearse Museum

St Enda's Park, Grange Rd, Rathfarnham ☎01/493 4208, ⊛www .heritageireland.ie. Note that, at the time of writing, the museum was closed for redevelopment until mid-2008. Museum: Feb–April, Sept & Oct 10am–5pm; May–Aug 10am–5.30pm; Nov–Jan 10am–4pm; closed 1–2pm; free. St Enda's Park: daily: Feb–March 10am–5.30pm; April, Sept & Oct 10am–7pm; May–Aug 10am–8pm; Nov–Jan 10am–4.30pm; free. Bus #16 from D'Olier Street. The informative Pearse Museum explores in detail the life and principles of **Pádraig Pearse** and is housed in the former **St Enda's School**, which he founded in 1910 with the aim of promoting Gaelic culture and Nationalist ideals. All classes were taught in Irish and students were encouraged to take part in Gaelic football and hurling. Pearse's renown, however, draws not from his educational work – the school recruited fewer pupils than expected and closed in 1916 – but from his role as one of the leaders of the **Easter Rising** (see p.126).

A visit best begins in the **back rooms** where displays focus on Pearse's background, including his birth in 1879 on Great Brunswick Street (now Pearse Street). Other rooms recount the school's history and Pearse's educational philosophy, a key part of which was "special attention to character building and the development of those elements which promote true manhood, honour and good citizenship". Upstairs, the original straw mattresses and rugged bed frames in the **dormitory** suggest that bodily comfort was not one of those elements. Pearse was also a reasonably successful playwright, but whether he was a good teacher was questioned by **James Joyce**, who took Pearse's Irish classes at University College but left after three months, deploring his tutor's attempts

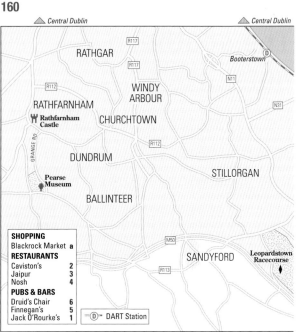

▲ Central Dublin   ▲ Central Dublin

RATHGAR

Booterstown

WINDY ARBOUR

RATHFARNHAM

♯ Rathfarnham Castle

CHURCHTOWN

DUNDRUM

STILLORGAN

Pearse Museum

BALLINTEER

SANDYFORD

Leopardstown Racecourse

SHOPPING	
Blackrock Market	**a**
RESTAURANTS	
Caviston's	2
Jaipur	3
Nosh	4
PUBS & BARS	
Druid's Chair	6
Finnegan's	5
Jack O'Rourke's	1

═Ⓓ➤ DART Station

to elevate the Irish language by denigrating English.

The museum has **tearooms** (May–Sept weekends only) and a nature study centre where you can acquire details of the trail around St Enda's Park. The park also offers pleasant riverside walks and a waterfall, as well as a walled **garden** which hosts summer outdoor concerts (call ☎01/493 4208 for details).

Rathfarnham Castle

Rathfarnham Rd, Rathfarnham
☎01/493 9462, ⓦ www.heritageireland
.ie. May–Oct daily 9.30am–5.30pm,
last entry 4.30pm; guided tours free.
Bus #16 or #16A from D'Olier Street.
A squat and chunky edifice constructed from limestone and brick, Rathfarnham Castle dates from the 1580s and was built for one **Adam Loftus**, a Yorkshire clergyman who rose through

the clerical ranks to become Archbishop of Dublin, and later Lord Chancellor of Ireland and the first Provost of Trinity College. The castle was besieged during the 1641 Rebellion and Cromwell's troops were based here during the English Civil War, which began the following year. The building subsequently passed through numerous hands, including those of William Conolly of Castletown renown (see p.180), until it was re-acquired by descendants of Loftus.

The castle's battlements were removed in 1720, but the building still retains a characteristic sixteenth-century appearance. Its innards, however, were much remodelled in the 1770s, under the direction of Henry Loftus, Earl of Ely, who employed notable architects

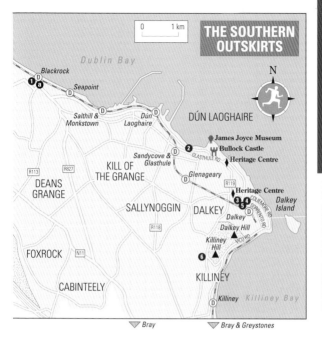

Dublin Bay

Blackrock
Seapoint
Salthill & Monkstown
Dún Laoghaire
DÚN LAOGHAIRE
James Joyce Museum
Bullock Castle
Heritage Centre
GLASTHULE RD
Sandycove & Glasthule
KILL OF THE GRANGE
Glenageary
R113 R827
DEANS GRANGE
R119
Heritage Centre
SALLYNOGGIN
DALKEY
Dalkey Island
Dalkey
Dalkey Hill
Killiney Hill
R118
FOXROCK N11
CABINTEELY
KILLINEY
Killiney
Killiney Bay

Bray   Bray & Greystones

PLACES The southern outskirts

and painters to produce suitably lavish interiors for his grand-scale society entertaining.

The castle later fell into serious decline and, in 1912, was purchased by property developers, but by the 1980s the building was semi-derelict. Hour-long guided **tours** concentrate very heavily on the renovation work that has subsequently taken place and draw attention to the changes in the building's structure uncovered by the process. The castle's **kitchen wing** has been fully restored, though work inside the main section is ongoing and now includes a room dedicated to temporary exhibitions of artwork.

The James Joyce Museum

Sandycove Point, Sandycove
℡01/280 9265. March–Oct Mon–Sat 10am–1pm & 2–5pm, Sun and public holidays 2–6pm; €7; €12 with Dublin Tourism combined ticket (see p.203).

▼ THE JAMES JOYCE MUSEUM

Sandycove & Glasthule DART station, then a 10min walk down Islington Ave, then east along the seafront; or bus #59 from Dún Laoghaire or Dalkey to Sandycove Ave and a couple of minutes' stroll northwards. This diverting memorial to Joyce is housed inside an impressive **Martello tower** overlooking the Irish Sea, one of fifteen such towers erected between Dublin and Bray in 1804–06 against the threat of invasion by Napoleon. Built with eight-feet-thick, circular, granite walls and an armoured door twelve feet off the ground as the only entrance, the towers never fired a shot in anger.

Joyce stayed here for just a week, in September 1904, a month before he left the country for Italy with Nora Barnacle. At the time, his host, the writer and wit **Oliver St John Gogarty**, was renting the tower from the War Office for £8 a year as digs during his medical studies. Joyce immortalized the tower as the setting for the opening chapter of his masterpiece, *Ulysses* – and Gogarty as "stately, plump Buck Mulligan" – and it's now the focus for readings and celebrations every year on June 16, **Bloomsday** (see p.142).

Opened in 1962 by Sylvia Beach, who first published *Ulysses* in Paris in 1922, the museum displays Joyce's guitar, waistcoat and walking stick, as well as one of two official **death masks** (the other is in Zurich, where he died in 1941). There are also copious letters and photos, as well as first and rare editions, notably a *Ulysses* beautifully illustrated by Matisse. On the first floor, Gogarty's Spartan **living quarters** in the former guardroom have been recreated as Joyce described

them, and you can climb up to the gun platform on the roof for panoramic **views** of Dublin Bay.

Just beyond the tower on the rocky headland is Dublin's most famous bathing spot, the **Forty Foot Pool** (so called because of a forty-foot-deep fishing hole off the coast here). It was traditionally for male nude bathers only, but nowadays hardy, dogged souls of both sexes jump-start their hearts here throughout the year.

Dalkey

DART to Dalkey. A fifteen-minute walk down the coast from Sandycove, Dalkey (pronounced "Dawky") is a pretty seaside suburb set against the tree-clad slopes of Dalkey Hill. In medieval times, it prospered as a fortified settlement and the main port of Dublin, until the dredging of the River Liffey in the sixteenth century took away its business. Nowadays, with the building of the railway, Dalkey's characterful old houses and villas are much sought after by well-to-do commuters, as well as celebrities seeking privacy (including U2's Bono).

Just down Railway Road from Dalkey DART station, Castle Street boasts two **fortified warehouses** from Dalkey's medieval heyday (if you make the walk from Sandycove to Dalkey, you'll pass a third fortification, Bullock Castle, on Ulverton Road, built by the Cistercians in the twelfth century to protect Bullock fishing harbour). Goat Castle, across the road from Archibold's Castle, serves as an attractive and well-designed **Heritage Centre** (℡01/285 8366, Ⓦwww .dalkeycastle.com; Mon–Fri 9.30am–5pm, Sat, Sun & public

▲ DALKEY

holidays 11am–5pm; €6). The detailed exhibition, with panels written by playwright and local resident Hugh Leonard, covers the town's history, especially its transport systems and literary associations, the latter including an exhibit on Joyce, who set the second chapter of *Ulysses* in Dalkey. The castle **interior** is impressive in itself, and fine views are to be had from the battlements. From May to October the entry price includes Living History **theatre tours** (every 30min: Mon–Fri 10am–4.30pm; Sat, Sun & public holidays 11.30am–4.30pm) in which suitably attired actors recount the lives and times of a selection of Dalkey's medieval residents.

The Heritage Centre regularly organizes interesting guided **historical tours** in the town (May–Aug Mon & Fri 11am, Wed 2pm; €4); for groups of six or more, guided literary walks of the town can be arranged during the same period and for the same price (call for details). The Centre also participates in Bloomsday (see p.142), re-enacting the Dalkey schoolroom scene in *Ulysses* and staging a special Joycean evening of entertainment.

If you want to take a trip out to tiny **Dalkey Island**, some 300m offshore, then your best bet is to make for Coliemore Harbour, down Coliemore Road from the southern end of the town, and negotiate a trip with one of the local fishermen (high season only). Once a Viking base, the island features the ruins of a seventh-century church, a Martello tower and gun battery from Napoleonic times, a herd of semi-wild goats and views of seals and a variety of seabird species.

Shopping

Blackrock Market

19A Main St, Blackrock. Sat 11am–5.30pm, Sun noon–5.30pm. Hugely varied and popular weekend market, just behind the high street of this southern suburb and close to the DART station. Antiques and bric-a-brac, books and CDs, crafts, jewellery, shoes and clothes are on sale.

Dalkey and Killiney Hills

A walk up adjoining Dalkey and Killiney Hills, before descending to Killiney DART station, offers panoramic views of the city and its environs, and can all be done in an hour and a half from **Dalkey** DART station at a moderate pace. From **Dalkey**, head southeast on Sorrento Road, and then either take the easier route to the right up Knocknacree and Torca roads, or continue along cliffside Vico Road (cited by Joyce in both *Ulysses* and, somewhat obliquely, *Finnegans Wake*), from where steps and a path ascend steeply. On Torca Road, Shaw fans might want to track down privately owned **Torca Cottage**, where GBS lived for several years as a boy and where he occasionally returned to write in later years. On the way to Dalkey Hill's summit, with its crenellated former telegraph station and fine views over Dublin Bay, you'll pass **Dalkey quarry**, which provided the granite blocks for the massive piers of Dún Laoghaire harbour below.

From here, follow the partly wooded ridge up to **Killiney Hill**, where a stone obelisk, erected in 1742 to provide work for the local poor, enjoys even more glorious **views**, north to Howth and south to Killiney Bay and the Wicklow Mountains. From the obelisk, you can quickly descend to the park gate on Killiney Hill Road and refreshment at the cosy *Druid's Chair* pub directly opposite; from there it's a fifteen-minute walk down Victoria Road and Vico Road through the leafy and exclusive borough of Killiney, to the DART station by the beach.

Restaurants

Caviston's

59 Glasthule Rd, Sandycove ☎01/280 9245, ⓦwww.cavistons.com. 3 lunch sittings: Tues–Fri noon, 1.30pm & 3pm, Sat noon, 1.45pm and 3.15pm. Handily placed between Sandycove and Glasthule

▼ BLACKROCK MARKET

DART station and the Joyce Museum, this restaurant works to a basic but hugely successful formula – the day's freshest fish and seafood, cooked simply. Booking is essential and there are a few outside tables in summer. Lunch will set you back €30–40 a head. The same company's next-door Food Emporium offers a wonderful selection of home-baked breads, a delicatessen and an extensive stock of fresh fish, among other delights.

Jaipur

21 Castle St, Dalkey ☎01/285 0552, ⓦwww.jaipur.ie. Closed lunchtime Mon–Wed. Branch of the excellent South Great George's Street Indian restaurant (see p.118); its early-bird menu (5.30–7.30pm, €21.75) is well worth sampling.

Nosh

111 Coliemore Rd, Dalkey ☎01/284 0666, ⓦwww.nosh.ie. Closed Mon. Simple, stylish contemporary bistro just off Castle Street,

▲ FINNEGAN'S

offering everything from linguini with smoked chicken to Thai green seafood curry in the evening, basic dishes such as fish pie and homemade burgers for lunch, and brunch on Saturday and Sunday.

Pubs and bars

Finnegan's
Railway Rd, Dalkey. Dalkey's watering-hole of choice,

handy for the DART station and tastefully smartened-up to reflect the neighbourhood's gentrification, but offering traditional hospitality and a fine pint of Guinness.

Jack O'Rourke's
15 Main St, Blackrock. Not just a comfortable place to admire your purchases from the adjacent market, but a purveyor of estimable Guinness and extremely good-value meals.

The northern outskirts

The northern outskirts from Glasnevin across to Howth hold an astonishing diversity of attractions, some of which can easily be combined on the same excursion. You'll want fine weather for a trip to the beautiful Botanic Gardens and the adjacent Glasnevin Cemetery, last resting-place for the major figures in Irish history since 1832, which is best appreciated on a guided tour. The exquisite architecture of the Casino at Marino and the fright-fest of the Bram Stoker Dracula Experience have quite different appeals, while the flora and fauna of North Bull Island's nature reserve can be appreciated by anyone. Half an hour from central Dublin at the end of the DART line, Howth is an attractive seaside village, with a good concentration of places to eat and drink and a fine cliff walk.

National Botanic Gardens

Glasnevin Hill, off Botanic Rd, Glasnevin ☎ 01/837 7596, ⬚ www.heritageireland.ie. Gardens: summer Mon–Sat 9am–6pm, Sun 10am–6pm; winter daily 10am–4.30pm; glasshouses: summer Mon–Fri 9am–5pm, Sat & Sun

▼ NATIONAL BOTANIC GARDENS

10am–5.45pm; winter daily 10am–4.30pm; free. Guided tour Sun 2.30pm; free. Bus #13 from Merrion Square or O'Connell St, or #19, #19A from South Great George's St or O'Connell St.

The Botanic Gardens' twenty hectares on the south bank of the River Tolka are a great place to wander on a fine day, while their magnificent Victorian wrought-iron **glasshouses** offer diversion and shelter whatever the weather. Laid out between 1795 and 1825 with a grant from the Irish Parliament, the gardens were, in 1844, the first in the world to raise orchids from seed and, in August of the following year, the first to recognize the potato blight that brought on the Great Famine.

Nowadays, a total of around twenty thousand species and cultivated varieties flourish here, including an internationally important collection of **cycads**, primitive fern-like trees. Outdoor highlights include the rose garden, collections of heather and rhododendrons, the Chinese shrubbery and the arboretum. Among the beautifully restored glasshouses, the **Curvilinear Range** was built by Richard Turner, a Dublin ironfounder who also built the Palm House at Kew Gardens in London, as well as the huge conservatories for the Great Exhibitions in London in 1851 and Dublin in 1853.

There's a pleasant self-service **café** with picture windows in the visitor centre, serving cakes, sandwiches, salads and simple hot meals.

Glasnevin Cemetery

Finglas Rd ☎01/830 1133, ⓦwww .glasnevin-cemetery.ie. Mon–Sat 8am–4.30pm or later, Sun 9am–4.30pm or later; free. Guided tours Wed & Fri 2.30pm; 90min; free. Bus #40, #40A/B/C from Parnell St.

Fifteen minutes' walk from the Botanic Gardens (down Botanic Road, then right into Prospect Way and Finglas Road) lies the entrance to Glasnevin Cemetery (aka Prospect Cemetery), which was founded as a burial place for Catholics by the nationalist political leader **Daniel O'Connell** in 1832. It's now the national cemetery, open to all denominations and groaning with Celtic crosses, harps and other patriotic emblems. O'Connell himself is commemorated near the entrance by a fifty-metre-high round **tower**, which managed to survive a Loyalist bomb in the 1970s. His corpse was interred in the tower's crypt in 1869, having been brought home from Genoa where he died (in fact, not all of his body is here: his heart was buried in Rome).

To the left of the round tower, O'Connell's political descendant,

▲ GLASNEVIN CEMETERY

Charles Stewart Parnell, who asked to be buried in a mass grave among the people of Ireland, is commemorated by a huge granite boulder from his estate at Avondale, County Wicklow. Other notable figures among the 1.2 million dead at Glasnevin – most of them gathered around O'Connell's tower – include Countess Markiewicz (see p.87), Éamon de Valera, prime minister, president and architect of modern Ireland, and his old rival Michael Collins, the most charismatic leader of the successful independence struggle. From the arts, there's poet Gerard Manley Hopkins (unmarked, in the Jesuit plot), W.B. Yeats's muse, Maud Gonne MacBride, playwright Brendan Behan and Alfred Chester Beatty (see p.109).

To the right of the tower is the **Republican plot**, with a memorial to hunger strikers, from Thomas Ashe who died in 1917 to Bobby Sands in

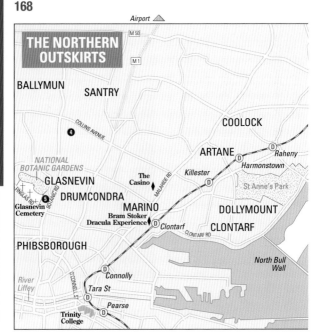

1981, while in front of the tower lie the recent graves of 18-year-old Kevin Barry and eight other Volunteers hanged by the British during the War of Independence; originally buried in Mountjoy Prison, their bodies were moved here with the full honours of a state funeral in October 2001.

The Casino at Marino

Cherrymount Crescent, off Malahide Rd, Marino ☎01/833 1618, ⊛www .heritageireland.ie. Guided tours Jan–March, Nov & Dec Sat & Sun noon–4pm; April Sat & Sun noon–5pm; May & Oct daily 10am–5pm; June–Sept daily 10am–6pm; last admission 50min before closing; €2.90; Heritage Card. Bus #20B, #27B from Eden Quay, or #27 from Talbot St; or DART to Clontarf, then a 15min walk. Sited in the now unpromising suburb of Marino,

the Casino is probably the finest piece of Neoclassical architecture in Ireland. It was commissioned by the first Earl of Charlemont, the leading intellectual figure of Georgian Dublin, shortly after he returned from eight years on the Grand Tour. Seeking to recreate an Italianate park with a *casino* ("little house" in Italian) as its focus, emphasizing the fine views of Dublin Bay that his estate then enjoyed, Charlemont turned to Sir William Chambers, the architect of Somerset House in London. Started in 1757, construction lasted nearly twenty years and cost £20,000 (equivalent to about €5 million today), almost bankrupting the estate.

The **exterior** is covered in exquisite carving in Portland

RESTAURANTS
Beshoff's 1
Casa Pasta 1
King Sitric's 2

LIVE VENUES
The Helix 4

PUBS & BARS
Abbey Tavern 3
Kavanagh's 5

stone, which reflects, notably in the ox skulls symbolizing animal sacrifice, the Enlightenment's preoccupation with pagan antiquity. To maintain the pristine Neoclassical appearance, Chambers disguised chimney pots as urns and used hollow Doric columns as drainpipes (with bronze chains inside to reduce the noise of the falling water). His most remarkable trick, however, was one of scale: from outside, the Casino appears to be a single-storey villa, but once inside you'll find three ingeniously designed floors containing a total of sixteen rooms.

The remarkable standards of craftsmanship characterize the **interior** too, with ornate plasterwork and beautiful wooden floors inlaid in geometric patterns. Nothing was allowed to mar guests' views: the entrance doors convert into a window, and a series of **tunnels** was built under the surrounding land, including one that ran to the main house (now demolished), so that the servants wouldn't blot the landscape.

▼ THE CASINO AT MARINO

The Bram Stoker Dracula Experience

Bar Code, West Wood Club, Clontarf Rd ☎01/805 7824, ⓦwww .thebramstokerdraculaexperience.com. Fri 4–10pm, Sat & Sun noon–10pm; €7, children €4. DART to Clontarf. Buried deep within a leisure centre, this well-designed attraction combines museum and fairground show, much to the delight of kids who love frights. It's run by a great Dracula enthusiast whose mission is to establish Stoker, born across the road on The Crescent in 1847 and educated at Trinity College, among the pantheon of Irish writers. Things begin fairly conventionally with some engaging display boards on Stoker's life and influences, but take an eerie turn with a disorientation tunnel; from here on, you walk through a series of ghoulish scenes – Dracula's lair, Renfield's lunatic asylum – punctuated by shocks and surprises.

North Bull Island

Interpretive centre at the end of the causeway road, by the beach in the centre of the island ☎01/833 8341. Mon–Fri 10am–4.30pm, Sat & Sun 10am–5.30pm; free. DART to Raheny, then a 30min walk to the interpretive centre, or bus #130 from Lower Abbey St along Clontarf Rd, then walk along North Bull Wall. Flanked by **Dollymount Strand**, a three-mile beach on its seaward side, North Bull Island is an impressive resource for nature-lovers – now designated a UNESCO Biosphere Reserve – just 8km from the city centre. Originally no more than a sandbank visible at low tide, the island grew in the tidal shadow of the North Bull Wall, which was built, along with the South Bull Wall, in 1821 on the advice of Captain William Bligh (of HMS *Bounty* fame) to prevent the mouth of the Liffey from silting up.

Besides golfers and day-tripping Dubliners, the island provides accommodation for up to 40,000 migrating **birds** from more than fifty species in winter, including a sixth of the world's population of Brent geese – it's one of the most northerly sites in Europe where the foreshore doesn't freeze. In summer, you'll see cormorants, oystercatchers and curlews wading on the mudflats.

Howth Cliff Walk

The best way to appreciate Howth, if the weather's fine, is to do the **Cliff Walk** around the peninsula, taking in great views south to the Wicklow Mountains and north to the Boyne Valley. The footpath runs for some 8km clockwise from the village round to the west-facing side of the peninsula, followed by a 3km walk by the sea along Strand Road and Greenfield Road to Sutton DART station; allow at least three hours in total.

You first head out east along Balscadden Road to the **Nose of Howth**, before the path turns south, crossing the slopes above the cliffs, which are covered in colourful gorse and bell heather in season; for refreshment on this stretch, the area known as **The Summit**, just inland from the path, has a pub and a café. The southeast point is marked by the Baily Lighthouse, which until March 1997 was the last manned lighthouse on Ireland's coastline. The path along the south-facing coast of the peninsula is the most spectacular part of the walk, providing close-up views of cliffs, secluded beaches and rocky islands.

▲ HOWTH HARBOUR

the DART station, **Howth Castle**, built in 1564 and now the oldest inhabited house in Ireland, is closed to the public, but a barn in the grounds has been turned into the **National Transport Museum** (Ⓦwww.nationaltransportmuseum.org; June–Aug Mon–Fri 10am–5pm, Sat & Sun 2–5pm; Sept–May Sat & Sun 2–5pm; €3), containing antiquated tractors, a horse-drawn fire engine and an old Hill of Howth tram.

As well as rich and varied **flora** – notably thrift, a mass of pink flowers in June, and several types of orchid – the grasslands behind sustain shrews, badgers and one of the few remaining large indigenous mammals, the much-harassed Irish hare.

Howth

DART to Howth station. Clinging to the slopes of a rocky peninsula and overlooking an animated fishing harbour, the village of Howth is a fine place to escape the rigours of the city centre. The windy walk along the harbour's east pier will blow away any Guinness-induced cobwebs and give you the chance to stare out **Ireland's Eye**, an island sea-bird sanctuary that shelters a ruined sixth-century monastery and a Martello tower; during the summer, boats from the pier run across to the island when they have enough takers.

To the west of the harbour, about ten minutes' walk beyond

Restaurants

Beshoff's

10 Harbour Rd, Howth Ⓦwww.beshoffrestaurants.ie. Well-run fish and chip shop, all gleaming chrome and tiles, serving great fishcakes, chunky chips, deep-fried fresh prawns and nice extras like garlic mayonnaise.

Casa Pasta

12 Harbour Rd, Howth ☎01/839 3823. Closed lunchtime Mon–Sat. Popular Italian restaurant with a buzzing, family-friendly atmosphere and views of the harbour. The moderately priced menu of pastas, salads and pizzas doesn't stray far from the usual suspects, but it's enlivened by daily specials and a few Chinese main courses.

King Sitric's Fish Restaurant

East Pier, Howth ☎01/832 5235, Ⓦwww.kingsitric.ie. Closed Sun. Excellent, plush restaurant with panoramic sea views, offering

▲ KAVANAGH'S

fish landed at the nearby pier, lobster from adjacent Balscadden Bay, and plenty of other delicious seafood and game. Though it's expensive, the set menus at lunchtimes are very good value. Smart bedrooms are available (doubles from €145) if you really want to push the boat out.

Pubs

The Abbey Tavern

Abbey St, Howth ☎01/839 0307, ⓦwww.abbeytavern.ie. Welcoming traditional pub, dating back to the sixteenth century and now smartly furnished with dark wood, flagstones and open fires, which is popular for its evening shows of Irish dancing and ballads in the back room (€20 with Irish coffee, €58 with a three-course meal). The bar serves decent lunches – soup, sandwiches, seafood salad and simple hot meals – and a good pint of Guinness.

Kavanagh's

Prospect Square, Glasnevin. One of the city's finest old pubs, aka *The Gravediggers*, a dimly lit classic of bare wooden floors, benches and trestles. Sandwiches are served Monday to Friday lunchtimes. Located just outside the old entrance to Prospect Cemetery, where it has consoled mourners (and changed little) since 1833, it's best reached from the present-day entrance by retracing your steps along Finglas Road and taking the first small lane on the left along the cemetery walls.

Live venues

The Helix

Dublin City University, Collins Ave, Glasnevin ☎01/700 7000, ⓦwww.thehelix.ie. *The Helix* is a modern, 1,250-seater venue, providing a very broad range of entertainment, including rock bands, jazz, classical music and ballet, musicals, ice shows and special events, plus a variety of performances in its smaller theatre.

Day trips

Within a fifty-kilometre radius of Dublin, there's some wonderful countryside and sights to explore. You can enjoy Neolithic discoveries at the awesome Brú na Bóinne, a UNESCO World Heritage Site, early Christian remains at Glendalough, set deep in the Wicklow Mountains, as well as several impressive Georgian mansions in gorgeous gardens and parkland. Alternatively, if you fancy the seaside experience, just head to Bray, which offers both cheap-and-cheerful and more refined delights. Efficient transport networks make it fairly easy – and not too expensive – to reach these outlying sights, though if you're short of time or feeling spoilt for choice, then taking a tour might be worth considering (see box, p.174).

PLACES Day trips

Bray

DART to Bray station. Just across the border in County Wicklow, the formerly genteel Victorian resort of Bray now draws a great influx of day-tripping Dubliners down the DART line on summer weekends, when the seafront amusement arcades and fast-food outlets go into overdrive. The attractive sand and shingle **beach**, however, dramatically set against the knobbly promontory of Bray Head, is long enough to soak up the crowds, and the enterprising town lays on a diverse roster of **festivals** to broaden its appeal, including the Bray Jazz Festival in May and the Oscar Wilde Autumn School in October (see p.208). Details of events are available from the **tourist office** (June–Aug Mon–Fri 9am–1pm & 2–5pm, Sat 10am–3pm; Sept–May Mon–Fri 9.30am–1pm & 2–4.30pm, Sat 10am–3pm; ☎01/286 6796), in the nineteenth-century former courthouse on Main Street, a ten-minute walk inland from the DART station. The attached **heritage centre** (same hours; €3) is devoted to local history, focusing on the achievements of Sir William Dargan, who built the Dublin–Kingstown (now Dún Laoghaire) railway, the world's first suburban line, in 1831–4, and helped to establish Dublin's National Gallery.

National Sea Life Centre

Strand Rd, Bray ☎01/286 6939, ⓦwww.sealifeeurope.com. Summer

▼ NATIONAL SEA LIFE CENTRE

Organized tours

Organized tours are especially useful if you want to take in more than one sight in a day; those which include Newgrange (see p.181) guarantee a place on the guided tour of the passage grave. It's best to book in advance, either directly or through a tourist office or your hotel. Admission charges are usually included in the price, though not lunch.

Bus Éireann (℡01/836 6111, ℗www.buseireann.ie) runs tours to Glendalough and Powerscourt (mid-March to Oct daily; Nov to mid-March Wed, Fri & Sun; 10am; 7hr 45min; €32) and Newgrange (May–Sept daily except Fri; Nov–April Thurs & Sat; 10am; 7hr 45min; €32), leaving from Busáras, Store Street.

Day Tours Unplugged (℡01/834 0941 or 087 272 0764, ℗www .daytoursunplugged.ie) runs a daily tour to Glendalough, via Sandycove and Dalkey (8hr; €26), departing from Gardiner Street (8.50am), with several other pick-up points, including the O'Connell Street and Suffolk Street tourist offices.

Dublin Bus (℡01/703 3028, ℗www.dublinbus.ie) operates a daily "South Coast and Gardens" tour from its office at 59 O'Connell St Upper, which runs along the coast to Bray and then to Powerscourt (11am; 4hr 30min; €25).

Gray Line (℡01/605 7705, ℗www.irishcitytours.com) runs a daily "Wicklow Mountains, Valleys and Lakes" tour from outside the tourist office on O'Connell Street Upper (9.45am), picking up at Trinity College (9.55am) and taking in Glendalough and the mountains (Mon & Fri–Sun €30, Tues–Thurs €25; 7hr). It also operates an excursion to Newgrange (Easter–Oct Mon, Tues, Fri & Sat 10am; 6hr; €32) from the Suffolk Street tourist office; and a "Grand Wicklow" tour, including Glendalough and Powerscourt (mid-March to mid-Nov Sun; 8hr; €38), from outside the tourist office on O'Connell Street Upper (10am), picking up at Trinity College (10.10am).

Mary Gibbons Tours (℡01/283 9973, ℗www.newgrangetours.com) takes in Newgrange, the Hill of Tara (seat of the Celtic High Kings of Ireland) and the Boyne Valley (Mon–Sat; 6hr 15min; €35), calling at *Pizza Hut* beside the Suffolk Street tourist office at 10.15am, as well as several leading Dublin hotels.

Over the Top Tours (℡1800 424252 or 01/860 0404, ℗www.overthetoptours .com) uses a minibus to visit Glendalough and the Wicklow Mountains (8hr; €26) leaving from outside *The Gresham Hotel*, O'Connell Street Upper, at 9.20am, calling at the Suffolk Street tourist office at 9.45am.

Railtours (℡01/856 0045, ℗www.railtoursireland.com) operates combined rail and coach tours, including the "Wicklow Mountaineer" (Mon–Sat 11.35am; 7hr; €39), which visits Glendalough. Tours depart from Connolly Station.

The Wild Wicklow Tour (℡01/280 1899, ℗www.wildwicklow.ie) explores Glendalough and heads off the beaten track into the mountains (8hr; €28), departing from outside the *Shelbourne Hotel*, St Stephen's Green, at 8.50am daily, and calling at the Suffolk Street tourist office at 9.10am and the *Gresham Hotel* at 9.20am.

daily 10am–6pm; winter Mon–Fri 11am–5pm, Sat & Sun 10am–6pm; last admission 1hr before closing. €9.95, children €7.50. Bray's main attraction, especially popular with children, is the National Sea Life Centre on the seafront, one of a Europe-wide chain of **aquariums** run by fishy enthusiasts, who lay on plenty of activities for kids, as well as informative display boards that'll keep adults interested. The full range of sea and freshwater habitats is covered – including "probably the largest shoal of piranhas in Ireland" – with a strong emphasis on the need for conservation. Inevitably, the more exotic, far-flung creatures provide the big thrills, notably the blacktips in the tropical shark tank, and the scary giant Japanese spider crab, a species which can grow to up to four metres from claw to claw.

Killruddery House and Gardens

Off Southern Cross Rd, Bray
⌖0404/46024, ⓦwww.killruddery .com. Gardens: April Sat & Sun 1–5pm; May–Sept daily 1–5pm; €6. House: May, June & Sept daily 1–5pm; €10 (gardens included). Bus #84, #184 or Finnegan's bus from Bray DART station, or a 20min walk from the southern end of the seafront (via Putland Rd, Newcourt Rd, Vevay Rd and

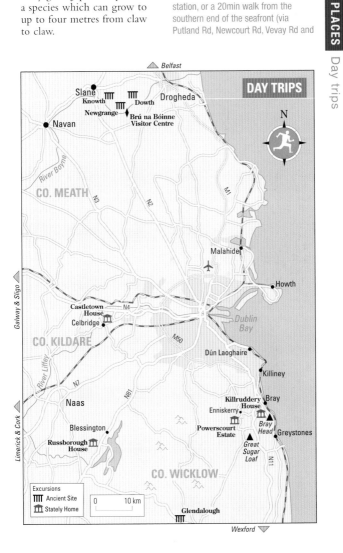

A walk over Bray Head to Greystones

There's an excellent two- to three-hour walk from Bray seafront south across Bray Head to **Greystones**, a small commuter town at the end of the DART line. You can follow the comparatively flat **cliff path** that runs above the rail tracks for most of the way, giving close-up views of rocky coves and slate pinnacles, lashed by magnificent waves on windy days. Alternatively, take on the steep climb over the top of **Bray Head** for great views of Killiney Bay and the cone-shaped hills inland known as Little Sugar Loaf and Great Sugar Loaf, with a distant backdrop of the Wicklow Mountains. The route ascends rapidly from the end of Bray seafront through pine woods and over gorse slopes to a large cross, erected to mark the Holy Year of 1950; from here a track winds across the ridge below the 240-metre summit of Bray Head, before you turn sharp left down to join the cliff path which will bring you into Greystones.

Southern Cross Rd). Used as a film location on many occasions, including for *My Left Foot* and *Becoming Jane*, the Killruddery estate is most notable for its **gardens**, which were laid out in the seventeenth century in early French formal style and added to in the eighteenth and nineteenth. As such, they're the oldest gardens in Ireland, featuring extensive walks flanked by hornbeam, beech and lime hedges, and an eighteenth-century "**sylvan theatre**" framed by a high bay hedge

▼ POWERSCOURT WATERFALL

and terraced banks, where plays are still staged in the summer, especially during the house's three-day arts festival at the end of June.

The two-hundred-metre-long twin ponds, once stocked with fish for the table, were designed as "water mirrors" in front of the main **house**. The latter, in Tudor Revival style, is still home to the Brabazon family (the earls of Meath), and boasts some fine plasterwork ceilings. When the house is open, you can get into the Orangery, which was built in the 1850s after the fashion of London's Crystal Palace, and restored in 2000 – so styling itself "Ireland's Millennium Dome". Killruddery features prominently in the Wicklow Gardens Festival from May to August every year (see p.207).

Powerscourt Estate

Enniskerry, Co. Wicklow ☎01/204 6000, ⊛www.powerscourt.ie. House and gardens: daily 9.30am–5.30pm; gardens close at dusk in winter; €9. Waterfall: daily: Jan, Feb, Nov & Dec 10.30am–4pm; March, April, Sept & Oct 10.30am–5.30pm; May–Aug 9.30am–7pm; closed two weeks before Christmas; €5. Bus #44 from Townsend St or #185 from Bray DART. In the northeastern foothills of the Wicklow Mountains, 19km south of Dublin and less than a kilometre beyond the village of Enniskerry, lies the massive Powerscourt Estate, where given fine weather you could easily pass a whole day. Although the estate is now something of an all-round leisure complex, with golf course, garden centre, craft shops and luxury hotel, the central attraction remains the formal **gardens**, whose spectacular design matches their superb setting facing Great Sugar Loaf Mountain.

In the late twelfth century, a castle was built on this strategic site by the Anglo-Norman le Poer (Power) family, from whom it takes its name. However, what you see today dates from the early eighteenth century, when Richard Wingfield, Viscount Powerscourt, employed Richard Castle to build a **Palladian mansion** – one of the largest in Ireland. The house remains impressive from a distance, but most of its interior was destroyed by a fire in 1974 (on the eve of a party to celebrate major refurbishment). Parts have since been recreated, notably the colonnaded, double-height **ballroom** upstairs, while an excellent **café** run by Avoca (see p.70) occupies part of the ground floor and a terrace that provides sumptuous views of the garden. The ballroom is accessible as part of an exhibition, which features displays on the house's former glories as well as short films on the estate's history and development.

The terraced **Italian Gardens** slope gracefully down from the back of the house. The uppermost terrace, with its winged figures of Fame and Victory flanking Apollo and Diana, was designed in 1843 by the gout-ridden Daniel Robertson, who used to be wheeled about the site in a barrow, clutching a bottle of sherry – the last of the sherry apparently meant the end of the day's work. A grand flight of steps leads down to a spirited pair of zinc winged horses, guarding the Triton Lake, whose central statue of the sea god (based on Bernini's fountain in the Piazza Barberini in Rome) fires a jet of water 30m skywards.

On the east side of the terraces are the curious Pepper Pot Tower (accurately modelled on the canister of the eighth Viscount Powerscourt's dinner set), surrounded by fine North American conifers, and a colourful **Japanese Garden** of maples, azaleas and fortune palms, laid out on reclaimed bogland.

To the west of the Italian Gardens lies the **walled garden**, with its rose beds, herbaceous borders and fine ceremonial entrances: the Chorus Gate, decorated with beautiful golden trumpeters, and the Bamberg Gate, which originally belonged to Bamberg Cathedral in Bavaria and features remarkable perspective arches as part of its gilded ironwork design.

The estate's final attraction is Ireland's highest **waterfall**, which leaps and bounds diagonally down a 120-metre rock face to replenish the waters of the River Dargle in the valley below. It's 6km further down the road from the main gate, but well signposted.

Glendalough

Co. Wicklow ☎0404/45325, ⊛www.heritageireland.ie. Site & visitor centre: daily: mid-March to mid-Oct

▲ ROUND TOWER, GLENDALOUGH

9.30am–6pm; rest of year 9.30am–
5pm. Visitor Centre €2.90 (Heritage
Card); site free. St Kevin's bus
service (☎01/281 8119, ⓦwww
.glendaloughbus.com) runs from
opposite the Mansion House on
Dawson Street, Dublin via Bray (Town
Hall, Main St) to Glendalough on Mon–
Sat at 11.30am & 6pm (7pm on Sat
in July & Aug), Sun 11.30am & 7pm
(€11 single, €18 return). Set deep in
a glaciated valley in the heart
of the Wicklow Mountains,
Glendalough, the "valley
of the two lakes", provides
a delightfully atmospheric
location for the striking
remains of one of Ireland's best-
preserved monastic sites. The
monastery was founded by
St Kevin in the sixth century
and played a vital role in the
development of learning in
pre-medieval Europe. You
can find out more about its
history via the **visitor centre**'s
informative displays and videos,
and all visitors are welcome
to join the informative, forty-
minute guided **tours** of the site
(included in the entry price)

that are laid on for large groups,
including a regular slot at 2pm
every day.

The site comprises no fewer
than five churches and an
impressive, though now roofless,
ninth-century **cathedral**,
containing slabs marking many
graves, as well as a **round
tower**, over 30m high, one of
the country's most noteworthy.
Just by the cathedral stands
St Kevin's Cross, one of the
most interesting relics from the
period, consisting of a granite
monolith decorated with an
eighth-century carving of a
Celtic cross superimposed
upon a wheel; unusually, the
quadrants of the cross have not
been pierced, which suggests
that it was left unfinished.
Above the doorway of the
nearby twelfth-century **Priests'
House**, which may have been
the site of Kevin's tomb-shrine,
are faint carvings of figures
believed to depict the saint and
two (later) abbots.

Downhill from here stands the
two-storey **St Kevin's Church**,
whose steeply pitched roof
and bell-turret so resemble a
chimney that the building is also
known as "St Kevin's Kitchen",
although it was almost certainly
an oratory.

Walking west from here
along the "Green Road", past
the Lower Lake, after about
twenty minutes you'll reach the
Upper Lake and the ruins of
the tiny Romanesque **Reefert
Church**, whose small cemetery
is thought to contain the graves
of local chieftains. From here
a path runs up to **St Kevin's
Cell**, a typically Celtic, corbel-
roofed "beehive" hut on a
promontory overlooking the
lake. Further up the cliff,
St Kevin's Bed is a small cave
into which the saint reputedly

moved to avoid the allures of an admirer called Caitlín; he's supposed to have offered the final resistance to her advances by chucking the poor woman into the lake.

Wicklow Mountains National Park Information Office

Glendalough, Co. Wicklow ☎0404/45425, ⓦwww .wicklownationalpark.ie. May–Sept daily 10am–5.30pm; Feb–April, Oct & Nov Sat & Sun 10am–6pm; Jan & Dec Sat & Sun 10am–4pm. At the eastern end of the Upper Lake at Glendalough is the Wicklow Mountains National Park Information Office, which provides information on the mountains and organizes free guided **nature walks** (see the website for the schedule). It also has details of local walking routes and conditions and sells a series of leaflets on the national park, including *The Walking Trails of Glendalough*, which suggests routes taking anything from 45 minutes to four hours.

Russborough House

Blessington, Co. Wicklow ☎045/865239, Erussborough @eircom.net. April & Oct Sun & public holidays 10am–5pm; May–Sept daily 10am–5pm; entry by guided tour only; €6. Maze: June–Aug daily 10am–5pm; €2. Bus #65 from Eden Quay or College Green – 6 or 7 times a day these buses continue beyond Blessington towards Ballymore Eustace, which will leave you much less of a walk to the house. Situated 3km south of Blessington, Russborough House is a lavish Palladian country house, designed by Richard Castle for Joseph Leeson, later the Earl of Milltown, the son of a wealthy Dublin brewer. Castle died before the end of the project, leaving Francis Bindon to oversee the fulfilment of

his grand design. Completed in 1751, the Wicklow granite building's 210-metre-wide **frontage**, with its curving colonnaded wings, is the longest of its kind in Ireland.

Russborough has gained widespread fame for its **art collections**, under both the Milltowns and latterly the Beits, who derived their fortune from the De Beers Diamond Mining Company and bought the house in 1952 (both families made substantial donations of artworks to the National Gallery in Dublin). Unfortunately, this fame has attracted the wrong kind of attention: the house was burgled on no fewer than four occasions between 1974 and 2002, though almost all of the stolen paintings have subsequently been recovered.

▼ RUSSBOROUGH HOUSE

At the moment, because of conservation work, none of the paintings are on show; to compensate, the guided **tour** currently takes in the first-floor bedrooms as well as the main, ground floor. However, it's planned to rehang works by Murillo, Bellotto and Gainsborough, among others; when that happens, there will probably be a choice of two guided tours: one of the ground floor and the paintings; the other, less frequently and less compellingly, of the first floor.

With or without the paintings, the **interior** of the house is sumptuous, featuring Baroque plasterwork ceilings by the Lafranchini brothers, notably in the saloon, depicting the four seasons, and in the music room, where the ingenious geometrical design seems to add height to the room. Further beautiful stuccowork, representing hunting and garlands, adorns the cantilevered main staircase, which was ornately carved out of dark Cuban mahogany by Irish craftsmen in the eighteenth century. Other highlights include the Italian marble fireplace in the dining room depicting Bacchus and vines, and a series of French clocks dating back as far as the fifteenth century, which are still wound every Tuesday.

The house has a pleasant **café**, while in the grounds are a maze and a 2km trail through the parkland, which will take you past a walled garden and a bog garden.

Castletown House

Celbridge, Co. Kildare ☎01/628 8252, ⓌＷwww.heritageireland.ie. Easter to Sept Mon–Fri 10am–6pm, Sat, Sun & public holidays 1–6pm; Oct Mon–Fri 10am–5pm, Sun & public holidays 1–5pm; entry by guided tour only; €3.70; Heritage Card. Bus #67 or #67A from Pearse St to Celbridge.

The oldest and largest Palladian country house in Ireland, Castletown is accessed by gates at the northern end of Celbridge's high street and then by a long avenue of lime trees. Its plain, grey but elegant facade, built in the style of a sixteenth-century Italian town palace, conceals a wealth of beautiful and fascinating interior detail.

▼ CASTLETOWN HOUSE

The house was built for **William Conolly**, son of a Donegal publican who, as legal adviser to William III, became the wealthiest man in Ireland by dealing in forfeited estates after the Battle of the Boyne, and was made Speaker of the Irish House of Commons in 1715. However, the project took an extraordinarily long time to complete – from 1722 till 1770, long after Speaker Conolly's death – and employed the designs of a range of architects, including Sir William Chambers, who built London's Somerset House.

The engaging hour-long guided **tours** highlight an impressive array of ornamentation, including stucco work depicting the four seasons by the Lafranchini brothers, alongside the impressive cantilevered staircase, which, built of Portland stone with solid brass banisters, weighs over ten tonnes. Perhaps the most ostentatious display of wealth and fashion at Castletown is the **Print Room**, whose walls were papered, painstakingly, over a period of six years, with black-and-white prints from London and Paris, portraying everything from landscapes and biblical scenes to famous actors of the day, complemented by decorative borders of swags, chains and masks. The upstairs **Long Gallery** contains busts of Greek and Roman philosophers, murals of classical scenes of love and tragedy and a false door, included for symmetrical effect, while its windows offer views of the **Conolly Folly**, some 3km north – an arcane, fifty-metre-high edifice consisting of an obelisk perched shakily on

▲ STAIRCASE, CASTLETOWN HOUSE

top of a cascade of arches. Attributed to Richard Castle, it was built as a monument to Speaker Conolly by his widow, and as a work scheme for the poor during the potato famine of 1739–41.

Brú na Bóinne

Donore, Co. Meath ☎041/988 0300, ⓦwww.heritageireland.ie. The valley of the River Boyne, some 50km north of Dublin, is scattered with Neolithic remains, the most important of which are the **passage graves** at Newgrange, Knowth and Dowth, although the last-named is still being excavated. Newgrange and Knowth are accessed from the impressive Brú na Bóinne Visitor Centre near Donore, which provides detailed information on the significance of the sites, their construction and artwork (as well as housing a tourist information desk and café). A footbridge crosses from the centre to the north side of the river, where the compulsory minibuses shuttle

Visiting Brú na Bóinne

Opening times

The Brú na Bóinne Visitor Centre is open daily: March, April & Oct 9.30am–5.30pm; May & second half of Sept 9am–6.30pm; June to mid-Sept 9am–7pm; Nov–Feb 9.30am–5pm. The last minibuses to Newgrange and to Knowth depart 1hr 45min before closing. Newgrange is open year-round, Knowth Easter–Oct only.

Admission prices

Admission to the visitor centre is €2.90; combined ticket with Newgrange €5.80; combined ticket with Knowth €4.50; all three €10.30. The Heritage Card is valid for all of these.

Getting there

Take Bus Éireann service #100 from Busáras to Drogheda (which is also served by suburban trains from Pearse, Tara Street or Connolly stations), and then the #163 bus to the visitor centre, which connects with the #100 5 or 6 times a day. Alternatively, a Newgrange shuttlebus operated by Over the Top Tours (see p.174; €18 return) leaves Suffolk Street tourist office daily at 8.45am & 11.15am, stopping outside the *Royal Dublin Hotel*, O'Connell Street Upper at 9am & 11.30pm, and departs from the visitor centre at 1pm & 4pm (though return times may vary in peak season); 45min; tickets can be purchased on board but it's better to book your seat in advance at any tourist office.

you to Newgrange and Knowth for guided tours.

Brú na Bóinne is one of Ireland's foremost attractions, and the numbers visiting each site daily are strictly limited. Booking by phone isn't possible, so it's advisable to arrive as early in the day as you can, especially at Easter or in summer, to book your places on the minibuses to Newgrange and Knowth, which have timed departures. Sunday mornings are generally the quietest time of the week. There's no point in arriving late in the day, as it takes at least three hours to see Newgrange, Knowth and the visitor centre.

Newgrange is unquestionably the most striking of the Brú na Bóinne mounds, not least because its façade of white quartz stones and granite boulders has been reassembled.

The quartz originally came from Wicklow, the granite from the Mourne and Carlingford areas, a mind-boggling feat of transportation. It has been estimated that the tumulus, which is over 75m in diameter, weighs 200,000 tonnes in total and would have taken around forty years to build. It was the final resting-place of a high-status Neolithic family, but seems also to have had a wider purpose as a ritual site or gathering place. The tomb's pivotal feature is a **roof-box** above the entrance whose slit was perfectly positioned to receive the first rays of the rising sun on the day of the winter solstice (December 21); the light first peeps into the burial chamber itself before spreading its rays along the length of the passage.

The fascinating guided **tour** provides an electrically

powered simulation of the phenomenon in the burial chamber, while tickets for the real thing are decided by lottery each year.

It's well worth signing up for the lively guided tour of **Knowth** too. Surrounded by eighteen satellite mounds, the main tumulus is pierced by two passages, aligned roughly with sunrise and sunset on the equinox days in March and September and leading to back-to-back burial chambers. Knowth is even richer in Neolithic art than Newgrange, with about 250 decorated stones discovered here, carved with spectacular but enigmatic crescents, chevrons and other geometric designs – over half of all known Irish passage-tomb art.

PLACES Day trips

▼ KNOWTH

Restaurants and pubs

The Hungry Monk

Church Rd, Greystones ☎01/287 5759, ⓦwww.thehungrymonk.ie. Restaurant: Wed–Sat 6.30–11.30pm, Sun 12.30–8pm. Wine bar: Mon–Sat 5–11pm, Sun 4–9pm. A fine, traditional restaurant, specializing in game in winter and seafood in summer, with an excellent, wide-ranging wine list; especially popular for Sunday set lunch (€30), served all day. A cheaper, simpler menu is available in the wine bar downstairs.

Castletown Inn

Upper Main St, Celbridge. A handy watering-hole a hundred metres from the main entrance to Castletown House that also serves exceptionally good bar meals in gargantuan portions.

Lynham's

Laragh, Co. Wicklow. Around 2km east of Glendalough, *Lynham's* is a welcoming pub where you can get excellent food in its lively bar and spruce restaurant or just sip a pint at one of its outdoor riverside tables.

The Porterhouse

The Strand, Bray ☎01/286 0668, ⓦwww.porterhousebrewco.com. A branch of the excellent Temple Bar microbrewery-pub, serving its own great stouts, lagers and ales, as well as good, basic fare such as Irish stew, salads and burgers. There's a beer garden overlooking the esplanade, and DJs play till late at weekends.

Accommodation

Hotels and guesthouses

Though Dublin has a plethora of accommodation possibilities, the city's hotels and B&Bs rank among Europe's most expensive; finding a bed can be especially problematic during July and August, major festivals and public holidays such as around St Patrick's Day, and at the time of major gigs or sporting events. Book with hotels directly or contact any Fáilte Ireland (Irish tourist board) or Northern Irish Tourist Board office, which will be able to book you a room for a fee of €4 or £2. Suburban B&Bs will generally charge around €60–80 for a double room, while their more upmarket central equivalents may charge anything from €100 to €300. As for hotels, prices range from the bargain to the extravagant, though good deals can be found by booking in advance via Gulliver (℡066 979 2030, ⓦwww.gulliver.ie), Dublin Tourism (ⓦwww.visitdublin.com) or through establishments' own websites, especially midweek in the city centre and, conversely, at weekends for places aimed at business travellers.

Trinity College, Grafton Street and around

The Westbury Harry St, off Grafton St ℡01/679 1122, ⓦwww.jurysdoyle.com. The glossy lobby of this five-star hotel is an indicator of the treats that lie in store. Its bedrooms are designed to pamper, and the range of facilities on offer includes a fitness centre, a sleek bar specializing in champagne cocktails, and underground parking. €449 official rate, but high-season bargains can be as low as €189; breakfast not included.

The Westin Dublin Westmoreland St ℡01/645 1000, ⓦwww.westin.com /dublin. Hiding behind the facade of the old Allied Irish Bank building just north of Trinity College, *The Westin* is a marvellously luxurious establishment. Its 163 elegant bedrooms (all non-smoking) are designed with character, and some now feature private workout facilities. The bar is housed in the former bank's vaults, and the lounge features a stunning glass roof. €254–539, depending on room size and facilities; breakfast not included.

Kildare Street and Merrion Square

Buswells Hotel 23–27 Molesworth St ℡01/614 6500, ⓦwww.quinnhotels .com. Popular with politicians due to its proximity to Leinster House, *Buswells* offers

A guide to prices

For hotels, guesthouses and B&Bs, the prices quoted in this chapter are for the cheapest double room in the summer high season, and include breakfast, unless otherwise specified; the majority of upmarket hotels do not include breakfast in their rates and this can cost anything from €5–€15. For hostels, prices are given for the cheapest dorm bed in high season, as well as for a private double or twin room, where available. A light breakfast is usually included; exceptions to that rule are noted in the text.

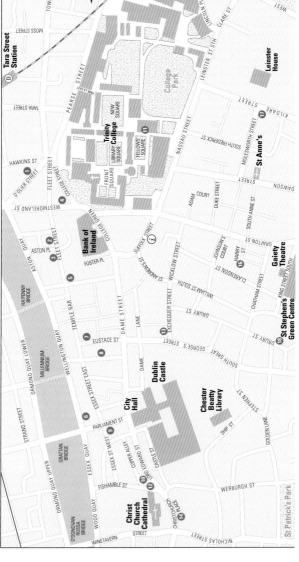

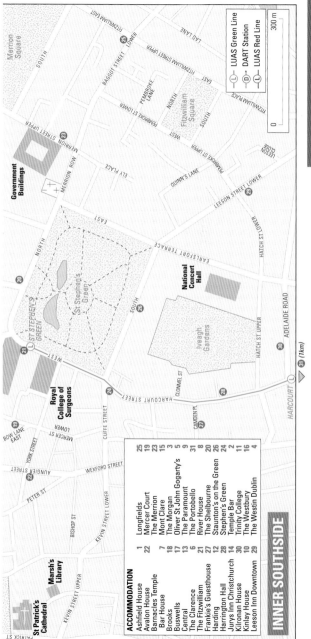

INNER SOUTHSIDE

ACCOMMODATION

Ashfield House	1	Longfields	25
Avalon House	22	Mercer Court	19
Barnacles Temple		The Merrion	23
Bar House	7	Mont Clare	15
Brooks	18	The Morgan	3
Buswells	17	Oliver St John Gogarty's	5
Central	13	The Paramount	9
The Clarence	6	The Portobello	31
The Fitzwilliam	21	River House	8
Frankie's Guesthouse	27	The Shelbourne	20
Harding		Staunton's on the Green	26
Harrington Hall	12	Stephen's Green	24
Jurys Inn Christchurch	28	Temple Bar	2
Kilronan House	14	Trinity College	30
Kinlay House	10	The Westbury	11
Leeson Inn Downtown	29	The Westin Dublin	4

Legend:
- Ⓛ — LUAS Green Line
- Ⓓ — DART Station
- Ⓛ — LUAS Red Line

0 — 300 m

67 pleasantly designed en-suite rooms in a converted Georgian town house. Ornate plasterwork and fireplaces testify to its origins and the hotel also has a splendid carvery/restaurant, its own bar and secure parking. €195.

Longfields Hotel 9–10 Fitzwilliam St Lower ☏ 01/676 1367, ⊛ www.longfields .ie. *Longfields* is a small hotel which fully proves the point that size isn't everything. Its 26 en-suite rooms are furnished and decorated to a high standard and include elegant drapes, prints and some four-poster beds. Run by a helpful team, there's also a cosy lounge, and the excellent breakfast is another bonus. €165.

The Merrion Hotel Merrion St Upper ☏ 01/603 0600, ⊛ www.merrionhotel .com. The Duke of Wellington's dismissal of his Irish connections – "being born in a stable doesn't make one a horse" – rings even hollower now that his birthplace at no. 24 is part of this very civilized luxury hotel. Four eighteenth-century town houses have been elegantly redecorated in Georgian style and hung with a superb collection of Irish art, overlooking a private landscaped garden. Facilities include the luxurious Tethra Spa (see p.35) and *Restaurant Patrick Guilbaud* (see p.85). Main House €565, Garden Wing €470; breakfast not included.

Mont Clare Hotel Merrion St Lower ☏ 01/607 3800, ⊛ www.ocallaghanhotels .com. Just off Merrion Square (and with its own secure car park), the *Mont Clare* offers over seventy recently refurbished, a/c rooms, providing a degree of comfort and an attractive location for which you might pay double elsewhere. Facilities include a bar and restaurant. €135.

St Stephen's Green to the Grand Canal

The Fitzwilliam Hotel St Stephen's Green ☏ 01/478 7000, ⊛ www .fitzwilliamhotel.com. With a grand, expansive foyer and swish rooms designed by Sir Terence Conran, the *Fitzwilliam* offers deluxe accommodation in a marvellous central location. The room rate ranges considerably depending on size and facilities (though all include free Internet

access, CD player and fresh flowers daily), and there's also a beauty salon, roof garden, bars, secure parking and restaurant. The Penthouse Suite (€3,200) boasts its own private bar and grand piano. €220.

Frankie's Guesthouse 8 Camden Place ☏ 01/478 3087, ⊛ www .frankiesguesthouse.com. By some distance the best gay- and lesbian-friendly guesthouse in Dublin, *Frankie's* occupies a fine mews location and offers a dozen rooms, including standard singles and doubles as well as en-suite doubles and twins – though note that at weekends there's a minimum stay of two/three nights for doubles/twins and singles respectively. The glorious roof garden and sumptuous breakfast are further draws. €90.

Harrington Hall 70 Harcourt St ☏ 01/475 3497, ⊛ www.harringtonhall. com. Occupying elegant Georgian premises and with equally stylish interiors, this guesthouse just south of St Stephen's Green has 28 thoughtfully furnished and spacious en-suite rooms, complete with double glazing and ceiling fans. Substantial discounts available in low season. €230.

Kilronan House 70 Adelaide Rd ☏ 01/475 5266, ⊛ www.dublinn.com. It would be hard to top the welcome at this fine Georgian town house, which features elegant decor, including Waterford crystal chandeliers, as well as orthopedic mattresses in all its rooms. €152 (though a small number of rooms, with shower /washbasin, but shared toilet facilities are as low as €110).

Leeson Inn Downtown 24 Leeson St Lower ☏ 01/662 2002, ⊛ www .leesoninndowntown.com. Some 250m from the southeast corner of St Stephen's Green, the *Leeson's* 28 tastefully furnished and well-accoutred en-suite rooms give respite from the city's hurly-burly – and at a reasonable price too. €149.

The Portobello Hotel 33 Richmond St South ☏ 01/475 2715, ⊛ www .portobellohotel.ie. Accessed via the canalside Charlemont Mall and with the reception on the first floor, this welcoming 24-room establishment has incredibly spacious and reasonably priced en-suite doubles. Most have views of the canal and the Dublin mountains beyond, and all have a bath as well as a shower. €79.

The Shelbourne 27 St Stephen's Green ☎01/663 4500, ⓦwww.theshelbourne .ie. The *grande dame* of Dublin hotels has recently been glitzily renovated and expanded. Highlights of the new look are the gilded lobby, where the old lift has been removed to reveal the grand staircase, and the *Saddle Room* restaurant (see p.92). The *Horseshoe Bar* (see p.93) and the *Lord Mayor's Lounge*, where you can tuck into traditional afternoon tea accompanied by views of the Green and the tinkling of a piano, have been refurbished but, mercifully, not reconstructed. A spa, pool and gym are planned. €265; breakfast not included.

Stauntons on the Green 83 St Stephen's Green ☎01/478 2300, ⓦwww.stauntonsonthegreen.ie. Set in an unbeatable location on the south side of the Green with its own private gardens, this is a splendidly equipped guesthouse whose thirty en-suite rooms offer levels of comfort and style befitting this Georgian building. €165.

Stephen's Green Hotel St Stephen's Green ☎01/607 3600, ⓦwww .ocallaghanhotels.com Swish, classy, yet thoroughly Modernist, this utterly enjoyable hotel occupies a spot overlooking the southwestern corner of the Green. As well as its lively bar, reasonably-priced bistro, fitness centre and Wi-Fi Internet, the hotel provides 68 spacious a/c double rooms and a number of even more luxurious suites (€435). €145.

Temple Bar

The Clarence 6–8 Wellington Quay ☎01/407 0800, ⓦwww.theclarence .ie. Formerly a bolt-hole for priests and lawyers up from the country, *The Clarence* retains the distinctive light oak panelling of its former incarnation, but has been transformed into a hip, informal, luxury hotel. Owned by Bono and The Edge of U2, it contains the *Tea Room* restaurant in the former ballroom (see p.102) and the stylish *Octagon Bar* (see p.103), as well as a two-storey penthouse suite used by sundry rock stars. All 45 rooms come with a state-of-the-art multimedia system. At the time of writing, plans were

afoot to expand the hotel, incorporating additional buildings on Wellington Quay. €179.

The Morgan 10 Fleet St ☎01/643 7000, ⓦwww.themorgan.com. Sheer bliss in terms of the quality of its accommodation, and crisply designed throughout, this establishment fully merits the term elegant. The hotel's 121 rooms vary in size and facilities, but none are anything less than extremely comfortable. €150.

The Paramount Hotel Parliament St ☎01/417 9900, ⓦwww.paramounthotel .ie. Situated at the eastern end of Temple Bar (and entered via Essex Gate), *The Paramount* combines deluxe accommodation – its 66 rooms decorated using tones and furnishings reminiscent of the 1930s – with thoroughly modern facilities. Its *Turks Head* bar is a stylish hangout and serves bistro-style meals throughout the day. €120.

River House Hotel 23–24 Eustace St ☎01/670 7655, ⓦwww.riverhousehotel .com. Tucked away on one of Temple Bar's quieter streets, the red-fronted *River House* is one of the few family-run establishments in the centre, with 29 stylishly decorated double rooms. Excellent breakfasts, which include freshly baked scones, add to the attraction. €125.

Temple Bar Hotel 13–17 Fleet St ☎01/677 3333, ⓦwww.templebarhotel .com. Tastefully designed throughout, from its bright and airy lobby to its attractive, modern en-suite bedrooms, the *Temple Bar* has a high reputation for service, though some of its front-facing rooms can suffer from late-night street noise. The hotel's *Buskers* bar is a popular spot, and there's reduced-rate secure car parking nearby. €145.

Dublin Castle and around

Brooks Hotel Drury St ☎01/670 4000, ⓦwww.brookshotel.ie. Compact, four-star boutique hotel, on a quiet road that's handy for Temple Bar and Grafton Street, with stylish, a/c bedrooms – some of which feature plasma-screen TVs and DVD players – as well as a small gym and sauna, and very friendly service. €170.

Central Hotel 1–5 Exchequer St ☎01/679 7302, ⓦwww.centralhotel.ie. Centrally located, as its name suggests, this hotel is one of the city's oldest, having been in business since 1887. The en suite rooms are stylishly furnished and most are sufficiently soundproofed to block out street noise, though some can feel a little cramped. The hotel's first-floor *Library Bar* is a popular spot for everything from morning coffee to pre-dinner drinks. €125.

Harding Hotel Copper Alley, Fishamble St ☎01/679 6500, ⊚**www.hardinghotel .ie.** Massively popular due to its budget-conscious high-season room rate and spacious rooms, the *Harding* also houses the atmospheric *Darkey Kelly's* bar (taking its name from an eighteenth-century Copper Alley brothel-keeper), supplying good food and a regular programme of live entertainment. €99; breakfast is an additional €6.50–8.50.

Jurys Inn Christchurch Christchurch Place ☎01/454 0000, ⊚**www.jurysinn .com.** Bang opposite the Cathedral (though don't compare the relative architectural merits), *Jurys* is popular with families thanks to its low room rates. Rooms are both restful and functional, and the hotel

offers a restaurant, café and bar. €122; breakfast not included.

The Liberties and Kilmainham

Hilton Dublin Kilmainham Inchicore Rd ☎01/420 1800, ⊚**www.hilton.co.uk /kilmainham; see map p.124.** Although it might look like a rejected design for social housing on the outside, there's no doubting the quality of the rooms and services provided inside, though this is a hotel aimed at business travellers, for whom proximity to the adjacent N4 is a bonus. En suite rooms are spacious and comfortable and have facilities such as Internet access and cable TV. Still, there's plenty a bargain to be found via the Internet and the hotel is very close to both Kilmainham Gaol and IMMA. €109.

O'Connell Street and around

Academy Plaza Hotel Findlater Place, Cathal Brugha St ☎01/878 0666, ⊚**www .academy-hotel.ie.** Tucked away behind O'Connell Street, this well-appointed hotel has recently been massively redeveloped and now boasts 285 tastefully furnished, a/c

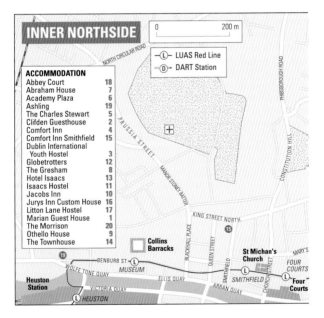

INNER NORTHSIDE

0   200 m

─Ⓛ─ LUAS Red Line
═Ⓓ─ DART Station

ACCOMMODATION	
Abbey Court	18
Abraham House	7
Academy Plaza	6
Ashling	19
The Charles Stewart	5
Clifden Guesthouse	2
Comfort Inn	4
Comfort Inn Smithfield	15
Dublin International Youth Hostel	3
Globetrotters	12
The Gresham	8
Hotel Isaacs	13
Isaacs Hostel	11
Jacobs Inn	10
Jurys Inn Custom House	16
Litton Lane Hostel	17
Marian Guest House	1
The Morrison	20
Othello House	9
The Townhouse	14

NORTH CIRCULAR ROAD

PHIBSBOROUGH ROAD

PRUSSIA STREET

MANOR STONEY BATTER

CONSTITUTION HILL

KING STREET NORTH

BLACKHALL PLACE

QUEEN STREET

SMITHFIELD

Collins Barracks

St Michan's Church

MARY'S

FOUR COURTS

BENBURB ST Ⓛ

WOLFE TONE QUAY

MUSEUM

ELLIS QUAY

CHURCH STREET

Four Courts

Ⓛ

Heuston Station

VICTORIA QUAY

ARRAN QUAY

Ⓛ HEUSTON

en-suite rooms and suites, as well as a fine range of breakfasts and a friendly bar, plus free Wi-Fi Internet access. €125.

The Gresham Hotel 23 O'Connell St Upper ☎01/874 6881, ⓦwww .gresham-hotels.com. *The Gresham* isn't just a splendidly equipped 4-star hotel, but one of Dublin's landmarks, a place where you don't have to be a guest to enjoy afternoon tea in the opulent surroundings of its lobby or sample the meals in its restaurant. Rooms are stylish and spacious, while the individually designed penthouse suites (€1500–2200) include one formerly occupied by Elizabeth Taylor and Richard Burton and another designed by "Spike" creator Ian Ritchie. €150.

Hotel Isaacs Store St ☎01/813 4700, ⓦwww.isaacs.ie. Though its setting – opposite Busáras – isn't exactly auspicious, *Isaacs'* tastefully designed interior, friendly staff and 99 well-accoutred bedrooms more than compensate. The hotel has its own attached Italian restaurant, *Il Vignardo*, as well as a suitably cosmopolitan café-bar, *Le Monde*. €119.

Jurys Inn Custom House Custom House Quay ☎01/607 5000,

ⓦwww.jurysinn.com. The riverside location really is hard to beat and the views of Dublin's developing docklands are staggering from rooms on the upper storeys. Rooms veer towards the functional, but are never less than comfortable. Facilities include a bar, café and restaurant. €108.

The Morrison Ormond Quay Lower ☎01/887 2400, ⓦwww.morrisonhotel .ie. Black remains the new black as far as this swish temple of minimalism is concerned. While that colour dominates the lobby and ultra-cool bar (see p.137), the luxurious rooms also feature chocolate and cream colour schemes using natural materials (fashion designer John Rocha was employed as consultant). The exclusive Penthouse Suite (€1100), offering lush decor and all manner of creature comforts, has spectacular riverside views. €165.

Othello House 74 Gardiner St Lower ☎01/855 4271, ⓦwww.othellodublin .com. A popular option on a busy street, this comfortable B&B provides 22 en-suite rooms, all equipped with TV, telephone and tea/coffee-making facilities, as well as an

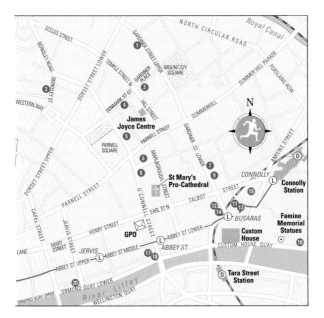

excellent Irish breakfast. Limited parking is available. €90.

The Townhouse 47–48 Gardiner St Lower ☎01/878 8808, ⓦwww .townhouseofdublin.com. This superbly converted Georgian house remains an oasis of calm in one of the city's busiest streets. Stylish rooms are fashionably decorated and have sizeable en-suite bathrooms. A buffet breakfast is served in an elegant dining room with a balcony and there are off-street parking spaces. €115.

North from Parnell Square

The Charles Stewart 5–6 Parnell Square ☎01/878 0350, ⓦwww .charlesstewart.ie. Despite its busy location, most of this budget hotel's rooms are well set back from the street, away from street noise. Though en-suite doubles and triples are well kept, if somewhat basic, some singles can be tiny, and plasterboard dividing walls do not block out the noise from adjoining rooms. Nevertheless, there are plenty of bargains to be had via the website, staff are helpful and friendly and a filling breakfast is served. €85.

Clifden Guesthouse 32 Gardiner Place ☎01/874 6364, ⓦwww.clifdenhouse .com. One of the Northside's most reliable options, this comfortable Georgian house is well maintained by very friendly hosts. Fifteen pleasant en-suite rooms include doubles as well as a triple and a family room, all tastefully decorated in keeping with its Georgian origins. Off-street parking is available. €110.

Comfort Inn Great Denmark St ☎1850/266 3678, ⓦwww .comfortinndublin.com. The *Comfort's* Georgian exterior houses a stylish modern hotel. Rooms are bright, airy and attractively furnished, and the hotel's bar, *The Belvedere*, is a popular meeting-place. Free broadband is available in all rooms, and the hotel is wheelchair accessible. Generous discounts available in low season. €89.

Marian Guest House 21 Gardiner St Upper ☎01/874 4129, ⓦwww .marianguesthouse.ie. Immensely popular due to its budget prices and warm welcome, the *Marian* offers five clean and comfortable en-suite double rooms, as well as one with bathroom in the corridor, plus a filling breakfast. Off-street parking is available and buses #16 and #41 stop just around the corner on Dorset Street Upper. €75.

From Capel Street to Collins Barracks

Comfort Inn Smithfield Village ☎01/485 0900, ⓦwww .comfortinnsmithfield.com. A great addition to the Smithfield area, this new-build hotel provides excellently equipped and furnished rooms, tastefully decorated using primary colours. There's also a good-value restaurant and secure parking nearby, and it's handily placed for music events at *The Cobblestone* (see p.153). €109.

Phoenix Park

Ashling Hotel Parkgate St ☎01/677 2324, ⓦwww.ashlinghotel.ie. Conveniently located near Heuston Station, this modern hotel offers 150 tasteful and comfortable bedrooms with plenty of space, as well as a pleasant bar and excellent breakfast.€150.

Hostels and student accommodation

Dublin has numerous hostels, and the majority of these offer both dorm beds (around €15–25, depending on the season) and private rooms, usually sleeping between two and four people (€25–45 per person), as well as a light breakfast included in the price. Private rooms are en suite and offer a standard of accommodation often equal to what you would expect in a B&B. Most hostels in Dublin belong to the IHH

(Independent Holiday Hostels of Ireland ⓦwww.hostels–ireland .com), though a few are members of the IHO (Independent Hostel Owners ⓦwww .independenthostelsireland .com). Additionally, several of the city's educational establishments open up their student accommodation to visitors during the summer vacation. Prices are generally higher than hostels (€45–70 per person), but still cheaper than many hotels in similarly central locations.

The majority of Dublin hostels now provide free Internet access.

Trinity College, Grafton Street and around

Ashfield House 19–20 D'Olier St ☏01/679 7734, ⓦwww.ashfieldhouse .ie. One of the centre's most popular options provides over 130 beds in bright and spacious rooms, all with en-suite facilities. Dorms come in a variety of sizes – mostly four- or six-bed – and comfortable doubles are also available, as well as a kitchen and Internet access. Dorms from €16, doubles €80.
Trinity College College Green ☏01/608 1177, ⓦwww.tcd.ie/accommodation /visitors/. The College opens its 800 residential rooms to visitors from mid-June to the end of September. Although not the cheapest budget option, the College does have an unbeatable, historic location. The single, twin and quad rooms (with en-suite bathroom and without) have access to a shared kitchen, and there's a campus restaurant, bar and sporting facilities. €57.60–69.60 per person.

St Stephen's Green to the Grand Canal

Mercer Court Campus Accommodation Mercer Street Lower ☏01/474 4120, ⓦwww.mercercourt.ie. Open from late June to late September during the Royal College of Surgeons' holidays, and just off St Stephen's Green, Mercer Court

has 100 en-suite bedrooms, all with TV, and continental breakfast is included in the price. €90.

Temple Bar

Barnacles Temple Bar House 19 Temple Lane ☏01/671 6277, ⓦwww .barnacles.ie. This modern hostel's lobby is strangely reminiscent of a sub-post office, but don't be dissuaded, because its en-suite rooms and facilities cover all essentials, including a sizeable kitchen and dining room. Dorms from €18.50, doubles €80.
Oliver St John Gogarty's 18–21 Anglesea St ☏01/671 1822, ⓦwww.gogartys .ie. Not to be recommended at weekends thanks to its popularity with British hen and stag parties, this well-equipped hostel has more than a 100 beds in a range of accommodation, including twins with en-suite bathroom and without, eight- and ten-bed dorms, as well as stylish one- to three-bed apartments. Kitchen and laundry facilities are available. Dorms €20, doubles €80, apartments €135–300.

Dublin Castle and around

Avalon House 55 Aungier St ☏01/475 0001, ⓦwww.avalon-house.ie. Five minutes' walk south of South Great George's Street, *Avalon House* occupies a former medical school and has dorms of various sizes and twin-bedded rooms. It's a large hostel (281 beds in total) and has a café, kitchen, Internet access, TV and games rooms. Dorms €20, doubles €60.
Kinlay House 2–12 Lord Edward St ☏01/679 6644, ⓦwww.kinlayhouse .ie. A very lively and busy hostel near Christ Church Cathedral, *Kinlay House* offers good-value private rooms as well as six-bed and 24-bed dorms. There's a large kitchen as well as a café, and residents qualify for discounts on bar meals at the adjacent *Darkey Kelly's* restaurant. Dorms €19, doubles €68.

The Liberties and Kilmainham

Brewery Hostel 22–23 Thomas St ☏01/453 8600, ⓦwww.irish-hostel .com. This IHO hostel's inauspicious location on The Liberties' main drag (see map p.124) is certainly mitigated by the friendliness of its welcome and all-round cosiness. More like a country hostel than its city-centre cousins, the bulk of this hostel's 70 beds are in small dorms, but there are also four private rooms. Facilities include a large lounge, a well-equipped kitchen and clean showers, plus a courtyard for alfresco conviviality. Dorms €18, doubles €75.

O'Connell Street and around

Abbey Court 29 Bachelors Walk ☎01/878 0800, ⊛www.abbey-court .com. Right next to O'Connell Bridge, this upmarket, well-designed hostel provides en-suite twins/doubles and dorms ranging from four to twelve beds. The hostel is very security-conscious: access is via keycards and there are lockers in every room. Other facilities include a café, kitchen, laundry, TV lounges, a conservatory and a barbecue area. Dorms €22, doubles €88.

Abraham House 82–83 Gardiner St Lower ☎01/855 0600, ⊛www .abraham-house.ie One of the larger Northside hostels, Abraham House has a friendly staff and atmosphere. As well as en-suite rooms, there are dorms of various sizes, sleeping from four to up to sixteen. There's also a kitchen, lockers, Internet access and a small car park. The stop for bus #41 to and from the airport is adjacent. Dorms €21, doubles €92.

Globetrotters 46 Gardiner St Lower ☎01/873 5893, ⊛www .globetrottersdublin.com. Under the same excellent management as The Townhouse (see p.194), this 94-bed hostel offers six- to twelve-bed dorms, equipped with some of the most comfortable bunks in Dublin. All are en suite, and there's a well-equipped kitchen too. Dorms €24.

Isaacs Hostel 2–5 Frenchman's Lane ☎01/855 6125, ⊛www.isaacs.ie. Dublin's oldest independent hostel, efficiently run and very welcoming, is still one of its best. Accommodation consists mostly of

eight- and ten-bed dorms, with some cosy twin-bedded private rooms, though none is en suite. Facilities include a high-quality kitchen, a café, a small garden hosting barbecues in summer, Internet access and live acoustic music on Fridays. Dorms €16, twins €72.

Jacobs Inn 21–28 Talbot Place ☎01/855 5660, ⊛www.isaacs.ie. Recently refurbished, this is Dublin's largest independent hostel which, despite its size, remains one of the most convivial, with a ground-floor café and first-floor common room with pool table and big-screen TV. En-suite private rooms are large and well-furnished, and the comfortable, twelve-bed dorms are en suite. Internet facilities are available and the hostel is wheelchair accessible. Dorms from €17, doubles €90.

Litton Lane Hostel 2–4 Litton Lane ☎01/872 8389, ⊛www.irish-hostel .com. Housed in a former recording studio in a quiet side street off Bachelors Walk, this popular and efficient hostel offers eight- and ten-bed dorms as well as comfortable private rooms and some self-contained apartments sleeping from two to four. There's a sizeable kitchen too, as well as a pool table. Dorms €19, doubles €78, apartments €90–120.

North from Parnell Square

Dublin International Youth Hostel Mountjoy St ☎01/830 1766, ⊛www .anoige.ie. A gargantuan 293-bed establishment in a somewhat grim Northside area, just west of the Black Church and Dorset Street Upper, this An Óige flagship is more homely inside than its forbidding exterior might suggest. Much of the accommodation is in largish dorms, though there are some private doubles and quads. Non-An Óige or International Youth Hostelling Association members are charged a supplement of €2. There's a reasonably-priced restaurant. Dorms €21, doubles €52.

Essentials

Arrival

No matter how you arrive, Dublin's efficient transport network means you'll soon be in the city centre, though bear in mind that journeys by road from the airport and ferry terminals may take much longer during rush-hour periods.

By air

Dublin Airport (☏01/874 1111, ⓦwww.dublinairport.com) is some seven miles north of the centre. The arrivals hall contains a tourist office (daily 8am–10pm), a travel information desk (Mon–Sat 8am–1pm & 2–5pm, Sun 10.30am–1pm & 2–4.30pm), a branch of the Bank of Ireland (Mon–Fri 10am–4pm, Wed until 5pm), a *bureau de change* (daily 5.30am–9pm, Mon until 8pm), several ATMs and a number of car-rental outlets.

Buses to the centre depart from outside the arrivals exit. The most direct are the **Airlink** bus #747 (every 10–15min Mon–Sat 5.45am–11.30pm, every 15–20min Sun 7.15am–11.30pm; €6 single, €10 return), which runs via O'Connell Street to Busáras, the central bus station; and #748 (every 30min Mon–Sat 6.50am–9.30pm, Sun 7am–10.05pm; same prices), which takes a similar route but continues to Heuston railway station. Alternatively, **Aircoach** (ⓦwww.aircoach.ie) operates two services – the first runs into the centre via College Green and onwards to hotels in Donnybrook and Ballsbridge (daily every 10–20min 4.30am–midnight, hourly midnight–4.30am; €7 single, €12 return); the second also takes in the centre and Donnybrook before continuing onwards to Stillorgan and Leopardstown (daily every 10–20min 4am–midnight, hourly midnight–4am; same prices).

The slower but cheaper option (€1.90) is to take one of the regular **Dublin Bus** services such as the #16A to O'Connell Street and College Green (every 15–30min Mon–Fri 6.50am–11.10pm, every 20–50min Sat 7.40am–10.20pm, every 25min–1hr Sun 8.30am–10.40pm) or the #41 to Abbey Street Lower, just off O'Connell Street (every 15–30min Mon–Sat 6.20am–11.50pm, every 30min–1hr Sun 7.15am–11.35pm). Additionally, the #746 (every 30min–1hr

15min Mon–Fri 9.15am–9.45pm, hourly Sat 9.45am–9.45pm & Sun 10am–7pm) runs to the centre and thence to Dún Laoghaire.

A **taxi** to the centre should cost from around €30.

By bus

Busáras, Dublin's central bus station, is on Store Street behind the Custom House, some ten minutes' walk east of O'Connell Street. It serves Bus Éireann express coaches from all parts of Ireland (North and South) as well as the Airlink service and coaches from Britain. City buses run into the centre along Talbot Street, a block to the north, while there are LUAS Red Line (see p.199) stops outside the bus station's northern exit or to the west on Abbey Street Lower. Alternatively, a taxi can usually be hailed on Beresford Place just south of Busáras.

Private coaches terminate at a variety of locations – check with the service operator for precise details.

By ferry

All services – except Stena Line's HSS (see below) – arrive at **Dublin Port**, two miles east of the centre. An unnumbered Dublin Bus service (€2.50) meets arrivals and runs directly to Busáras. The return service leaves Busáras daily at 6.45am (Sun 7am), 7.30am, 1.15pm and 8pm. Stena Line HSS ferries arrive at **Dún Laoghaire**, nine miles southeast of the city centre. The DART (see p.199) station is directly opposite the terminal and trains (€2) run every 20 minutes to the centre (including the central Pearse, Tara Street and Connolly stations). Alternatively, bus #46A (Mon–Sat every 5–15min, Sun every 10–40min; €1.90) runs from outside the Crofton Road entrance to the station via Donnybrook to St Stephen's Green and O'Connell Street. The Dún Laoghaire ferry terminal has a tourist office (Mon–Sat 10am–1pm, 2–6pm).

By train

Trains from Belfast, Sligo, Wexford and Rosslare terminate at **Connolly Station** on Amiens Street, fifteen minutes' walk east of O'Connell Street via Talbot Street and connected to the centre by regular buses and LUAS trams. The station is also on the DART line. **Heuston Station**, on the south bank of the Liffey, two miles west of the centre, serves trains from Ballina, Cork, Galway, Kilkenny, Killarney, Limerick, Tralee, Waterford and Westport. Heuston is connected to the centre by LUAS trams and buses #90 and #92. Two other Southside stations, **Tara Street** and **Pearse** serve DART and suburban railways. Information on train services and timetables is available from ☎01/836 6222, ⊛www.irishrail.ie.

By car

Almost all major trunk roads entering Dublin are linked by the M50 motorway which runs in a semi-circle around the city's outskirts. The M1/N1 (from Belfast and Drogheda), N2 (Derry and Monaghan) and N3 (Cavan) eventually converge on Dorset Street, just north of Parnell Square and O'Connell Street. The N4 (from Sligo, linking with the N6 from Athlone) runs past Heuston Station and thence along the Northside Quays of the Liffey. The N7 (from the southwest, linking with the N9 from Waterford) runs along Crumin Road, entering the centre via Patrick Street and Christchurch. Lastly, the N11 (from the southeast, linking with the N21 from Dún Laoghaire) runs through Ballsbridge and on to Merrion Square.

City transport

Getting around the city couldn't be easier, thanks to an extensive system of buses, trams and railway services, as well as many taxis.

Buses

Dublin Bus (⊛www.dublinbus.ie) operates a network of routes covering just about everywhere in the city and extending far beyond its boundaries into Dublin county, as well as counties Kildare, Meath and Wicklow. Most of its bus stops display route maps. A free guide to the services, plus timetables and an excellent, free visitors' map are available from the company's offices at 59 O'Connell St Upper (Mon 8.30am–5.30pm, Tues–Fri 9am–5.30pm, Sat 9am–2pm, Sun 9.30am–2pm), while travel information is also available from ☎01/873 4222. If your mobile is connected to an Irish network you can also send **text message** enquiries to ☎53503 – type "BUS" followed by the route number (such as "BUS46A") to receive details of the next three buses in each direction. You can also specify different times using the 24-hour clock (such as "BUS19 2100" or even "BUS15 0830 TOMORROW").

All bus **fares** are exact-change only and regular ticket prices range from €1 for a short ride to €1.90 for the longest journeys (child fares €0.70–0.90), though there's a flat €0.60 shopper's fare for short-hop journeys within the city centre. If you do not have the exact fare and pay more than required, you will receive a refund voucher from the bus driver; this and your bus ticket should be presented at the Dublin Bus office (see above) to obtain a refund.

Most services operate around 6.30am–11.30pm on weekdays, starting later and finishing earlier on Sundays. Special **Nitelink** buses run in the small hours (Tues–Fri 12.30–2am; Sat & Sun 12.30–4.30am; every 30min. These buses run from College Street, D'Olier Street and Westmoreland Street, all routes carry the suffix "N" (eg 46N) and tickets cost a flat-fare rate of €4 for the shorter routes and €6 for longer journeys to places such as Ashbourne and Maynooth.

LUAS

Introduced in 2004, LUAS (Irish for "speed"; ⊛www.luas.ie) currently operates two overground **tramway** routes (more are in the pipeline) which are much quicker than buses and avoid traffic congestion. The Red Line runs from Connolly Station along Abbey Street to Collins Barracks before crossing the river at Heuston Station, then heads southwest to the suburb of Tallaght; while

Travel passes

A bewildering range of **travel passes** is available from the Dublin Bus office (see p.199), newsagents and other shops displaying the Dublin Bus sign, and from DART and suburban railway stations. Bus-only **Rambler** passes are accepted on all routes except Airlink and Nitelink and cover one day (€5), three (€11), five (€17.30) and seven (€21) days. Alternatively, the "Rambler Handy Pack" (€18.30) consists of five one-day passes and is useful if you don't intend to travel every day, while the "Family One-day Rambler" (€8.50) covers travel by two adults and up to four children.

The three-day **Freedom** ticket (€25) includes travel to and from the airport on the Airlink service (so is best bought at the airport's travel information desk), all Dublin bus services (including Nitelink) and the company's hop-on and -off city tour (see p.200).

One-day passes for the **LUAS** service (see p.199) cost €4.80 and a seven-day pass is €17.20 when purchased from station vending machines, but they're cheaper (€4.50 and €15.50) when bought from shops bearing the LUAS sign (usually found near stations). A combined one-day bus and LUAS pass is €6.50 and a seven-day pass is €25 (with no reduction in price if buying from a LUAS agent).

The price of most **DART** railway/suburban rail passes depends on the starting and finishing points of your journey. A three-day pass ranges from €7.40 to €14.20 and a seven-day pass from €15.30 to €26. Alternatively, to roam more widely around the network, a one-day pass is €7.20 and a one-day family pass is €12.40, while a three-day adult pass is €15.30. A combined bus/DART/suburban rail one-day pass costs €8.80, rising to €17.30 for three days and €30 for seven, and a one-day family pass covering these services is €13.50. A one-day LUAS and rail pass is €8.20 (there is no family pass for this combination). All of these passes can only be used in the short-hop zone (the entire DART network and suburban rail services as far as Balbriggan to the north, Maynooth and Celbridge to the west and Kilcoole to the south).

the Green Line commences at St Stephen's Green, then heads down Harcourt Street before cruising along to the southeastern suburbs of Dundrum and Sandyford. Trams run every 5–15 minutes (Mon–Fri 5.30am–12.30am, Sat 6.30am–12.30am, Sun 7am–11.30pm); singles cost €1.40–2.10 and returns €2.70–4 (children €1 and €1.90 respectively). Tickets are bought from vending machines at the tramway stops.

DART and suburban trains

The trains of the Dublin Area Rapid Transit system or **DART** (Mon–Sat 6.20am–midnight, Sun 9.20am–11.40pm; ⓦ www .iarnrodeireann.ie/dart/home) link Howth and Malahide to the north of the city with Bray and Greystones to the south via places such as Blackrock, Dún Laoghaire and Dalkey. It's certainly the quickest option for visiting some of the outlying attractions

(see Day trips, p.173). Single fares range from €1.20–3.70 with returns at €2.05–6.90 (children's fares €0.75–1.60 and €1.30–2.90), though buying a travel pass (see above) is a cheaper option. The suburban train services operated by Iarnród Éireann (ⓦ www.iarnrodeireann.ie/home) utilize the same tracks as the DART, but stop at fewer stations (Connolly, Tara Street and Pearse in the centre, the new Docklands station just east of the centre, Dún Laoghaire and Bray to the south and Howth Junction to the north). The Northern Commuter line from Pearse Station via Tara Street and Connolly is the quickest means of making day trips to Malahide and to Drogheda for Brú na Boinne.

Taxis

Dublin's taxis vary in shape and size from London-style black cabs and saloon cars to people carriers, though all are readily identifiable by an illuminated box on the roof displaying the driver's taxi licence number. Taxis can be hailed on the street, but it is often easier to head to one of the ranks, such as at the northwest corner of St Stephen's Green, next to the Bank of Ireland on College Green, outside *The Westin Hotel* on Westmoreland Street, in front of *The Gresham Hotel* on O'Connell Street, or on the western branch of Parnell Street.

Finding a taxi after 11pm on a busy night can be arduous, especially at weekends in the city centre, so it's advisable to book one earlier. Conversely, if you're heading back to the centre from the suburbs, it can often be easy to hail a cab returning the same way. City Cabs (℡01/872 7272), Satellite Taxis (Northside ℡01/836 5555, Southside ℡01/454 3333) and Eurocabs (℡01/623 4100) are all generally reliable options. Eurocabs can also supply a wheelchair-accessible taxi if booked at least one hour in advance.

As for **fares**, a short hop will usually cost around €6–9, while a trip from the centre to one of the closer suburbs, such as Clontarf or Ballsbridge, will cost around €10–13. Metered taxis tend to be cheaper than the flat-fare variety and can use the city's bus lanes.

Cars and parking

Dublin's rush hour covers 7–10am and 4–7pm on weekdays, and some areas, such as The Quays and Dame Street, are best avoided at all times. As for **car parks**, a good Southside option is the Royal College of Surgeons multi-storey off the west side of St Stephen's Green. On-street spaces are hard to find, but Merrion Square and Fitzwilliam Square are usually sure bets. If you're parking in the centre expect to pay at least €2–3 per hour.

Unless you're planning to use the city as a tour base there's no need to **rent a car** in Dublin, but if you do so, several outlets are based at the airport and at the Dublin Tourism Centre, Suffolk Street. The cost of a week's rental ranges from around €200–300 depending upon vehicle size and insurance costs, though major reductions can be found by advance Internet booking.

Tours

From open-top bus tours to river cruises to literary jaunts, there are plenty of ways to see the sights.

Open-top bus tours

One of the simplest ways of seeing the sights if time is short is to take a ride on one of the hop-on-hop-off **open-top bus tours**. Commentary is provided either by the driver (some of whom also readily break into appropriate songs), an on-board guide or a pre-recorded tape.

All tours follow roughly the same **route**, covering Parnell Square, Trinity College, St Stephen's Green, Dublin Castle, the cathedrals, the Guinness Storehouse, the Irish Museum of Modern Art (or Kilmainham Gaol), Phoenix Park and Collins Barracks. The full circular tour lasts around 1hr 15min, depending upon traffic congestion, and tickets are valid for 24 hours from the time of first use. All tickets offer a range of discounts to the city's attractions.

Dublin Bus (℡01/873 4222, ✇www .dublinbus.ie) offers the daily Dublin City Tour, commencing from Cathal Brugha St, off O'Connell St Upper (daily every 10min 9.30am–3pm, every 15min 3–5pm and also April–Oct every 30min 5–6.30pm). Tickets cost €14 and can be purchased from the Dublin Bus office (see p.197) or from the driver, and from some hotels. The company also operates a Ghost Bus Tour (Mon & Thurs 8pm, Fri 8pm & 8.30pm, Sat 7pm & 9.30pm; 2hr15mins; €25; not suitable for under-14s), visiting the city's spookier spots.
Irish Tours (℡01/605 7705 or 01/458 0054, ✇www.irishcitytours.com) operates a City Sightseeing Tour (daily every 10–15min: April–June 9.15am–5pm, July–Sept 9.15am–5.30pm, Oct–March 9.30am–4.30pm; €15). Tickets can be purchased from the driver, tourist information offices and some hotels. Tours depart from outside 14 O'Connell St Upper.

Land and water tour

The award-winning **Viking Splash** tour (64–65 Patrick St ☎01/707 6000, ⊛www.vikingsplash.ie) uses reconditioned World War II amphibious vehicles known as Ducks and guides in Norse costume to provide a lively tour of the centre, culminating in a voyage from the Grand Canal Basin (daily: mid-Feb to mid-March & Nov 10am–4pm; mid-March to Oct 9.30am–5pm; 1hr 15min; tours depend upon demand – call for times). Tours operate from both Bull Alley Street (next to St Patrick's Cathedral) and St Stephen's Green North. Tickets (€20) can be purchased at the departure points or by telephone.

River cruises

A waterborne trip along the River Liffey is provided by **Liffey River Cruises** (☎01/473 4082, ⊛www.liffeyrivercruises .com). Sailings depart from Bachelors Walk (daily: March–Nov 11am, noon, 1.45pm & 2.45pm, also March–Oct 4pm and April–Sept 5pm), or you can board at Custom House Quay (March–Nov 11.35am & 2.20pm, also April–Sept 4.35pm). The 45-minute tour includes guided commentary and costs €12.

Sea cruises

Two companies offer exhilarating trips around **Dublin Bay**, lasting 1hr15min, taking in views of islands such as Ireland's Eye and possible sightings of seals and porpoises as well as a host of birdlife. **Sea Safari** (☎01/855 7600, ⊛www.seasafari .ie) runs two cruises in open inflatable boats (waterproof clothing and lifejackets are provided), running from Dublin City Moorings, near the IFSC on Custom House Quay, or from Malahide harbour. Tours cost €30 and are not suitable for children under eight. **Dublin Sea Tours** (☎01/492 5919, ⊛www.dublinseatours.ie) operates from Poolbeg Marina, Seán Moore Rd, Ringsend, just east of the East Link Bridge (buses #2 or #3 from O'Connell St) and Dún Laoghaire Harbour East Pier. Trips are in a covered, heated boat (no special clothing needed) and cost €35; children must be over six years of age.

Advance booking for all cruises is essential. Though there may be up to six cruises daily in high season, their frequency is always subject to weather conditions.

Walking tours

Historical Insights (☎087/688 9412 or ☎087/830 3523, ⊛www.historicalinsights .ie) operates a two-hour tour run by Trinity

---

Tourist passes

Available at any tourist information office or online at ⊛www.dublinpass.com, the **Dublin Pass** provides free entry to more than thirty attractions as well as a range of other special offers, plus a one-way journey from the airport on the Aircoach service (see p.197). A one-day pass costs €31 with two-, three- and six-day passes at €49, €59 and €89 respectively. It can also be worth acquiring a **Heritage Card** (€21) run by the Heritage Service (☎01/647 2453, ⊛www.heritageireland.ie), for free entry to attractions across the whole of the Republic, such as the Casino at Marino, Kilmainham Gaol, Dublin Castle, Rathfarnham Castle, Phoenix Park Visitor Centre and, further afield, Glendalough Visitor Centre, Castletown House and Brú na Boinne. Cards are available from Heritage Service sites and tourist offices.

The €5.99 Heritage Island brochure (☎01/236 6890, ⊛www.heritageisland.com) contains **discounts** to a range of sights across the whole of Ireland. Participating Dublin attractions include the Chimney Viewing Tower, Christchurch Cathedral, City Hall, Dalkey Castle, Dublinia, the GAA Museum, the Guinness Storehouse, the James Joyce Centre, the Old Jameson Distillery and St Patrick's Cathedral, plus Powerscourt and Russborough House further afield.

A **combined ticket** covering any two of the five attractions operated by Dublin Tourism (Dublin Writers Museum, Fry Model Railway, James Joyce Museum, Malahide Castle and the Shaw Birthplace) costs €12, a saving of €2, and can be purchased at each site.

history graduates covering Dublin's development and major events in its history. Tours (April & Oct daily 11am, May–Sept daily 11am & 3pm; Nov–March Fri–Sun 11am; €12) start from Trinity College's front gate.

The 1916 Rebellion tour (☎086/858 3847, ⓦ www.1916rising.com) covers the events leading up to the Easter Rising, the rebellion itself and its aftermath. Tickets cost €12 and tours commence inside the *International Bar*, Wicklow Street (Nov to mid-March Sat 11.30am, Sun 1pm; mid-March–Oct Mon–Sat 11.30am, Sun 1pm; 2hr).

For something more bookish, the Jameson Dublin Literary Pub Crawl (☎01/670 5602, ⓦ www.dublinpubcrawl.com)

commences upstairs at *The Duke* on Duke Street and involves actors performing extracts from major works in a number of pubs with literary connections (April–Nov daily 7.30pm, Sun also at noon; Dec–March Thurs–Sun only, same times; 2hr 15min; €12).

The Traditional Irish Music Pub Crawl (☎01/475 3313, ⓦ www.discoverdublin .ie/musicalpubcrawl.html) sees two musicians guide you on a tour of half a dozen pubs, performing songs and music while recounting Ireland's musical history. Tours (April–Oct daily 7.30pm, Nov–March Thurs–Sat only, same time; 2hr 30min; €12) begin upstairs at *Oliver St John Gogarty's*, Fleet Street.

Information

Tourist offices

The main Dublin Tourism Centre (Mon–Sat 9am–5.30pm, July & Aug until 8pm, Sept until 7pm, Sun and Public Holidays 10.30am–3pm; ⓦ www.visitdublin.com) occupies the former St Andrew's Church on Suffolk Street, a short distance west of the Grafton Street junction with Nassau Street. A numbered-ticket queuing system operates for information and accommoda- tion reservations (see p.187 for more on the latter) and there are also desks for currency exchange, car rental and events tickets. Outside is a touch-screen infor- mation console that accepts credit card accommodation bookings. Dublin Tourism's other offices are at the airport (see p. 197), Dún Laoghaire ferry terminal (see p. 197), 14 O'Connell St Upper (Mon–Sat 9am– 5pm) and Baggott Street Bridge (Mon–Fri 9.30am–noon & 12.30–5pm).

If you have an iPod, you can download one of a dozen or so free guided iWalks podcasts, providing a range of walking tours with commentary provided by local author and historian Pat Liddy (ⓦ www.visitdublin.com/multimedia /dublinpodcasts).

Newspapers and listings magazines

The heavyweight daily Irish Times (€1.60) and the Evening Herald (€1) are both useful sources of information, including cinema and theatre listings, and the former also produces a weekly listings supple- ment, The Ticket, on Fridays. The most comprehensive free listings magazine is the fortnightly Event Guide (ⓦ www.event- guide.ie); others include Mongrel (monthly; free) which also has articles on the local arts scene, while Connected (monthly; free) offers detailed music-oriented listings. These can be picked up in bars, cafés, CD shops and shopping malls. Music listings can also be found in the fortnightly rock and style magazine Hot Press (€3.50), while traditional music is covered by the monthly Irish Music (€2.95). An inherent drawback of all of these is the absence of addresses for the venues listed, so check the telephone directory in your hotel or ask locally for information.

The O'Connell Street Lower branch of Eason's (see p.134) stocks just about every magazine published in Ireland, along with all Irish and British newspapers.

Dublin on the Internet

Dublin Tourism's ⓦ www.visitdublin.com site is a useful entry point, particularly for details of attractions, events and booking accommodation. If you want to catch up with local bloggers, then check ⓦ dublin .metblogs.com.

ⓦ **www.browseireland.com** A massive all-Ireland portal with plenty of useful Dublin links.

ⓦ **www.ddda.ie** Events and activities both on the water and in the surrounding Docklands.

ⓦ **www.dublin.ie** A city-based portal with information on everything from events to the local environment.

ⓦ **www.dublinpubscene.com** Pub review site with details of live music and comedy nights.

ⓦ **www.entertainment.ie** Bucketloads of information about the latest shows, screenings and events.

ⓦ **www.templebar.ie** Everything that's happening around this vibrant area.

Entertainment

Cinema

Mainstream cinemas include Cineworld, 17 Parnell St ☏ 1520/880444, ⓦ www .cineworld.ie; Savoy, 17 O'Connell St ☏ 0818/776776, ⓦ www.savoy.ie; and Screen, Townsend Street ☏ 01/672 5500, ⓦ www.screencinema.ie. Fans of world and independent cinema should head for the Irish Film Institute (see p.98).

For information on the city's film festival, see p.204.

Music

The National Concert Hall (Earlsfort Terrace ☏ 01/417 0000, ⓦ www.nch.ie) is Dublin's largest classical music venue, featuring weekly concerts by the resident RTÉ National Symphony Orchestra as well as visiting orchestras and soloists, and a varied programme of jazz and traditional music.

Other places regularly staging classical music events include Bewley's Café Theatre (☏ 086/878 4001; see p.69); the Coach House, Dublin Castle (☏ 01/671 9429); The Helix (see p.172); The Hugh Lane Gallery (see p.140); the National Gallery, Merrion Square West (see p.81); the Project Arts Centre (see p.98); St Mary's Pro-Cathedral (see p.133); and St Patrick's Cathedral (see p.113).

There is also a wealth of venues for lovers of traditional music, as well as plenty of places dedicated to live rock, pop and indie. Major venues are listed throughout the guide, but J.J. Smyth's (see p.121) is the place for blues and jazz-fusion, The Cobblestone (see p.153) hosts traditional music nights, the Temple Bar Music Centre (see p.104) gives space to left-field and indie bands, while Crawdaddy (see p.94) puts on a range of live acts, including world and indie bands.

Theatre

The most renowned theatres are the Abbey (see p.132) and the Gate (see p.139). Others worth seeking out include Gaiety Theatre, King Street South ☏ 01/677 1717, ⓦ www.gaietytheatre.net; The Helix (see p.172); Olympia Theatre (see p.104); Pavilion Theatre, Marine Road, Dún Laoghaire ☏ 01/231 2929, ⓦ www .paviliontheatre.ie. Theatres showing fringe or experimental theatre include Liberty Hall, Eden Quay ☏ 01/872 1122; New Theatre, 43 Essex St East ☏ 01/670 3361, ⓦ www .thenewtheatre.com; Peacock Theatre (see p.133); and SFX City Theatre, 23 Upper Sherrard St ☏ 01/855 4090, ⓦ www.sfx.ie.

Also of note is the Lambert Puppet Theatre (5 Clifton Lane, Monkstown ☏ 01/280 0974, ⓦ www.lambertpuppettheatre.com), which stages daily shows during May and June (call for times) and performances on Sat & Sun at 3.30pm year-round, as well as an international puppet festival in mid-September.

For information on the city's theatre festival, see p.207.

Sporting venues

Croke Park St Joseph's Ave ☎01/836 3222, ⓦwww.gaa.ie. The home of the Gaelic Athletic Association hosts both hurling and Gaelic football matches and other major events (see p.144), as well as both rugby and association football international matches while the Lansdowne Road stadium in Ballsbridge is being redeveloped.

Donnybrook Stadium Donnybrook Rd, Donnybrook ☎01/269 3224, ⓦwww .leinsterrugby.ie. Top quality rugby matches each weekend featuring the Leinster province side against the best clubs in Ireland, the UK and France.

Shelbourne Park Greyhound Stadium South Lotts Rd, Ringsend ☎01/668 3502, ⓦwww.shelbournepark.com. Greyhound racing every Wed, Thurs & Sat 8pm (€10). Alternatively, there's also Harold's Cross Stadium, off Harold's Cross Road (☎01/497 1081), Mon, Tues & Fri (same time and price).

Horse racing

There are several racetracks within easy reach of Dublin, and Bus Éireann (☎01/836 6111, ⓦwww.buseireann.ie)

lays on special services on race days, leaving from Busáras (see p.197).

The Curragh 31 miles southwest of the capital, near Kildare town ☎045/441205, ⓦwww.curragh.ie. Home to the flat-racing classics: the Irish 2000 Guineas and 1000 Guineas in May, the Irish Derby in June, the Irish Oaks in July and the Irish St Leger in September. Trains from Heuston Station stop at The Curragh on big race days.

Fairyhouse Ratoath, 15 miles northwest of Dublin – on the R155, 2 miles east of its junction with the N3 – ☎01/825 6167, ⓦwww.fairyhouseracecourse.ie. Venue for the Irish Grand National on Easter Monday.

Leopardstown in the southern suburb of Foxrock ☎01/289 0500, ⓦwww .leopardstown.com. Races are held at weekends at various points of the year and on Wed evenings during June and July, but the main events are the four-day Christmas Festival starting on St Stephen's Day (Dec 26), and the Hennessy Cognac Gold Cup in February. LUAS to Sandyford station then a 15min walk.

Punchestown 25 miles southwest of Dublin near Naas in County Kildare ☎045/897704, ⓦwww.punchestown.com. Home to the five-day Irish National Hunt Festival in April.

Festivals and events

Temple Bar Trad Festival ☎01/677 2397, ⓦwww.templebartrad.com. Four days and nights of traditional music pub sessions, concerts, instrument workshops and more, in the heart of the city.

February

Jameson Dublin International Film Festival ☎01/672 8861, ⓦwww.dubliniff .com. Held at cinemas and other venues across the city centre for ten days in mid-February. While screening the latest in new Irish cinema, the festival also has a decidedly international flavour and its hundred or so films include themed offerings and retrospectives.

RTÉ Living Music Festival ☎01/208 2617, ⓦwww.rte.ie/music. Three days of contemporary classical music concerts

and events, featuring leading Irish and international figures, held in mid-February at a variety of central venues.

March/April

Easter Rising Commemorations take place on Easter Sunday, featuring speeches and a march from the General Post Office to Glasnevin Cemetery (see p.167).

St Patrick's Festival ☎01/676 3205, ⓦwww.stpatricksfestival.ie. Running for five days on and around St Patrick's Day (March 17), this city-wide festival includes a parade, a funfair, light shows, concerts, films, exhibitions and a *céilí mór* (thousands of locals and visitors fill the streets in a traditional dance-athon).

Poetry Now Festival ☎01/205 4873, ⓦwww.dlrcoco.ie/arts. A major three-day

event, held over the first weekend in April at The Pavilion Theatre, Dún Laoghaire, the festival features readings by well-known Irish and international poets, master classes, exhibitions and children's events.
Handel's Messiah Festival ☎01/677 2255, ⓦwww.templebar.ie. A week-long festival in mid-April celebrating Handel's visit to Dublin in 1742, featuring free concerts, workshops and talks held in various venues around Temple Bar and Dublin Castle.

May

Heineken Green Energy ☎0818/719 300, ⓦwww.ticketmaster.ie. Major music acts play outdoors in the grounds of Dublin Castle over the first weekend in May; previous performers have included The White Stripes, Lou Reed, Faithless and Kasabian.
Bray Jazz Festival ☎01/287 3992, ⓦwww.brayjazz.com. Three days of gigs, featuring international singers and musicians at more than a dozen venues over the first weekend in May.
International Dublin Gay Theatre Festival ☎01/677 8511, ⓦwww.gaytheatre.ie. Almost three weeks of drama, comedy, cabaret and musical theatre – with international and Irish casts – at a variety of city-centre locations, plus a post-performance Festival Club at The Dragon (see p.120).
Wicklow Gardens Festival ☎0404/20070, ⓦwww.visitwicklow.ie. A variety of privately owned gardens close to Dublin throw open their gates to the public between May and August.

June

Wicklow Gardens Festival see May.
Diversions Temple Bar ☎01/677 2255, ⓦwww.templebar.ie. This series of free outdoor events runs from June to September in and around Meeting House Square and includes film screenings, music performances, circus acts, family fun days and other entertainment.
Docklands Maritime Festival ☎01/818 3300, ⓦwww.ddda.ie. Tall ships welcome visitors to their decks over the first weekend in June at North Wall Quay, plus there's a market, street theatre, trips along the Liffey and a variety of events for children.
Dublin Writers Festival ☎01/222 7848, ⓦwww.dublinwritersfestival.com. Major Irish and international writers and poets take part

in five days of readings, discussions and other events around the centre in mid-June.
Bloomsday ☎01/878 8547, ⓦwww.jamesjoyce.ie. The James Joyce Centre organizes a week of events in mid-June, culminating in Bloomsday itself (June 16), the day on which Joyce's *Ulysses* is set.

July

Wicklow Gardens Fesival see May.
Diversions Temple Bar see June.
Howth Peninsula Fesival ⓦwww.howthpeninsula.com. A plethora of fun events, from tug-of-war competitions to a fun fair, displays and a variety of music, held in the harbour area and other locations around the peninsula during the first weekend in July.

August

Wicklow Gardens Festival see May.
Diversions Temple Bar see June.
GAZE – The Dublin International Lesbian and Gay Film Festival ⓦwww.gaze.ie. Takes place at the Irish Film Institute (see p.98) over four days in early August and has a strong programme of new feature and documentary works.
Dublin Horse Show ☎1850/882883, ⓦwww.dublinhorseshow.com. Five days of equestrian events in early August at the RDS arena in Ballsbridge, with major international showjumpers participating in the Nations Cup.
Dún Laoghaire Festival of World Cultures ☎01/230 1035, ⓦwww.festivalofworldcultures.com. The last weekend in August sees more than 150 (mostly free) events in over forty venues around town, featuring major international acts and a host of lively outdoor activities.

September

Diversions Temple Bar see June.
All-Ireland Senior Hurling and Gaelic Football finals Two of Ireland's major sporting events are staged at Croke Park (see opposite) in September: the hurling final on the second Sunday and the football final on the fourth.
Dublin Fringe Festival ☎01/677 8511, ⓦwww.fringefest.com. Ireland's biggest performing arts festival takes place over more than two weeks during mid-September and features all manner of music, dance, street theatre, comedy and children's events.

Public holidays

New Year's Day; St Patrick's Day (March 17); Good Friday, Easter Monday; first Monday in May, June and August; last Monday in October; Christmas Day; St Stephen's Day (December 26). Virtually all attractions are closed on Good Friday and from Christmas Eve to St Stephen's Day.

ESSENTIALS Directory

Puppet Festival
Lambert Puppet Theatre (see p.203) attracts international puppeteers to its festival, which runs for roughly two weeks in mid-September.
Dublin Theatre Festival ☎01/677 8899, ⓦwww.dublintheatrefestival.com. A major celebration of theatre, held during the last few days of September and the first two weeks in October, this includes performances of new and classic drama at various city-centre venues.

October
Dublin Theatre Festival see September.
Oscar Wilde Autumn School ☎01/286

5245. Six days in Bray (see p.173) devoted to the dramatist, novelist and man of letters, set around Wilde's birthday (Oct 16), with shows, lectures, readings, walks and musical events, including some activities geared towards children. The venue for indoor events is usually the Mermaid Theatre.
Dublin City Marathon ☎01/623 2250, ⓦwww.dublincitymarathon.ie. Featuring 10,000 entrants, the race takes place on the last Monday in October and involves a roughly circular course starting from Kildare Street, crossing the Liffey and taking in Phoenix Park and the Grand Canal Basin before terminating at Merrion Square West.

Directory

ATMs Virtually all banks have ATMs which accept cards bearing the Cirrus, Maestro, Switch or Visa symbols.
Banks and exchange Most banks open Mon–Fri 10am–4pm, Thurs until 5pm. The majority of bank branches will change travellers' cheques and there are also foreign exchange desks at the airport, at Thomas Cook, 118 Grafton St (Mon–Sat 9am–5.30pm, Thurs until 8pm), and at the Dublin Tourism Centre, Suffolk Street (Mon–Sat 9am–5pm).
Disabled travellers Both the government agency Citizens Information Board (7th Floor, Hume House, Dublin 4 ☎01/605 9000, ⓦwww.citizensinformationboard.ie), and Dublin Tourism (see p.202) offer advice and information to people with disabilities visiting Ireland. The latter's annual accommodation guide (available from all offices) indicates which of the city's establishments are wheelchair-accessible. The Irish Wheelchair Association, Áras Chúchulain, Blackheath Drive, Clontarf, Dublin 3

(☎01/818 6400, ⓦwww.iwa.ie) also provides advice on accessible accommodation and other amenities in Ireland, and its website lists contact details of companies offering wheelchairs for hire. In terms of transport, Dublin Bus (see p.198 and ⓦwww.dublinbus.ie /your_journey/accessibility.asp) operates low-floor, fully accessible buses on almost seventy routes and on some of its tours. With advance notice, Iarnród Éireann (☎01/836 6222, ⓦwww.iarnrodeireann .ie/your_journey/disabled_access.asp) will make sure that staff meet and assist you on your DART or railway journey. For information on taxis, see p.199.
Electricity The standard electricity supply is 220 volts and three-pin plugs are the norm. Northern American appliances will need a transformer and a plug adapter (available from most electrical suppliers and airport shops). Those from Australia, New Zealand and South Africa will only require an adapter.

Embassies Australia, Seventh Floor, Fitzwilton House, Wilton Terrace ☎01/664 5300; Canada, 65 St Stephen's Green ☎01/417 4100; South Africa, Alexandra House, Earlsfort Centre, Earlsfort Terrace ☎01/661 5553; UK, 29 Merrion Rd ☎01/205 3700; USA, 42 Elgin Rd ☎01/668 8777.

Emergencies Dial ☎112 or ☎999 for emergency medical assistance, fire services or police.

Gay and lesbian travellers *GCN* (Gay Community News; ⊛www.gcn.ie) is a free monthly magazine with events listings – copies can usually be found at gay venues or at Books Upstairs (see p.70). Outhouse, 105 Capel St (☎01/873 4932, ⊛www.outhouse.ie) is a gay and lesbian resource centre with a café (Mon–Fri 1.30–5.30pm, Sat 1–5pm, also Tues 6.30–9.30pm & Thurs 7–10pm – women only, and Fri 7–10pm – men only) and a small library. Gay Switchboard (Mon–Fri 7.30–9.30pm, Sat 3.30–6pm; ☎01/872 1055, ⊛www.gayswitchboard .ie) provides advice and information. Useful websites include ⊛www.queerid.com for events and news, and ⊛www.gaire .com for information, message boards and online chat.

Hospitals Hospitals with accident and emergency departments include: Beaumont Hospital, Beaumont Rd (☎01/809 3000); Mater Misericordiae, Eccles St (☎01/803 2000); St James's, James St (☎01/410 3000); and St Vincent's, Elm Park (☎01/269 4533). For dental emergencies there is the Dublin Dental School and Hospital, Lincoln Place ☎01/612 7200.

Internet Central Internet cafés include Central Cyber Café, 6 Grafton St; Global Internet Café, 8 O'Connell St Lower; Internet Exchange, 3 Cecilia St, Temple Bar; and Oz Cyber Café, 39 Abbey Street Upper. Access costs from as little as €1–3 per hour.

Left luggage Luggage lockers are available in Busáras (in the station basement; €6–10) and on the concourse of Connolly Station (€4–6) and Heuston Station (€1.50–5); prices are per item, per night, and vary depending on the size of the locker.

Lost property Dublin Bus ☎01/703 1321; Bus Éireann ☎01/836 6111; Connolly Station ☎01/703 2362; Heuston Station ☎01/703 2102; Airport ☎01/814 5555.

Opening hours For details on opening hours of restaurants, cafés and shops, see p.6.

Pharmacies Central pharmacies include branches of Hickey's at 55 O'Connell St Lower (Mon–Wed 7.30am–10pm, Thurs & Fri 9am–9pm, Sat 8am–10pm, Sun 10am–10pm; ☎01/873 0427) and 17 Westmoreland St (Mon–Wed 8.30am–7pm, Thurs & Fri 8.30am–8pm, Sat 8.30am–6.30pm; ☎01/677 8440).

Police The main police station (Garda Síochána) is on Harcourt Terrace (☎01/666 9500). The Irish Tourist Assistance Service (☎01/478 5295, ⊛www.itas.ie) offers support to tourist victims of crime.

Post offices The largest is the General Post Office on O'Connell Street Lower (Mon–Sat 8am–8pm, ☎01/705 7000). There are also central branches at St Andrew's St (by the Suffolk St Tourism Centre), Ormond Quay Upper and Clare St. For enquiries call ☎1850/575 589. Many newsagents sell postage stamps.

Smoking You cannot smoke in any enclosed workplace in the Republic of Ireland, including all bars and pubs, clubs, cafés and restaurants. However, many establishments provide outdoor spaces for smokers.

Swimming pool Markievicz Leisure Centre, Townsend St ☎01/672 9121, ⊛www.dublincity.ie.

Tax-free shopping Visitors from outside the EU can claim a VAT refund on all goods bought in Ireland, as long as these are taken out of the country within three months of purchase. Retailers who participate in the scheme will display a

---

Fly Less – Stay Longer!

Rough Guides believes in the good that travel does, but we are deeply aware of the impact of fuel emissions on climate change. We recommend taking fewer trips and staying for longer. If you can avoid travelling by air, please use an alternative, especially for journeys of under 1000km/600miles. And always offset your travel at ⊛www.roughguides.com/climatechange.

sticker; for more information see
ⓦ www.globalrefund.ie.

Telephones Public phones are widely
available and making a local call costs a
minimum €0.50. Most phones will also
accept pre-paid cards which can be bought
from post offices and newsagents. Mobile
phones from the UK usually switch to
an Irish network automatically on arrival
(though you should check call costs with
your network provider); US cellphones need
to be GSM compatible. For operator
assistance, including reverse-charge calls,
dial ☏ 10 for Ireland and the UK and
☏ 114 for the rest of the world. For
directory enquiries dial ☏ 11811 for Ireland
and ☏ 11818 for everywhere else.

Time Ireland, like Britain, is on Greenwich
Mean Time and operates a similar daylight
saving scheme, putting clocks forward by
one hour in March and back again at the
end of October.

Tipping It's usual to reward good
restaurant service with a tip of 10–15
percent, a sum expected by most taxi
drivers too. A growing number of
restaurants and hotels automatically add a
discretionary service charge to your bill.

Toilets Public toilets are relatively scarce,
but can be found in shopping malls and
some major department stores. Note that
the Irish words *fir* (men) and *mná* (women)
may appear on some establishments'
toilet doors.

Chronology

Chronology

c.150 AD ▶ The Greek cartographer Ptolemy's map of the world marks a place named Eblana, where Dublin now stands.

837 ▶ Viking incursions into Dublin Bay include an attack on a monastic settlement at Dubh Linn ("dark pool", the origin of the city's English name), and lead to their takeover of the surrounding area.

902 ▶ Defeated in battle by the King of Leinster, the Vikings withdraw, but return in 917 to establish the renascent Dublin as a trading centre, building wooden houses on what is now Wood Quay and the surrounding area.

1014 ▶ The High King of Ireland Brian Ború defeats the Vikings at the Battle of Clontarf, dying in the process, but his victory leads to the assimilation of the Norsemen into Irish culture.

1170 ▶ A spate of Irish in-fighting drives the defeated King of Leinster, Dermot MacMurrough, to seek aid from the English king Henry II to regain his throne. Henry offers the assistance of Richard Fitzgilbert de Clare (aka Strongbow), whose army of Welsh knights reclaims MacMurrough's lands. Henry then sails to Dublin himself to assume ascendancy over Ireland, granting a charter to the developing town and establishing a court there.

1348 ▶ Europe-wide pandemic, the Black Death (a virulent form of bubonic plague) strikes Dublin and similar, though less devastating outbreaks will affect the town over the next 300 years.

1487 ▶ The Fitzgerald clan (Earls of Kildare), dominant force in Irish politics, occupy Dublin during the War of the Roses. Ten-year-old Lambert Simnel is proclaimed King of England and crowned in Christ Church Cathedral, but the Fitzgeralds' rebellion is soon quelled by Henry VII.

1534 ▶ Another Fitzgerald, Silken Thomas, besieges Dublin in the mistaken belief that his father had been imprisoned by the English while in London. A large force dispatched by Henry VIII dispels the rebellion, and direct rule is imposed by the appointment of Leonard Grey as Lord Deputy of Ireland.

1592 ▶ Trinity College is founded by Elizabeth I as a university for the sons of the Protestant gentry.

1649 ▶ A coalition army of Irish Catholics and Royalists is routed by Dublin's Parliamentarian garrison at the Battle of Rathmines.

1742 ▶ Handel's *Messiah* is premiered in Dublin.

1757 ▶ The Wide Streets Commission is created to encourage the city's gentrification. The peak period of Georgian housebuilding follows and during the subsequent decades City Hall, the Four Courts and the Custom House are erected, as well as the western frontage of Trinity College.

1791 ▶ The Society of United Irishmen is founded by middle-class Protestants in Belfast, but soon attracts wider support for its demands for democratic reforms and Catholic emancipation.

1793 ▶ After England declares war on France, French aid is sought for Irish independence and a Dublin barrister, Theobald Wolfe Tone, is dispatched to Paris to seek military support.

1798 ▶ A major Irish rebellion is brutally suppressed by the English. Most of its leaders are captured and Tone commits suicide in prison rather than face execution.

1801 ▶ The Act of Union dissolves the Dublin parliament and direct rule of Ireland is reinstated.

1803 ▶ Robert Emmet leads a poorly organized rebellion in Dublin which is quickly defeated.

1829 ▶ The English parliament grants Catholic Emancipation.

1840 ▶ Daniel O'Connell is elected as the first Catholic mayor of Dublin. His mass rallies, calling for a repeal of the Act of Union, result in his imprisonment for sedition.

1845–1851 ▶ The Irish potato crop, the main source of sustenance for many of its 8.5 million inhabitants, is devastated by blight. The Great Famine ensues, resulting in the deaths of 1.5 million people, and the emigration of a similar number to Britain, the Americas and Australia.

1882 ▶ The Home Rule campaign is undermined when two British government officials are assassinated in Phoenix Park.

1904 ▶ Founded by W. B. Yeats and Lady Gregory, the Abbey Theatre stages its first performance.

1912 ▶ A Home Rule Bill is passed by the British parliament, but suspended when war with Germany breaks out in 1914.

1916 ▶ Irish rebels led by Pádraig Pearse and James Connolly seize government buildings on Easter Monday, and Pearse delivers the Proclamation of the Irish Republic from the steps of the General Post Office. However, after six days' fighting, the leaders surrender and are executed, except for Éamon de Valera who has US citizenship.

1918 ▶ Sinn Féin is hugely successful in the General Election, but its members refuse to take their seats at Westminster, instead convening in Dublin as Dáil Éireann ("Ireland's parliament") and issuing a declaration of independence.

1919 ▶ A bloody War of Independence begins in September and drags on until a truce is declared in 1921.

1921 ▶ Elections for the new Dublin-based parliament see another victory for Sinn Féin. De Valera demands a 32-county state, but a delegation he sends to London is forced to agree to partition. The Anglo-Irish Treaty, signed in December, grants Ireland independence as the Irish Free State, at the cost of partition.

1922 ▶ Pro- and anti-Treaty forces become involved in a bitter civil war. Fierce fighting takes place on the streets of Dublin and across the country, but the Republicans are eventually forced to surrender in May, 1923. Meanwhile, in Paris, James Joyce's *Ulysses* is published.

1926 ▶ De Valera splits from Sinn Féin and founds the Fianna Fáil ("Soldiers of Destiny") as a separate Republican political party. Radio Éireann is established.

1938 ▶ Douglas Hyde becomes Ireland's first President and takes occupancy of the former viceregal lodge in Phoenix Park, now known as Áras an Uachtaráin.

1948 ▶ A coalition government led by the Fine Gael party passes the Republic of Ireland Act, establishing the country as a republic from the following year.

1953 ▶ The central bus station Busáras is constructed, becoming the capital's first Modernist building.

1966 ▶ Republicans blow up Nelson's Column on O'Connell Street in commemoration of the fiftieth anniversary of the Easter Rising.

1972 ▶ Rioters attack and burn down the British Embassy in Dublin in protest at the shooting dead of thirteen civilians by British troops in Derry on "Bloody Sunday".

1974 ▶ As the Troubles in Northern Ireland escalate, Loyalists detonate car-bombs in Dublin, killing 26 people.

1976 ▶ 14-year-old drummer Larry Mullen forms a band at his Clontarf school which will go through various changes of name, from Feedback to The Hype, before finally settling upon U2, releasing its first single in 1979.

1979 ▶ Pope John Paul II visits Ireland and celebrates Mass with a congregation of more than a million people in Phoenix Park.

1990s ▶ After a decade of recession, Ireland's economy enjoys an upswing, giving rise to the nickname "Celtic Tiger". The city sees the beginnings of a huge building boom, the most notable change being the redevelopment of Temple Bar.

1991 ▶ Mary Robinson becomes Ireland's first woman president.

1994 ▶ The Eurovision Song Contest, staged in Dublin, includes a seven-minute showstopper fusion of traditional dance and contemporary music, spawning the full-length show *Riverdance*, which becomes an international phenomenon.

2000s ▶ Irish political life is racked by a series of scandals involving financial corruption at the highest level. The Flood Commission is established to investigate.

2007 ▶ Dubliner Bertie Ahern, leader of Fianna Fáil, becomes the first Irish Taoiseach ("prime minister") to win three successive general elections.

Travel store

Available from all good bookstores   D: Rough Guide DIRECTIONS

For more information go to www.roughguides.com

Rough Guides To A World Of Music

'stick to the reliable Rough Guide series' The Guardian (UK)

Music has always been an essential part of Irish culture, and the musical traditions of Ireland – focused around pub sessions – remain amongst Europe's most enduring and vibrant. Songs (sung in Irish and English) hold a special place in Irish life and exemplify the vivacity of the Irish singing tradition and its wide range of subjects. This all-new second edition of *The Rough Guide To Irish Music* provides an extensive introduction to Ireland's musical landscape, from the driving music of Donegal and the foot-stomping polkas and slides of Kerry and Cork to the work of those exploring the borders between traditional music and other genres.

Celtic music has captured the ears and hearts of people all over the world with bittersweet a cappella ballads and lively jigs and reels. Although most commonly associated with Irish and Scottish music, Celtic musical influences are also scattered across northern France, USA, England, northern Spain, Canada, Wales and beyond. Crammed with swirling fiddles, flutes, pipes, harps, guitars and mandolins performed by some of the best musicians from across the diaspora, *The Rough Guide To Celtic Music* explores the common connections between the Celtic traditions.

Hear sound samples at WWW.WorldMusic.Net

Rough Guides Radio Now you can visit www.worldmusic.net/radio to tune into the exciting Rough Guide Radio Show, with a new show each month presenting new releases, interviews, features and competitions.

Available from book and record shops worldwide or order direct from
World Music Network, 6 Abbeville Mews, 88 Clapham Park Road, London SW4 7BX, UK
T. 020 7498 5252 F. 020 7498 5353 E. post@worldmusic.net

Visit us online
www.roughguides.com

Information on over 25,000 destinations around the world

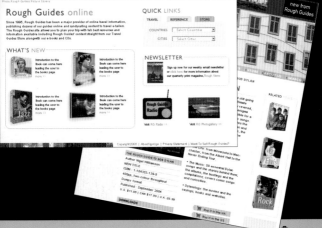

- **Read** Rough Guides' trusted travel info

- **Access** exclusive articles from Rough Guides authors

- **Update** yourself on new books, maps, CDs and other products

- **Enter** our competitions and win travel prizes

- **Share** ideas, journals, photos & travel advice with other users

- **Earn** points every time you contribute to the Rough Guide
  community and get rewards

BROADEN YOUR HORIZONS

Listen Up!

"You may be used to the Rough Guide series being comprehensive, but nothing will prepare you for the exhaustive Rough Guide to World Music . . . one of our books of the year."

Sunday Times, London

Rough Guide Music Titles

The Beatles • Blues • Bob Dylan • Classical Music
Elvis • Frank Sinatra • Heavy Metal • Hip-Hop
iPods, iTunes & music online • Jazz • Book of Playlists
Led Zeppelin • Opera • Pink Floyd • Punk • Reggae
Rock • The Rolling Stones • Soul and R&B • World
Music Vol 1 & 2 • Velvet Underground

NOTES

NOTES

NOTES

NOTES

small print & Index

A Rough Guide to Rough Guides

In 1981, Mark Ellingham, a recent graduate in English from Bristol University, was travelling in Greece on a tiny budget and couldn't find the right guidebook. With a group of friends he wrote his own guide, combining a contemporary, journalistic style with a practical approach to travellers' needs. That first Rough Guide was a student scheme that became a publishing phenomenon. Today, Rough Guides include recommendations from shoestring to luxury and cover hundreds of destinations around the globe, including almost every country in the Americas and Europe, more than half of Africa and most of Asia and Australasia. Millions of readers relish Rough Guides' wit and inquisitiveness as much as their enthusiastic, critical approach and value-for-money ethos. The guides' ever-growing team of authors and photographers is spread all over the world.

In the early 1990s, Rough Guides branched out of travel, with the publication of Rough Guides to World Music, Classical Music and the Internet. All three have become benchmark titles in their fields, spearheading the publication of a range of more than 350 titles under the Rough Guide name, including phrasebooks, waterproof maps, music guides from Opera to Heavy Metal, reference works as diverse as Conspiracy Theories and Shakespeare, and popular culture books from iPods to Poker. Rough Guides also produce a series of more than 120 World Music CDs in partnership with World Music Network.

Visit www.roughguides.com to see our latest publications.

Rough Guide travel images are available for commercial licensing at www.roughguidespictures.com

Publishing information

This second edition published May 2008 by
Rough Guides Ltd, 80 Strand, London WC2R 0RL.
345 Hudson St, 4th Floor, New York,
NY 10014, USA.

Distributed by the Penguin Group
Penguin Books Ltd, 80 Strand, London WC2R 0RL
Penguin Group (USA), 375 Hudson Street, NY
10014, USA
14 Local Shopping Centre, Panchsheel Park,
New Delhi 110017, India
Penguin Group (Australia), 250 Camberwell Road,
Camberwell, Victoria 3124, Australia
Penguin Group (Canada), 10 Alcorn Avenue,
Toronto, ON M4V 1E4, Canada
Penguin Group (NZ), 67 Apollo Drive, Mairangi Bay,
Auckland 1310, New Zealand
Typeset in Bembo and Helvetica to an original
design by Henry Iles.

Cover concept by Peter Dyer.

Printed and bound in China
© Paul Grey, Geoff Wallis 2008

ISBN 978-1-85828-285-5

1   3   5   7   9   8   6   4   2

Help us update

We've gone to a lot of effort to ensure that the second edition of Dublin DIRECTIONS is accurate and up-to-date. However, things change – places get "discovered", opening hours are notoriously fickle, restaurants and rooms raise prices or lower standards. If you feel we've got it wrong or left something out, we'd like to know, and if you can remember the address, the price, the phone number, so much the better.

Please send your comments with the subject line "Dublin DIRECTIONS Update" to ©mail@roughguides.com. We'll credit all contributions and send a copy of the next edition (or any other Rough Guide if you prefer) for the very best emails.

Have your questions answered and tell others about your trip at ®community.roughguides.com

Rough Guide credits

Text editor: Natasha Foges
Layout: Ankur Guha
Photography: Michelle Bhatia, Mark Thomas
Cartography: Jasbir Sandhu

Picture editor: Mark Thomas
Proofreader: Camilla Cooke
Production: Rebecca Short
Cover design: Chloë Roberts

The authors

Paul Gray has been a regular visitor to Dublin since 1990 and lived in the city for three years until 2004. He is co-author of the *Rough Guide to Ireland* and the *Rough Guide to Thailand*, and has edited and contributed to many other guidebooks, including updating his native Northeast for the *Rough Guide to England*.

Geoff Wallis is a freelance writer on travel, music and sport and a regular contributor to magazines such as *fRoots*, *Songlines* and *When Saturday Comes* as well as a wide range of Irish and UK newspapers. Co-author of the *Rough Guide to Ireland*, the *Rough Guide to Irish Music* and the *Rough Guide to Family Fun in Ireland* he has also compiled several commercial CDs of Irish music. He lives in rural bliss in Ireland and is currently writing another book on traditional music.

Acknowledgements

The authors would like to thank: Emma Gorman and John Lahiffe at Tourism Ireland; Sinead Barden and Sam Johnston at Dublin Tourism; Heritage Ireland; Heritage Island; and our editor, Natasha Foges.

Paul would also like to thank: Jacobs Inn, the Merrion and the Shelbourne; Alexia, Andy, Sarah, John and Kate Grier; and Bill Gray.
Geoff would also like to thank: Joanie McDermott, Finbar Boyle, Éamonn Jordan and Mireille Cambier.

Readers' letters

Thanks to all those readers of the first edition of Dublin Directions who took the trouble to write in with their amendments and additions. Apologies for any misspellings or omissions.
Shane Cahill; Barbara and David Cross; Rebecca George; Sarah Nicholls; Laura Norton; Gaylene Reisima; Jane Williams

Photo credits

All images © Rough Guides except the following:

Front cover: Barrels, The Guinness Storehouse © Chloë Roberts.
Back cover: Buses, O'Connell Street © Michelle Bhatia/Rough Guides
p.5 The River Liffey at night © Jon Arnold Images/Alamy.
p. 13 *The Singing Horseman*, Jack B Yeats © The National Gallery of Ireland/DACS.
p.13 Gold collar, Glensheen, Co Clare Courtesy of the National Museum of Ireland.
p.13 *Akbar discourses with two priests* by Narsingh, India © Chester Beatty Library.
p.14 Bloomsday © Richard T Nowitz/Corbis.
p.17 Oysters © Rougemont Maurice/Corbis.
p. 19 U2 © Getty Images.

p. 21 Newman House. Courtesy of Newman House.
p.28 Glendalough © Atlanpic/Alamy.
p.32 Robert Emmet death mask Courtesy of The National Museum of Ireland.
p. 34 *Merrion Hotel* spa. Courtesy of the *Merrion Hotel*.
p.35 Interior, *Restaurant Patrick Guilbaud*. Courtesy of *Restaurant Patrick Guilbaud*.
p.35 *The Clarence*. Courtesy of *The Clarence*.
p.36 Swimming in the Forty Foot Pool © Michael St Maur Sheil/Corbis.
p.37 Curlew © David Tipling/Alamy.
p. 38 The Dublin Marathon © Brandon Moran/Sportsfile.
p. 38 Rugby at Donnybrook © Sportsfile.

Selected images from our guidebooks are available for licensing from:
ROUGHGUIDESPICTURES.COM

Index

Maps are marked in colour

INDEX

He's covered. Are you?

ROUGH GUIDES
Travel Insurance

Visit our website at **www.roughguides.com/insurance** or call:

- ☎ UK
- ☎ Spa
- ☎ Aus
- ☎ Nev
- ☎ Wo
- ☎ USA

Please

Cover f